Texas Ranger Tales

Stories That Need Telling

By
MIKE COX

Republic of Texas Press

Published by Republic of Texas Press
An imprint of The Rowman & Littlefield Publishing Group, Inc.
4501 Forbes Boulevard, Suite 200
Lanham, MD 20706

Distributed by NATIONAL BOOK NETWORK

Library of Congress Cataloging-in-Publication Data

Cox, Mike.
    Texas Ranger tales : Stories that need telling / Mike Cox.
       p. cm.
    Includes bibliographical references and index.
    ISBN 1-55622-537-7 (pbk)
    1. Texas Rangers—History—Anecdotes. 2. Texas Rangers—Biography—Anecdotes.
3. Frontier and pioneer life—Texas—Anecdotes. 4. Texas—History—1846-1950—
Anecdotes. 5. Texas—History—1951- —Anecdotes. I. Title

F391.C78   1997   97-6899
976.4—dc21   CIP

™
ⓒ The paper used in this publication meets the minimum requirements of American
National Standard for Information Sciences—Permanence of Paper for Printed Library
Materials, ANSI/NISO Z39.48-1992.

Manufactured in the United States of America.

*For my daughter, Hallie Dorin Cox, and
again, for my wife, Linda, who helped me
survive the roughest gunfight of my life and
then fought one of her own . . .*

Contents

Contents

Foreword

by Leon C. Metz

A mystique hovers over the Texas Rangers, a mystique giving them a quality unlike other warriors or lawmen. They are seen at once as brave, resourceful, intrepid, and straightforward. They have a reputation as men who keep a-coming and never back up.

Because they have always been a team, scant Rangers have become household names. Out of the thousands who have served, only a few such as James J. Gillett, John R. Hughes, and Big Foot Wallace have achieved any notable fame. Few singular Ranger exploits have echoed down through the meandering corridors of history. To most people, Rangers are simply obscure men behind the badge, men who did their duty, men who avoided the limelight.

Oddly, while Texas historians rarely write Texas chronicles without including Rangers in one form or another, up until the 1930s the Rangers never had a history to call their own. Then along came a singular book, *The Texas Rangers: A Century of Frontier Defense*, by Walter Prescott Webb.

Since then numerous biographies have been written about individual Rangers. Now Mike Cox has taken the subject another step forward with one of the most alluring Ranger books to date.

Mike Cox, who is Chief of Media Relations in the Public Information Office of the Texas Department of Public Safety, has done considerable research. He recognizes good anecdotes, and he knows how to weave a plot. Cox writes not only about specific Rangers, he also digs into the stories behind the stories. Furthermore, his characters are not only

Rangers, they are human beings capable of broad ranges of intelligence, shrewdness, emotions, bravery, and sometimes weaknesses.

What makes Cox different from the average Ranger historian and biographer is that several of his accounts are relatively contemporary. He knew some of the Rangers involved; he had access not only to the records, but to the individuals. And while a whole lot of shootin' goes on in these pages, the narrative also dispenses fascinating Ranger humor. Even more so, however, Cox provides an in-depth history and analysis of the Ranger aura varying from the dynamic personalities and events to the badge.

Altogether, this information accounts for twenty-seven factual chapters extending from Samuel Walker, inventor of the Walker Colt, to the Phantom Killer of Texarkana. Cox discusses Tom Mix, the famous Ranger who wasn't, and "Rangers Make 'Em Die Laughing." And how's this for a title with flair: "Rx for Keeping the Peace: Laxatives and a .45."

Cox's book isn't a history of the Rangers in the complete sense of the word. However, it advances a cross section of Ranger waggery, valor, dedication, and day-to-day life. A superb book rarely tenders more than that.

Stories That Need Tellin': An Introduction

1. Frank Dobie used to say that a story belongs to the person who tells it best.

If that's true, then a lot of stories belonged to him.

But my grandfather, the late L.A. Wilke, was a pretty fair storyteller himself. I trace my interest in storytelling, and the beginning of any talent I have in that field, to Granddad.

I heard my first stories about the Texas Rangers from Granddad, who knew some of the old-time Rangers well, men like John R. Hughes, Ira Aten, Frank Hamer, Tom Hickman, "Lone Wolf" Gonzaullas and others. He had a story or two about each of these men. Some of these stories I've used in this book.

Later, during a twenty-year newspaper career, I met quite a few modern Texas Rangers myself while covering oilfield strikes, bank robberies, murders, and the 1974 incident in which a noted San Antonio heroin dealer named Fred Gomez Carrasco took eleven people hostage in the library at the Walls Unit of the state prison in Huntsville. Now, as Chief of Media Relations for the Texas Department of Public Safety, which includes the Rangers, I deal with the Rangers nearly every day and count many of them as my friends. Someday, I hope, my daughter, Hallie, will pester me for details of my experiences with these law enforcement officers, just like I warted my grand-dad to tell me about the old horseback Rangers he had known.

Maybe Hallie will ask me about an adventure I had with a Ranger on February 18, 1991. Joaquin Jackson, then a Ranger stationed at Alpine, went with me in search of a desolate spot where seventy-five years earlier, a Texas Ranger and another officer were killed in an ambush by Mexican bandits.

Our destination was a remote ranch in Presidio County. Though not far from the border as the eagle flies, the ranch was surrounded by mountains. In fact, the only way onto the property by vehicle was to drive through an abandoned railroad tunnel drilled through one of those mountains. This ranch and the area around it remains one of the most isolated spots in the continental United States.

The unpaved road we had to take to get to this ranch, Ranger Jackson informed me, was a rough route by our standards—but considered a virtual freeway by north-bound marijuana and cocaine smugglers. No nicely landscaped roadside parks grace this highway, however.

Before we headed south from Marfa in a four-wheel-drive vehicle loaned us by the Presidio County sheriff, the Ranger handed me a lever-action .30-30 rifle.

"Keep this next to you," Jackson said. "We're going where there isn't any 9-1-1."

Actually, we were going back into the nineteenth century. Not only was there no three-digit emergency telephone number to dial if the need arose, there was no telephone. We were on our own, even out of range of the sheriff's department two-way radio.

As we drove toward the ranch where Rangers on horse-back had lost a gunbattle in 1915, I began to realize what it must have been like to carry a badge and a gun in that era. It made me appreciate even more the toughness of those early-day Rangers in the wide open country of the Trans-Pecos—or anywhere else where there was too much trouble and too little law.

Rangers always have been tough, but I'm not saying they were perfect. They did not always do the right thing. They did not win every fight they got in. They were not always fair and impartial officers of the law. But they were right more than they were wrong. And they prevailed more often than they lost.

Texas Ranger Tales certainly is no attempt at a definitive history of the Rangers, though I believe a reading of these stories will give a general idea of their overall story. The more I have dug into Ranger history, the more convinced I am how hard a job a definitive study of the Rangers would be. I do not believe the story could be done justice in a single volume. Consider Walter Prescott Webb's classic *The Texas Rangers: A Century of Frontier Defense.* His book, first published in 1935, is 584 pages long, and it stops with the transfer of the Rangers to the then newly created Texas Department of Public Safety. The Rangers now have another sixty-plus years of always colorful and sometimes controversial history behind them.

For this book, I've aimed my literary Winchester at two types of stories: First, they had to be interesting. Second, I wanted to concentrate on lesser-known Ranger tales. When I did decide to include one of the more familiar Ranger stories, such as the search for the Depression-era outlaws Bonnie Parker and Clyde Barrow, I looked for unusual new angles. Some Texas Ranger stories just keep getting told and retold. I wanted to go after fresh meat.

The stories which follow are for the most part arranged chronologically, but all twenty-seven are freestanding. This is a book you can read from cover to cover, or browse through at your leisure.

In the 1870s the Texas Adjutant General published a list of fugitives, from horse thieves to murderers, wanted by the state. The publication came to be informally called "The Book of Knaves." Rangers carried the book in their saddlebags, jokingly referring to it as their Bible. Whenever they encountered a suspicious person or group, out came "The Book of Knaves." To recognize the folks who helped me most with my book, I don't need a "Book of Knaves."

All I have to do is round up the usual suspects: My mother, retired librarian and now free-lance editor, Betty Wilke Cox, and my wife, Linda Aronovsky Cox. As with almost all my writing projects, my mother was a one-person reference staff and editor. Wife Linda also, as with other projects, read and commented on the manuscript. More important, she kept the campfire going and the beans simmering while I was out on the literary scout. A new addition to my list is one of my brothers-in-law, Sam Aronovsky, an electronics engineer and computer expert who rescued me from a near ambush by my laptop computer. He headed the sons of glitches off at the pass, so to speak, saving my Rangers from cyberdeath.

Also helping out in various ways was my father, Bill Cox, longtime newsman and now book author, and these other folks: The Amarillo Public Library; Judith Blackwell, Austin; Fred Bonavita, San Antonio *Express-News*; The Center for American History, University of Texas at Austin; Waynne Cox (no relation), San Antonio; Peggy Coleman of the Former Texas Rangers Association, San Antonio; Randy Hall, Texarkana; Frank Hamer Jr., San Marcos; Jeff Heard, Austin; Lynn Highley, San Antonio; Casey King, Kingsville; Brad Newton, Fort Stockton; Chuck McCarthy, Austin; Jerome Preiss, Floresville; Jeanne Pruett, Ranger, Texas; Margaret Rose, Corpus Christi Public Library; and Frank Wagner, Corpus Christi.

The old Rangers used to say that some men just need killin'. Well, I think the stories in *Texas Ranger Tales* just need tellin'. I hope you enjoy reading them as much as I've enjoyed rounding them up.

Mike Cox
Austin, Texas

Samuel Walker's Last Fight

An arctic cold front had whipped through San Antonio the day before, sharply dropping temperatures and bringing the slight possibility of a rare South Texas snow.

On the near east side, in the old Oddfellows Cemetery on Powder House Hill off North Monument and North Pine Streets, the north wind rattled the fronds of a nearby palm tree and the blue plastic tarp covering a mound of dirt heaped between two weathered columns of stone as gray as the sky above.

Dead for nearly a century-and-a-half, Texas Ranger Samuel Hamilton Walker once again was about to be right in the middle of a fight. But this time the battle would be on the pages of a newspaper and in a courtroom—the ammunition would be rhetoric and the law, not Indian arrows or Mexican lead.

Born on February 24, 1817, in Toaping Castle, Maryland, the red-headed, blue-eyed Walker lived only thirty-two years. Yet he left an enduring legacy—a slender man of average height, he played a major role in the development of the worldwide reputation of the Texas Rangers and had a hand in perfecting a powerful weapon that would bear his name and help win the West, the Walker Colt.

Walker's forebears fought in the American Revolution, so it was natural that when he learned of the massacre of more than one hundred U.S. soldiers by Seminole Indians in Florida that he would sign up hoping to join the fray. Mustered into the Washington City Volunteer Company in May 1836, Walker and his fellow soldiers soon were on their way to the swamps of Florida. After a fight with Indians in January 1837, he was promoted to corporal in recognition of "exceptional courage" shown in the engagement. By 1838 Walker was out of the military, but he stayed on in Florida until 1841, serving as a civilian military scout and later as a superintendent for the Alabama, Florida and Georgia Railway.

In January 1842, like many other young adventurers, Walker came to the Republic of Texas, landing at Galveston. He may have come to Texas hoping to acquire land or start a business, but for the rest of his life his principal business would be fighting. He was good at it, too, but after being taken prisoner in Mexico following an overly ambitious Texas invasion five years after Sam Houston's defeat of General Antonio Lopez de Santa Anna, and suffering wounds in three separate Indian fights as a Texas Ranger, he picked up the nickname "Unlucky Walker."

But when the Mexican government ordered the execution of every tenth man among the Mier Expedition prisoners, Walker drew a white bean. Seventeen of his fellow prisoners pulled black beans from the jar and ended up standing before a firing squad.

Back in Texas on September 9, 1843, after escaping from Mexican custody along with two other Texans—including the man who would one day deliver his eulogy—Walker soon signed up to ride with the legendary Ranger Captain John Coffee Hays. In the words of a contemporary writer, Texas was "then embroiled with the abrasions of the great Camanche [Comanche] race and the minor tribes strewn

Engraving of Samuel H. Walker made for *Graham's Magazine*
by A.B. Walter in 1848 from a daguerreotype by M.P. Simons.

along her northern frontier." Mindful of these "abrasions," in January 1844 the Congress of the Republic of Texas authorized Hays to organize "a Company of Mounted Gun-men, to act as Rangers."

Hays recruited his men in February and March and went to work on the frontier. All the Rangers were armed with a new weapon, originally purchased by the Republic for its navy: a five-shot revolver manufactured by a Connecticut gunsmith named Samuel Colt. Walker and the other Rangers soon got a chance to use the new pistols.

On June 8, 1844, near a creek in the Pedernales River watershed, at a point Hays later described as about fifty miles north of Seguin (no other communities existed in the area at the time), the Rangers—including Walker—tangled with seventy to eighty Comanche and Waco Indians. Hays reported some Mexicans also were in the party.

This is how Hays described the fight in his official report:

> After ascertaining that they could not decoy or lead me astray, they came out boldly, formed themselves, and dared us to fight. I then ordered a charge; and, after discharging our rifles, closed in with them, hand to hand, with my five-shooting pistols, which did good execution. Had it not been for them, I doubt what the consequences would have been. I cannot recommend these arms too highly.

The Rangers killed twenty-three of the hostiles, badly wounding another thirty. Hays lost one Ranger to Indian arrows with Walker, Robert Addison Gillespie, and another Ranger suffering wounds.

Walker later assessed the fight in this light:

> Col J C Hays with 15 men fought about 80 Comanche Indians, boldly attacking them upon

their own ground, killing and wounding about half their number. Up to this time these daring Indians had always supposed themselves superior to us, man to man, on horse . . . the result of this engagement was such as to intimidate them and enable us to treat with them.

This battle changed the history of the West. It marked the first time Rangers had been able to fight the Comanches with an effective close range weapon that did not have to be reloaded after each shot. In firing an estimated 150 rounds, Hays and his men shot 53 Comanches in a running battle. The Rangers had the frontier equivalent of the atomic bomb on their side.

The Comanches, though clearly at a disadvantage in weaponry, still were extremely competent in using their bows and arrows and lances.

"In this encounter," *Graham's Magazine* reported only a few years later, "Walker was wounded by a lance, and left by his adversary pinned to the ground. After remaining in this position for a long time, he was rescued by his companions when the fight was over."

Walker was taken to San Antonio, where he recovered from his wounds. Despite his close call, Walker stayed with Hays until the Ranger company ran out of funding. In 1845 he served in another Ranger company, this one led by Gillespie. On March 28, 1846, Walker was honorably discharged from the "Texas Mounted Rangers." But more rangering lay ahead.

When the United States annexed Texas, General Zachary Taylor led an army into the new state. Taylor set up camp at Corpus Christi and Walker, looking for action, organized a Ranger company to serve as scouts for the federal troops. When war broke out with Mexico in May 1846, the Ranger provided Taylor invaluable intelligence in scouting between Point Isabel, Taylor's supply point near the Gulf of Mexico, and Fort Brown, opposite Matamoros, Mexico. News accounts of Walker's early exploits so impressed the people of New Orleans, Louisiana, that they shipped him a fine horse, Tornado. Regular Army officers under Taylor passed the hat and gave him $1,000 in appreciation of his efforts. As the American army began its invasion of Mexico that summer, Walker joined a regiment of Rangers headed by Hays. After the Battle of Monterrey, Walker accepted a commission as captain in the Regular Army.

In the fall of 1846 Walker left the theater of war and traveled to Washington and New York to procure weapons and recruit men for his new unit, the First U.S. Mounted Rifles.

When Colt heard that Walker was in New York, he wrote a letter inviting the young combat veteran to his shop in

Patterson, New Jersey: "I have [heard] so much of [Col. Hays] & your [exploits] with the Arms of my invention that I have long desired to know you personally & get from you a true narrative of the [various] instances where my arms have proved of more than ordinary utility."

Walker replied to Colt three days later, writing on hotel stationery what amounted to a product endorsement letter of the first order. Walker recounted the already famous battle with the Comanches in the summer of 1844. In that fight, he continued, and in several "other Skirmishes . . . I can safely say that you deserve a large share of the credit for success." He concluded: "Without your pistols we would not have had the confidence to have undertaken such daring adventures."

When they met in person, Walker told Colt he would like to take some of his pistols back to Mexico. Colt said he had no more Patterson Colts in stock. Over a bottle of brandy—or two—the inventor of the five-shot revolver got invaluable feedback from a man who had used the pistol in life or death situations. A new weapon was born, a heavier, larger caliber revolver that would fire six shots instead of five. With those changes and a few other improvements, the revolver would be called the Walker Colt.

Before Walker headed back to Mexico in the spring of 1847, the U.S. Army had contracted with Colt to produce 1,000 of the new pistols at $25 each. Colt, who had gone bankrupt in 1842 and had no plant of his own, in turn contracted with Eli Whitney of cotton gin fame to manufacture the weapons.

In a gesture of appreciation for his design input, and the military contract, Colt shipped Walker two of the new six-guns in early October. On October 5 Walker wrote his brother: "There is not an officer who has seen them but what speaks in the highest terms of them and all of the Cavalry officers are determined to get them if possible."

Ironically, the awesome firepower Walker carried on his hips proved useless when the enemy had the advantage of shooting first from a concealed position. Four days after writing his brother to express his delight with the new pistols that bore his name, Samuel Walker would be dead. Though legend—and a sensationalized engraving made after his death—had him run through with a lance thrust by a leering Mexican soldier, Walker's death came from rifle fire.

By the fall of 1847 American troops had raised the stars and stripes over Mexico City and the Mexican government had collapsed with the resignation of Santa Anna as president. But the self-styled "Napoleon of the West" continued as commander of what was left of his army. On October 9 General Joseph Lane's force of some 1,000 men faced Santa Anna at Huamantla in what would be the Mexican general's last battle.

Walker led a vanguard of four companies of cavalry into the pueblo only to find themselves trapped in a counterattack personally led by Santa Anna. The captain was overseeing the movement of his men and two captured cannon into a walled churchyard when, as First Lieutenant Thomas Claiborne later recalled:

> I looked out of a side window and saw Walker with his right hand braced against the jam of the gateway, his left foot on the stone steps his left hand on his knee, looking to the right along the line of the wall. As I observed him, he fell, shot through from left shoulder blade to right nipple. In a few minutes he was dead.

Another Mexican War veteran later wrote that:

> "[A] . . . Mexican . . . from the window or housetop, fired and shot him through the head while

another one shot him through the breast from
behind a corner. He then fell in the arms of our
surgeon Reynolds."

Two versions of Walker's last words were circulated in
the years after the battle:
"I am gone boys. Never surrender! Never surrender!
Hand me my six-shooter!"
Or:
"I am dying boys, you can do nothing for me now. I'll
never see Texas again. Carry me back to San Antonio and
bury me with Ad Gillespie."
If the head shot came first, Walker probably did not
have time to say anything before he crumpled in death.
Still, Walker's admiration of and friendship with his old
Ranger comrade Gillespie, who had fallen on September
22, 1846, during the Battle of Monterrey, was well known.
Perhaps, mindful of his previous close calls in combat and
the sobriquet they had earned him, Walker had made
known his desire to be buried next to Gillespie in the event
he died in Mexico.
When the rest of Lane's soldiers reached the village, they
carried the day. One of those soldiers, Albert G. Brackett,
later described what happened after the fighting ended:

> ... Placing our killed and wounded in wagons,
> we marched out of the city. Captain Walker's
> body was carried back to the hacienda in a coach
> belonging to Catholic priests of Huamantla ...
> At the hacienda, the dead men of our com-
> mand, were laid out in a row in a room. I went in
> and there lay Walker with the dried blood in
> streams over his face, and his faithful slave David
> who was killed with him, not far off ... We had

no coffins, and a large pit was dug in which all the dead men were placed.

Captain Walker was buried alone.

Colonel F.N. Wynhoop presided at the funeral for the fallen Walker. An honor guard of Ohio Volunteers fired three volleys over his grave. Many of Walker's men had wept openly when they heard of his death, and they soon exacted a terrible revenge against, as one American soldier put it, "all Mexicans found with firearms in their hands." No prisoners were taken in a slaughter that in a later era would have resulted in mass court martials.

Walker was an American war hero. His death was national news, spreading across the world with the fastest clipper ships.

In January 1848 *The Illustrated London News* carried a story headlined, "The Late Samuel Hamilton Walker, Captain of the Texas Rangers." The author, shown only as "J.B.W." said of Walker:

> He was much esteemed, and beloved by those friends who watched, with intense anxiety, his gallant achievements, in the most hazardous undertakings; and now that he rests in the grave of a soldier, his name is respected, and his daring deeds admired, even by the war-made enemy.

The former Ranger's remains did not stay in Mexico much longer than the conquering army he had fought for. After the war, Walker's body was exhumed and shipped to San Antonio, where he was buried in the old City Cemetery.

Nine years later, plans were made to move Walker again, this time to the Oddfellows Cemetery, next to the grave of his old Ranger colleague Ad Gillespie. On April 21,

1856—San Jacinto Day—Walker's remains were reinterred amid elaborate ceremonies in the Alamo City.

Two monuments were put up. The larger of the two was an obelisk on a pedestal with the inscription "To the Memory of Capt. R.A. Gillespie & Capt. S.H. Walker by their Comrades in Arms." A smaller monument, to the rear of the larger one marked Walker's grave.

Mier Expedition veteran James Charles Wilson, one of the men Walker had escaped with from Mexico, delivered a stirring patriotic oratory at Walker's graveside. Since the event marked the twentieth anniversary of Sam Houston's decisive victory over Santa Anna at Buffalo Bayou, Wilson spent more time talking about the Texas Revolution than Walker and Gillespie. His speech was a classic stemwinder in an era where a long speech was considered far more important than a short one.

When Wilson did get around to the two Mexican War heroes, he used the still popular technique of contrasting and comparing the two Rangers.

"I think that Gillespie was more universally a favorite with his comrades," Wilson said, "while Walker was more devotedly loved by the few friends who thoroughly knew him, though both were highly esteemed and respected by all their associates, and most highly by those who knew them best."

Gillespie, he continued, was always "the cheerful comrade and gallant solider" while Walker "in ordinary service seemed quite an ordinary man; retiring, silent, mild, apathetic, and rather melancholy performing his duties merely from a sense of duty and not that he delighted in them; yet never failing to perform them well."

But when the ordinary became the extraordinary, so did Walker.

"Walker was rapid, untiring, terrible," Wilson said. "[In action] he seemed to change his whole character and appearance, and arise a new being, entirely superior to himself. Gillespie was brave. Walker had no sense of fear. Gillespie did not shun danger... Walker seemed to seek danger; to love it for itself."

Gillespie, Wilson said in assessment, probably would lose fewer men in a military campaign. Walker would take chances "which perhaps neither Gillespie nor any other leader in Texas, save himself, would attempt."

In the midst of flying arrows or singing lead, Wilson continued, "Gillespie was a brave man and a good soldier; Walker was a hero."

When he spoke those words in the Oddfellows Cemetery that antebellum spring day, Wilson probably thought Walker's memory would live on forever, at least as long as the bluebonnets bloomed in Texas. But in time, the old veterans who knew him or knew of his exploits died off. San Antonio continued to grow and the area around the cemetery became a rough part of town. The cemetery, as were other graveyards in the older part of the city, was neglected, vandalized, and virtually forgotten. Guidebooks to historic sites in the Alamo City did not even mention the Oddfellows Cemetery and the graves of Gillespie and Walker.

Though Walker never married, and thus had no direct descendants, he came from a proud family which traces its roots to the fighting clans of Scotland. Bilateral descendants were not pleased with how Walker's gravesite had been allowed to deteriorate.

In 1994 Tom Burks, then curator at the Texas Ranger Hall of Fame and Museum in Waco, was approached by one of the Walker relatives with a proposition.

"We were asked if we would accept the remains [of Walker] and look after them, and we agreed to," Burks later said. "We did not initiate the action... the Walker family did."

A San Antonio funeral home was contacted and arrangements were made to exhume Walker on January 7, 1995. A Waco funeral home agreed to store the Ranger's well-traveled remains pending a formal reburial of Walker's bones next to the grave of Ranger Captain Thomas H. Barron, the Indian fighter who established Fort Fisher on the west bank of the Brazos River in 1837. In the late 1960s the site of the Ranger post was chosen as the home for the Texas Ranger Hall of Fame and Museum.

The story broke about the intended move of Walker to Waco in the San Antonio *Express-News* two days before the planned exhumation. Workers had already removed some of the dirt between the two grave markers and covered the hole with plywood.

"This catches us in a situation that we are not able to cope with," Jim Ables, then president of the Former Texas Rangers Association, told the newspaper. The exhumation of Walker, he continued, would be "a loss to San Antonio and a loss to us."

Ables said the San Antonio-based association he headed would like to locate the graves of all former Rangers and mark them with a plaque, but "We just don't have the money now."

San Antonio historian Bob Dale was more direct in his comments on the proposed move of Walker's bones.

"The city of Waco has attempted to do this to the city of San Antonio on the sly," he said. "This is a part of San Antonio's history that Waco is stealing from us."

One of the people reading the newspaper that day was Lee Spencer of Spring Branch, president of the Alamo Defenders Descendants Association. She was horrified by a color photograph showing a mound of dirt between the graves of Gillespie and Walker because she knew something most other San Antonio residents did not: The dirt probably contained bone fragments of some of the men who died in the Alamo.

Spencer packed an overnight bag, grabbed a shotgun, and drove to San Antonio. (She later explained that the shotgun was only for personal protection in case she had to spend the night by herself at Walker's gravesite.) That Friday, one day before the planned exhumation, Spencer got a district judge to sign a fourteen-day temporary restraining order. The state judge set a hearing on a motion for a permanent injunction for January 20.

The petition filed with the court cited a 1906 San Antonio newspaper story in which August Bzensenbach, then City Clerk, said that as an eight-year-old in 1856 he witnessed the exhumation of ashes, bones, and bone fragments of Alamo victims from a site near St. Joseph's Church on what is now East Commerce Street. These remains, he said, had been buried near where the bodies of the Alamo defenders were burned by Santa Anna's soldiers. Bzensenbach said the remains were reinterred in 1856 "midway between the monuments to Capt. R.A. Gillespie and S.H. Walker."

All of this had nothing directly to do with Walker and his old Ranger partner, but Spencer's court action would delay the scheduled reinterment of Walker until an archeological survey of the site could determine if there were any Alamo victims buried between their grave markers.

Meanwhile, based on the publicity and a promise from the city of San Antonio that the gravesite would be cleaned up and protected, Walker's family decided to let the Ranger stay in the Oddfellows Cemetery next to his friend.

When the temporary injunction against disturbing the gravesite was lifted on January 16, at the request of Spencer and with the permission of the Walker family, San Antonio archeologist Waynne Cox and twelve volunteers from the

South Texas Archeological Society met at the cemetery to screen the disturbed dirt between the grave markers.

Archaeologists working at gravesite of Samuel Walker.
(Author's photo)

The archaeologists sifted an estimated seven yards of soil and then refilled the excavation made before the injunction was issued. They did not do any additional digging. "It was determined that no evidence of any remains from the funeral pyres were present, but several fragments of human bone were collected," Cox reported. A few coffin nails and a remnant of a gold epaulet also were found.

Cox said the bone fragments, which he believed to be Walker's because they showed no evidence of having been burned, were reinterred at the request of Walker's descendants. In a summary of the incident prepared for the

15

archeological association's February newsletter, Cox wrote: "As one old-time Texan observed, 'Walker was a Texas Ranger, if he'd awanted to go to Waco, he'd awalked.'"

Sources

Coburn, James. "Consent sought to sift for Alamo defenders." San Antonio *Express-News*, Jan. 9, 1995.

Cox, Waynne, letter to author, Oct. 28, 1996.

_____. Interview with author, Oct. 26, 1996.

Gonzalez, Susie Phillips. "Ranger's grave yields fragments." San Antonio *Express-News*, Jan. 17, 1995.

"Ranger Stays in Alamo City: Walker's Descendants Have Change of Heart." Fredericksburg *Standard*, Jan. 18, 1995.

Robinson, Fayette. "Captain Samuel Walker." *Graham's Magazine*, Vol. XXXII, No. 6, June 1848, pp. 301-303.

Rybczk, Mark Louis. *San Antonio Uncovered*. Plano: Wordware Publishing, Inc., 1992, pp. 271-272.

Sibley, Marilyn McAdams. Edited with an introduction by. *Samuel H. Walker's Account of the Mier Expedition*. Austin: Texas State Historical Association, 1978.

Spurlin, Charles. "Ranger Walker in the Mexican War." *Military History of Texas and the Southwest*, Vol. 9, No. 4, pp. 259-279.

Winingham, Ralph. "Ranger's relatives to relocate remains: Mexican War hero's grave to grace Waco." San Antonio *Express-News*, Jan. 5, 1995.

Young, Kevin B. letter to Glo Stuart, Sept. 18, 1979. Former Texas Ranger Association Collection, San Antonio, Texas.

Young, Kevin B. to Editor, *True West Magazine*, Oct. 10, 1979. Former Texas Ranger Association Collection.

"Legs" Lewis Loses a King-dom

Come sweet Alice, come with me,
Where the zephyrs wander free;
All, so fair and calm above,
'Tis the witching hour of love.

—From *The Katy-Did Song*, popular tune in 1855.

The King Ranch. Not only is it the largest ranch in Texas, it is one of the biggest spreads in the world.

This sprawling South Texas enterprise, made up of four separate divisions covering more than 825,000 acres, easily could have been known by two names instead of the short, single bold word brand it has, a famous name that rings of royalty and in fact does represent a Texas dynasty. But hyphenated nomenclature for this vast ranch would never be, owing to a bad case of roving eye afflicting the former Texas Ranger who, along with Richard King, was co-founder of the ranch. A Corpus Christi doctor prescribed a remedy of two measures of buckshot, administered sub-cutaneously. Unfortunately for the unwilling patient, the doctor's dosage brought on an acute case of frontier lead poisoning.

The amorous Ranger's story is a favorite of retired Ranger Casey King—no relation to THE Kings—of Kingsville. The King Ranch was in his district when he was a Ranger and he spent a lot of time on the ranch.

"Ever heard of 'Legs' Lewis?" King began. "I don't know if that was his given name or just a nickname that described one of his interests. If things had worked out differently, for 'Legs,' we'd probably be calling the King Ranch the King-Lewis Ranch."

Gideon K. Lewis was born in Ohio in 1823. By rights, his nickname—up to a certain point—should have been "Lucky," not "Legs."

Lewis grew up in New Orleans, where as a boy he worked as a newspaper printer's devil, melting lead type for reuse. When Texas was penetrated by a Mexican force in the spring of 1842, he enlisted in a volunteer company and went to help the nascent Republic defend itself against the country it had violently separated from only a few years earlier. When the Louisiana company disbanded, Lewis joined Ewen Cameron's volunteer outfit to help repel the invasion of Mexican General Adrian Woll.

In the fall of 1842 President Sam Houston reluctantly agreed to allow a Texas force to march on Mexico in retaliation. After barely a week in Mexico, during which time the Texans had taken the cities of Laredo and Guerro, Texian General Alexander Somervell ordered the army back across the Rio Grande. But nearly half the force, including "Legs" Lewis, wanted to keep fighting and refused to leave Mexico. Less than two weeks later, at the city of Mier, the Texans were badly defeated in their third fight. Taken prisoners, they were marched toward Mexico City. At Salado, 193 of the Texas invaders escaped, but 176 were recaptured, including Lewis.

Of those recaptured, every tenth man was ordered executed. Who would face the firing squad was determined by drawing. Those who fished a white bean out of a clay pot would survive. Anyone drawing a black bean would not. Lewis drew a white bean.

Released from Perote Prison in mid-September, Lewis returned to the relative civilization of what was then Texas' largest city, Galveston—a smaller version of New Orleans. There he managed a theater and worked for the Galveston *News.*

In June 1846, shortly after the Mexican War broke out, Lewis again went south. Along with pioneer Texas printer Samuel Bangs, he started a newspaper, the *Reveille,* in the Mexican city of Matamoros across from Brownsville. Lewis soon discovered that the First Amendment—the right of freedom of the press—did not extend beyond the Rio Grande. General Zachary Taylor, irritated by something in the paper, soon shut down Lewis and Bangs' sheet. Since there was a war on anyway, Lewis returned to his other avocation, fighting. He rode in Mexico with Samuel H. Walker's Texas Rangers and later reenlisted under Walter P. Lane, serving until the summer of 1848. He was

"Legs" Lewis survived the Mexican War only to die from a shotgun blast inflicted by a jealous husband.

wounded in action several times. When he mustered out, he was a captain.

Lewis spent some time in Brownsville after the war, but judging from surviving newspaper coverage of his activities, he was well known from New Orleans to Mexico and throughout South Texas. At various times he was in San Antonio, Corpus Christi, and on the border.

He seems to have liked to see his name in print and was concerned about his reputation.

On December 23, 1848, the Corpus Christi *Star* printed a long letter from Lewis in which he attacked a rumor that he had participated in a robbery in the Mexican town of Sabinas the previous July 17. Writing from San Antonio, where he said he intended to make his home, Lewis declared that he had spent three months and traveled hundreds of miles to clear his good name, collecting affidavits to show that he had been nowhere near Sabinas at the time of the raid. Why Lewis was so concerned about his rumored involvement in a criminal act in a foreign country was not evident in his letter. Some may have concluded from the published missive that he protested his innocence a little too vigorously to be entitled to full credibility in the matter. After all, he had been held prisoner in and later fought against Mexico. Few people on the Texas side of the river even cared what happened south of the border, and anyway Lewis was safe from prosecution as long as he stayed on Texas soil.

Lewis settled in Corpus Christi and went back to newspapering, starting a paper he called the *Nueces Valley* to compete with the *Star*. The two weeklies did not have a very large circulation base to fight over. The 1850 census found only 698 residents in Nueces County, and 149 of them were listed as illiterate. A year later, in 1851, Lewis ran unsuccessfully for a seat in the U.S. Congress.

Though sparsely populated, Corpus Christi had its share of boosters, the prime mover being Henry Lawrence Kinney, a Pennsylvania-born adventurer who had founded a trading post at the future site of Corpus Christi in 1839. He envisioned a glorious future for Corpus Christi as a seaport and trade center. Kinney ran ads in distant newspapers touting Corpus Christi as "the Naples of the Gulf" and planned a grand fair for May 1852 to promote the area and attract additional settlers.

"Legs" Lewis was a member of the committee Kinney put together to organize the fair. No doubt relying on the experience he gained as a showman when he managed a theater in Galveston, Lewis helped plan an event like nothing else Texas had ever seen. An agent was sent to Europe to tout Corpus Christi and the fair. Buildings were constructed. A band and a circus company would be imported from New Orleans. Kinney spent more than $3,000 to buy prizes to be presented to winning exhibitors.

When the fair opened, Kinney expected as many as 30,000 visitors to his version of Naples. Fewer than 2,000 people actually showed up, but they must have had a good time. From cockfights to lectures on philosophy, Kinney's fair offered something for everyone, including plenty of whiskey.

Among the visitors to the fair were some friendly Comanches and Lipan Apaches, but most of the Indians along and below the Nueces River were not interested in fostering Anglo growth in the area. Depredations were frequent, and the U.S. Army did not seem to be able to do much about it.

"All our rangers are either mustered out or are being mustered out of the service, which renders the frontier entirely exposed at this time," the *Star* had reported on July 26, 1848.

Indians and "bands of marauders" had practically free reign in South Texas, the newspaper lamented. The editorial writer proposed a solution: "A few companies of energetic rangers would regulate this on the whole line from the mouth of the Rio Grande to the Presidio, and leave American and Mexican citizens to pursue their avocations in quiet and safety."

At a town meeting in Brownsville on April 8, 1850, Lewis was selected to make a direct appeal to the U.S. Congress for assistance with the Indian problem. At the meeting, according to the *Rio Grande Sentinel*, "The horrors of Indian warfare were truthfully depicted by men who have been eye-witnesses ... "

The American military responded to Indian attacks with infantry, but what the frontier needed was experienced horseback fighters, the only force capable of dealing with "an enemy whose movements are as fleet almost as the winds!" as the *Sentinel* put it.

One man who had been pretty successful as an Indian fighter was Kinney. But he was not having much luck in business. The Lone Star Fair bankrupted him, and in the summer of 1852, Lewis bought Kinney's half-interest in the Corpus Christi *Star* and a tract of bayfront lots.

Lewis went back to rangering on September 1, 1852. He was named captain of a company of Texas Mounted Volunteers charged with patrolling the area below the Nueces. His service continued through March 14, 1853. Shortly after leaving the ranger company, Lewis turned his attention from Indian fighting to ranching.

Though the Lone Star Fair had proven a financial bust, it had one profound effect: Steamboat captain Richard King of Brownsville met Lewis at the event and struck up a friendship. As Tom Lea later wrote in his classic history of the King Ranch, "The exact circumstances that brought 'King's Rancho' to birth went unrecorded at the time ....

[But] before King's return to the Rio Grande, a ranching partnership evolved. Lewis probably proposed the original arrangements."

King and Lewis set up a fortified cow camp on high ground near a spring at the head of Santa Gertrudis Creek on an old Spanish land grant about 45 miles west of Corpus Christi. King bought the 15,500-acre tract on July 25, 1853, for $300—less than two cents an acre. On November 14 King sold Lewis an undivided half-interest in the land for $2,000.

Lewis bought some additional land nearby and in turn sold King half-interest. "In two years," Lea wrote, "their undivided partnership interests grew into a complicated set of ramifications." By the spring of 1854 King and Lewis had acquired 53,000 more acres of grassland. They expanded their ranch headquarters, purchased more livestock, and hired more cowboys. The first ranch account book reflects that $5.50 in ranch funds were used to buy Lewis a new pair of boots.

Rip Ford, like Lewis, had been a newspaperman and a Ranger. In fact, as a Ranger he and his men had camped at the future site of the King-Lewis Ranch headquarters. Ford later wrote of King and Lewis and their ranch: "The men who held it were of no ordinary mould. They had gone to stay. It was no easy matter to scare them." Lewis, as events would show, perhaps was too brave for his own good.

Lewis and King were only a few months apart in age. King was married to twenty-two-year-old Henrietta Chamberlain of Brownsville on December 9, 1854—a happy ending to a four-year courtship. Lewis continued as a bachelor, but as Lea wrote, the former Ranger captain "was notably gifted with the ladies. When Legs Lewis went to town, any town, his gifts did not go unused."

One of the ladies Lewis charmed was the wife of a Corpus Christi physician, Dr. J.T. Yarrington. Hoping he would be popular with the electorate as well, Lewis decided to run again for Congress. He began his second campaign in the spring of 1855.

Corpus Christi historian Frank Wagner said Lewis:

> was not particularly popular around Corpus Christi during his lifetime. Capt. King got along with him pretty well, but he was not generally liked. Captain King got along with nearly everybody.... [Lewis] was a rough and tough fellow...

As Lewis stumped for Congress and operated the ranch with King, in addition to overseeing retail and real estate interests in Corpus Christi, he apparently conducted an unpublicized and winning campaign for the affections of Mrs. Yarrington. The doctor, self-diagnosing the problem, intercepted letters "from both parties," which convinced him of "improper and familiar freedom" with Mrs. Yarrington by Lewis.

The doctor ordered his wife out of their house. At least that's one side of the story.

According to Wagner:

> Dr. Yarrington was a wife-beater, and caused his poor wife considerable grief. She did not have enough money to get a divorce (at the time, bills of divorce had to be passed by the Texas State Legislature). She persuaded a friendly lawyer to bring a civil suit against Dr. Yarrington, evidently on a *pro bono* basis and she obtained a large enough judgment to allow her to institute proceedings for a divorce. Meanwhile, she entertained former Texas Ranger... Lewis.

The Galveston *Journal* reported the next development: "They lived separately for a short time, when Lewis, hearing that Dr. Yarrington held in his hands such and such letters, came to the Doctor's office and demanded them. Yarrington refused to deliver them, whereupon a wordy altercation ensued, attended however by no serious result, and the parties separated."

Lewis went to the doctor two more times to demand the letters, the *Journal* reported.

"At the third visit Yarrington told him that 'if he came again it would be the last time.' [Lewis] called again, and prepared with a double-barrelled shot gun, Yarrington shot him down. The unfortunate man lived but a short time after the discharge."

The newspaper did not report whether Yarrington, mindful of the Hippocratic Oath, attempted to treat the mortally wounded Lewis as the gunsmoke still hung in the air. But the doctor apparently felt badly about what he had done. Three days after the shooting, he wrote the newspaper in Gonzales, reporting that he "had the misfortune to kill Capt. G.K. Lewis at Corpus Christi on the 14th inst." He had done so, he continued, because Lewis had "seduced Mrs. Yarrington from me and my children, then added insult to injury by continually coming to my house, and also trying to steal my children from me, and for trying to force from my possession certain letters, which I intercepted, addressed to my wife."*

Lewis was well known among Texas journalists, who were quick to lament his passing.**

"Capt. Lewis was a young man not yet 30 [he may have been about two years older], yet an old ranger, and his exploits had rendered him noted for courage and fearlessness," the *Texas State Gazette* in Austin remarked on April 28. The paper said the events which allegedly led to Lewis' death were "of a melancholy character, and we hope that it will be proved that he was not the reckless and licentious citizen which they would indicate. His gallantry in the field had won him the present of a sword, and it is unfortunate that the circumstances of his death should thus dim the lustre of so much patriotism."

The San Antonio *Herald* eulogized Lewis on May 2:

> But few braver men could be found where all were daring, than G.K. Lewis. Deeply imbued with a love of adventure and justifiable pride in Texan chivalry, he was always ready to defend the home of his adoption. While the mantle of charity is thrown over his errors, let us drop a tear to the memory of the boy-prisoner of Mier.

According to Wagner, not everyone shed a tear at Lewis' death. "Some of the boys in John Harney's Ruby Saloon are reputed to have given [Dr. Yarrington] a vote of thanks" after the shooting, Wagner wrote.

"Legs" Lewis had penned hard-hitting newspaper editorials and flowery love letters, but as a young man in the prime of life, the former Ranger had never bothered to write a will. Having no heirs, his complicated estate was settled in Nueces County's Probate Court. On July 1, 1856, Lewis' holdings were sold at public auction in Corpus Christi. King was high bidder on Lewis' interest in the Santa Gertrudis land and a friend of King's, clearly operating in the former riverboat captain's behalf, purchased Lewis' undivided half-interest in another large tract of ranchland owned with King.

The King-Lewis Ranch would from then on be known as just the King Ranch.

••••• ⭐ •••••

Sources

Briscoe, Eugenia Reynolds. *City by the Sea: A History of Corpus Christi, Texas, 1519-1875.* New York: Vantage Press, 1985, pp. 73, 91-92, 148.

Coker, Caleb. *The News from Brownsville: Helen Chapman's Letters from the Texas Military Frontier, 1848-1852.* Austin: Texas State Historical Association, 1992, pp. 346-47, 369.

Corpus Christi *Star*, July 26, 1848; Dec. 23, 1848.

Lea, Tom. *The King Ranch.* Boston: 1957, Vol. 1, pp. 91, 98-102, 104-105, 110, 120, 127, 131-136.

Rose, Margaret. Letter to author, Nov. 30, 1996.

Texas State Gazette. Austin, Texas, April 28, 1855.

Wagner, Frank. Letter to author, Nov. 14, 1996.

Notes

* Like "Legs" Lewis, Jacob and Anna Maria Yarrington came to Texas from New Orleans, where they had been married February 22, 1836.

They came to Texas in November 1848. They are listed in the 1850 Census as residents of Bexar County. Yarrington's age in 1850 was shown as 44, his wife, 29. The couple had two sons at the time. Later they had a third child, a daughter. On January 10, 1855, they moved to Corpus Christi. According to the divorce petition Mrs. Yarrington filed on February 27, 1855, she had been physically and verbally assaulted by her husband twice since moving to Corpus Christi. A jury trial resulted in the granting of a divorce on June 17, 1857, the panel finding that Yarrington used abusive language to his wife, "often charging her with having Negro blood . . . and applying to her the epithet of whore and strumpet." What happened to Jacob and Anna Maria and their children after the couple were divorced remains a mystery. None of them show up in the 1860 Census for Nueces County. As Margaret Rose, special collections librarian with the Corpus Christi Public Library put it, "it appears that Yarrington's one claim to fame is that he killed Lewis." It also is unclear what, if any, legal action was taken against Yarrington in connection with the Lewis slaying. The sheriff took him to Galveston immediately after the shooting, but it seems he may have been no-billed by a grand jury or acquitted.

** Lewis' grave has not been located. The oldest cemetery in Corpus Christi is Bayview (established in 1846) but records of burials from 1846 to 1896 have been lost. A published survey of readable grave markers in the cemetery does not list his name. If Lewis is buried there, his grave marker has been lost. It is remotely possible his body was shipped to New Orleans for burial.

Ropin' the Bear Was the Easy Part

Orders were orders, but Ranger Bob Tedford was in a fix.

Tedford and several other Rangers were scouting the headwaters of the Llano River, looking for Indians. In the early 1870s the Rangers were under strict orders not to fire a shot unless they came up on Indians. Whether this was a precaution to keep their presence on the Indian scout undetected or was a cost-saving measure to prevent the waste of ammunition on such frivolous things as target practice or hunting was not explained.

The shoot-only-at-Indians order must have been mildly irritating to young men on the frontier, but it was no big problem until, while crossing a hill, Tedford and his fellow Rangers rode up on a bear.

As fellow Ranger Frank G. Kaiser later recalled, "We asked ourselves, and each other, what to do with him. Someone suggested roping him—which no sooner said than we began to try it."

At first, the bear indignantly grabbed the rope at each toss and threw it off. But Tedford finally got out a big enough loop for the bear to run through. The Ranger quickly tightened the rope and had the bear roped around its middle.

Unfortunately, the Rangers had not discussed what to do with the bear once they had it roped. But the bear had his own ideas.

"Mr. Bear began to march off, dragging Tedford and horse towards a deep ravine," Kaiser remembered.

Thinking quickly, Kaiser and Ranger Henry Gray landed their loops around the bear, forcing the brute to pull against three horses and their riders. But even that did not hold the bear, who acted as if he had urgent business elsewhere.

Mindful of their orders not to shoot, the two Rangers dismounted and attacked the bear with their knives in the courageous manner of the late Davy Crockett. Not intimidated by the flashing steel, the bear was still winning the fight.

Finally, knowing their officers were waiting for them and that they might soon be encountering Indians, Gray pulled his revolver and violated orders. The shot echoed across the hills, audible for miles.

The bear went down.

"We got our ropes and scampered," Kaiser later wrote. "We expected a dishonorable discharge but the captain didn't say anything [and] we were careful not to let anything like that happen again."

Kaiser and his bear-roping colleagues had been sworn in as members of Company C, Texas Rangers, on August 25, 1870, in Austin. This was the result of an act by the Twelfth Texas Legislature, which on June 13, 1870, had passed a law providing for protection of the frontier. The act provided for the creation of twenty companies of Texas

Rangers, their operations funded by the issuance of $750,000 worth of bonds at seven percent interest.

Unfortunately, in an economy still suffering from the effects of the Civil War, not enough investors sufficiently trusted the reconstruction state government to buy the Ranger bonds. Only fourteen Ranger companies, including Kaiser's Company C, were raised. Kaiser left the Rangers on May 30, 1871, and by June 15 all of the Ranger companies had been disbanded for lack of funding. But Kaiser did collect his back pay, $430.

For the time being, the Indians—and the bears—were safe from the Texas Rangers.

★

Sources

Farrow, Marion Humphreys. *The Texas Democrats: Early Democratic History in Texas*. San Antonio: The Naylor Co., 1944, p. 51.

Kaiser, Frank G. A.E. Skinner, ed. *Reminiscences of a Texas Ranger*. Austin: Privately published, 1967, pp. 13-15, 37.

"He Said Rangerin' Was a Easy Life"

The ex-Ranger rode grimly into San Antonio in 1873, trailing the man he planned to kill.

Sixty-some years later, old and no longer bent on violence, he told an Amarillo newspaper reporter his story. The journalist typed up the fellow's recollections and ran it as a first-person piece with the author shown as Anonymous.

"I first saw the Texas Panhandle in 1872, when I was a Texas Ranger," the old man began. The captain of his company had "picked out six of us he didn't care whether got killed or not" to assist the U.S. Cavalry in the military campaign that finally forced the Comanches onto a reservation in Indian Territory.

This Ranger's job was to carry sealed orders for the military. The mission was considered so dangerous, the same orders were dispatched in the care of three Rangers on the grim assumption that one or more of them might not survive. "To say I 'saw' the Panhandle then ain't right," the old-timer said, "for I was ridin' nights [and] hidin' in the daytime" carrying orders.

"I ain't no hero and don't try to make me out none," he told the reporter years later. "All I knowed about the Panhandle was that it was d--- good country to stay out of."

The Ranger and his family had moved to Dallas from Georgia shortly after the Civil War, "General Sherman havin' burnt my daddy's farm and everything else he had."

In 1871, at 18, the young man went to Denton County and hired on with "Old Man" [Daniel] Waggoner as a cowboy "ridin' line." Everything went along fine, he recalled, until an Indian "squall" blew up. That's what settlers called an Indian raid, he told the reporter.

"I was drafted to go out and fight with the Rangers," he continued. "While I was out with the Rangers one of them lied to me and talked me into joinin' 'em."

The recruiter painted a pretty picture:

"He said Rangerin' was a easy life, lyin' around in camps, goin' to dances, and drawin' pay. There was no danger he said, as long as you didn't get too close to the Comanches, which was the only true thing he said."

The sales pitch was enough for the young Georgian, who enlisted for $12.50 a month, a horse, chuck, and ammunition. Rangers were required to furnish their own weapons. As a Waggoner cowboy, he recalled, he had been making $30 a month, "which is how much a damn fool I was."

Not only was his change in jobs earning $18 less each month, he quickly found that the "Rangerin'" life was not the leisurely outdoor experience he had been led to believe.

"We didn't go to no dances, except when the Indians was around, and then we danced lively gettin' away from 'em," he said. "The horses was crowbaits, and the grub was what you could shoot with the ammunition they furnished."

The cowboy-turned-Ranger spent the spring of 1872 criss-crossing desolate Indian country as a messenger for the military "during the last campaign against the Comanches."* He rode from Fort Sill to Camp Supply to Fort Sumner in New Mexico to Fort Concho in San Angelo, traveling at night and making cold camps to avoid Comanches, sometimes covering as many as fifty miles a day.

He quickly developed a finely honed set of survival skills on the desolate plains:

"I'd hide my horse in trees every day, givin' him a light feed of corn and lettin' him eat what grass he could reach. I'd ride away from water before sunup, figurin' if there was any Indians around they'd be camped on water. At night I'd ride toward where I figured where water'd be."

The redundancy of sending three Rangers with the same set of orders proved to have been an over-precaution. They all made it to Fort Concho in good health, if a little tired and saddle weary.

"When we got to Fort Concho we was afraid we'd have to come back up [to the Panhandle] with the soldiers, but we didn't. We reported back to our company, stationed at the time in Knox County," he said.

Discharged in 1873, the ex-Ranger lit out for San Antonio, gunning for the smooth-talking fellow who'd signed him up as a Texas Ranger.

"I looked around for him but found out he was gone to Kansas with a trail herd," the old Ranger told the reporter. "So I went to Kansas, but I couldn't find him."

While in Kansas he met up with a group of Texas trail drivers from Clay County and signed on with them as a cowboy again—at his old salary of $30 a month. Fortunately for the man who'd talked him into riding with the Rangers, the two never crossed paths again.

•••••• ⭐ ••••••

Sources

Anonymous. "'I Joined the Rangers'," Amarillo *News-Globe*, Aug. 14, 1938.

Sowell, A.J. *Rangers and Pioneers of Texas*. Austin: State House Press, 1991, p. 345.

Notes

* Following the Civil War, and prior to the creation of the Frontier Battalion in 1874, the state of Texas organized Ranger companies on an as-needed basis. They operated until the job was done or money ran out. The unknown Ranger quoted here never said who his captain was, but a year prior to the time he said he served as a Ranger, several members of Captain David P. Baker's company, which operated from November 1870 to July 1871, spent some of their time as couriers for the U.S. Cavalry.

  The company operated for a time in Wise County, not far from where Anonymous would later sign on.

  Anonymous' memory was faulty about this being the last campaign against the Comanches, though it was without question the beginning of the end. General Ranald Slidell Mackenzie would not have the Panhandle clear of these Plains Indians until 1875, at the conclusion of the so-called Red River War.

"Pass the Coyote, Please!"

The Rangers rode hard.

Indians, probably Comanches, had attacked settlers in Coleman County in West Texas and stolen a baby. Now the raiders were headed for the Red River and sanctuary on their reservation in the Territory.

Rangers trailed the Indians westward through Runnels and Coke Counties, and into Nolan County before making a grim discovery. About eight miles south of present-day Sweetwater, the Rangers reined in their horses when they came up on a blanket hanging from a tree. Inside the blanket was the abducted child, dead either from exposure or from having been smothered.

Finding the baby made the Rangers even more determined to catch up with the Indians, but they had pushed themselves nearly as far as they could. Neither the Indians nor their pursuers had taken time to hunt for food and they were getting hungry.

Their energy lagging from lack of food, and possibly believing the Rangers would give up the chase now that they knew the baby they had wanted to rescue was dead, the raiders stopped in what is now known as Mulberry Canyon. Finding no game, they were forced to kill and cook a colt.

Not seeing any buffalo or antelope, and needing all their horses to continue their pursuit, the Rangers turned in desperation to the only source of meat around: They shot a coyote and barbecued it.

Years later, Norman Rogers, one of those Rangers, recalled that his partner, a Ranger named Elkins, was so hungry he ate a half-quarter of the coyote.

Accounts do not reflect whether the Rangers enjoyed their meal, but the barbecued coyote gave them enough energy to take up the trail again.

More determined than ever to catch up with the Indians, the Rangers traced the renegades through Fisher and into Kent County. There they discovered that the Indians had made it across the Double Mountain Fork of the Brazos just before a flood crest swept downstream. The frustrated Rangers were trapped on the other side of the river as the Indians got away.

Ironically, the Comanches would have starved before eating a coyote. Some Plains Indians did eat dog meat—the Cheyennes considered coyote pups a delicacy—but not the Comanches. They realized that dogs were kissing cousins of coyotes, which were demigods to them. Killing and eating a dog or coyote would have been very bad medicine for the Comanches.

Anglos, on the other hand, had no religious convictions concerning coyotes, but, as far as is known, this 1874 incident is the only recorded account of coyotes being used as a food source by frontier Texans. On at least one other occasion, though, some Rangers got so hungry they were beginning to think about coyote as an entree.

Former Ranger A.J. Sowell remembered years after his Indian-chasing days an occasion when his company, sixty miles into the frontier beyond Fort Griffin, was running low of the essentials—flour, bacon, coffee, and tobacco. Not only that, an icy norther was blowing and the Rangers only had two tents. On top of all that, it was Sowell's turn to stand guard, hungry and cold, while the other men tried to sleep.

As Sowell sat alone in the cold, his rifle about to freeze to his hands, "It seemed as if all the coyotes and wolves that roamed these vast solitudes had collected, and taken their position on the hills around our camp, to serenade us with dismal howls and yelps."

Sowell did not write whether he thought about shooting some of the coyotes for breakfast, but it would be a violation of orders to shoot at one at night. The other Rangers might think Indians were attacking, and that could be more dangerous than an empty stomach.

Having some fresh coyote meat would not have done much good in this case. The Ranger did not have any firewood, either.

"Without wood; our provisions nearly exhausted; with no chance of getting any, unless we could eat coyotes, we were in a sad fix. Coyotes by the million," Sowell wrote.

The Rangers turned to head back to Fort Griffin, but it took another couple of cold, hungry days to reach the fort. At their next camping spot they did find wood for a fire and grass for their horses, but no game. They were living on coffee and half-rations of bacon. By the time they set up camp near Fort Griffin, they were not far from the point of cooking some coyote when a detail of Rangers rode in to the fort to get some fresh supplies.

J. Frank Dobie wrote a book on coyotes, but devoted only a footnote in that 386-page volume to a consideration of coyote as food. A lover of classic literature, Dobie began his note with an appropriate quote from Dr. Samuel Johnson, a man who enjoyed pondering the unusual, though he knew only of wolves, not coyotes: "It is not easy to fix the principles upon which mankind have agreed to eat some animals and reject others; and as the principle is not evident, it is not uniform."

The only mention Dobie found of men of European descent eating coyote meat on the Western frontier came in *The City of the Saints*, in which author Richard Burton reported that mountain men, when pickings were slim, resorted to coyote or wolf meat. "Wolf mutton" was "by no means bad," Burton wrote.

Far more common on the frontier as survival food was panther meat, which, Dobie said "is excellent." This reads like a conclusion Dobie reached from experience, though no further details were offered.

While acknowledging that "the meat of a grown dog-coyote is as rank as that of the rankest billy goat," Dobie continued, "when times get hard enough, any meat is good."

· · · · · · ⭐ · · · · · ·

Sources

Dobie, J. Frank. *The Voice of the Coyote*. Boston: Little, Brown and Company, 1950, p. 91.

Sowell, A.J. *Rangers and Pioneers of Texas*. Austin: State House Press, 1991, pp. 248-253.

Wade, Lelia Jeanette. *Our Community: Organization and Development of Nolan County*. Sweetwater: Watson-Focht Co., 1960, pp. 73-75.

Fight at the Haunted Lake

For ten days it had been raining, but now, as the Rangers rode a trail along the swollen Nueces, a full moon hung in the South Texas sky.

This was J.K. Fisher's country. Better known as "King" Fisher, the twenty-five-year-old outlaw was a stealer of cattle and horses and a killer of men. Earlier in the year, Captain Leander H. McNelly's rangers had arrested Fisher and nine members of his gang in Eagle Pass. But due to the "King's" reputation and local connections, he was released without prosecution.

Fisher was famous for the sign he supposedly put up at a crossroads near Eagle Pass, not far from his ranch, the Pendencia: "This is King Fisher's Road—Take the other."

The Rangers wanted another shot at Fisher—literally, if possible. McNelly was sick in San Antonio, fighting the consumption that would soon kill him. Now it was McNelly's sergeant, John B. Armstrong, who was after the flamboyant Fisher, a good-looking young cowboy gone bad who dressed like a dime novel outlaw. He wore a big Mexican sombrero, a buckskin jacket embroidered with gold, a red sash, pearl-handled, silver-plated six-shooters, and tigerskin chaps on his legs. Despite his regal getup, Armstrong figured the "King" needed deposing.

Near Carrizo Springs, the Rangers captured a known horse thief named Noley Key, a suspected member of Fisher's gang. Key told Armstrong that Fisher and his men had left the area, but with twenty-five men, Armstrong surrounded the house where Fisher and his gang had been staying. They found that the outlaw had been telling the truth. Fisher and his men were gone, having left their women and children behind.

The Ranger sergeant took Key some distance out in the brush and had a private conversation with him. When the sergeant came back, he told his men that some of Fisher's associates were camped at Lake Espantosa, only six or so miles away.

With Key as their guide, the Rangers rode as quietly as they could toward the lake. Despite whatever persuasive techniques Armstrong had used on the prisoner, Key talked pleasantly with one of the Rangers, who even gave him some tobacco.

Lake Espantosa was a small natural water hole on the old road from Mexico to San Antonio, a route used since the time Texas was a Spanish colonial province. How much border Spanish the Rangers knew is not recorded, so whether these men understood what *espantosa* meant is open to speculation. Judging from the later misspelling of the name in his report, Armstrong probably did not.

The lake was in the as yet unorganized Dimmit County. Savvy travelers and the few residents of Carrizo Springs, five miles from the lake, knew an eerie fog sometimes formed over its waters after dark. Tales floated around of waylaid travelers, alligator attacks, ghostly apparitions, and buried treasure dating back to the time of the Spanish *entradas*. The word *espantosa* was Spanish for "fearful" or "horrid."

The Rangers working their way toward this lake may or may not have heard Lake Espantosa's stories, but they were about to add to its legend. What was about to happen there on this moonlit night fit the name perfectly.

After about an hour, near midnight on the last day of September in 1876, the riders turned off the trail into an oak motte and dismounted. Armstrong ordered Rangers T.N. Devine and Thomas J. Evans to stay with the horses and guard their "guide."

Former Ranger John B. Armstrong

In a low voice, Armstrong addressed the remaining four Rangers—George Boyd, L.P. Durham, N.A. Jennings, and A.L. Parrot.

"Boys, we are going to capture those thieves or kill them."

The Ranger sergeant explained his reasoning for approaching the horse thieves with so few men: The outlaws were more likely to stand and fight, which was exactly what Armstrong wanted. "If they only fire on us, we can rush in on them and kill them all. Nothing but that will break up this gang."

Creeping through the brush, their carbines at the ready, the Rangers emerged into a clearing near the lake. A campfire flickered in the distance. Slowly they eased closer to the camp.

The Rangers got within 75 feet of the camp before one of the rustlers finally noticed the lawmen advancing in the shadows.

"Here they come, boys! Here they come!"

The outlaw giving the alarm snapped off a round in the general direction of the Rangers as his colleagues jumped to their feet and grabbed for their guns.

"Damn you," Armstrong shouted, "you'll shoot at an officer, will you?"

Muzzle blasts lit up the night like giant fireflies gone berserk. Inside four minutes, at least two hundred rounds were fired.

As Ranger Jennings approached the outlaw camp, one of the brigands emptied his six-shooter at the lawman, slinging a barrage of curses in his direction for good measure. A bullet from the Ranger's rifle took off part of the outlaw's jaw and he collapsed.

Thinking the outlaw was dead, Jennings looked for another target but of the four outlaws the Rangers had jumped, three were lying still on the ground. The fourth was locked in a knife fight with Boyd, which the Ranger soon won.

Jennings was bending over to look at the man he had killed when he saw his eyes move.

"For God's sake, gentlemen, don't kill me," the man moaned, pleading the same thing a second time.

"No one wants to kill you," Jennings said. "We are not murderers. Would you like some water?"

The Ranger picked up a tin cup near the campfire and went to the lake to fill it. Returning with the water, Jennings gently lifted the man's head and placed the cup against the man's smashed and bloody mouth. Besides the trauma to his face, the outlaw had been hit in the leg and maybe elsewhere.

Jennings thought the man was going to die, but he recovered—a bit of good fortune for the outlaw that the Ranger would later come to regret.

Armstrong's official report on the fight, which Jennings said he helped write, is not as action-packed as Jennings' account, which he published in a book more than twenty years after the one-sided gunbattle.

The sergeant, in a communication to Captain McNelly, reported that the confrontation occurred about midnight, and that his men were within twenty yards of the outlaw camp when fired on by two outlaws, not one as Jennings later wrote.

"We responded promptly [to the gunfire] and a lively little fight ensued, resulting in the death of three of them and the wounding of another in five places. We subsequently learned from the wounded man that there were but four of them in camp, the balance having left. They had received information of our coming and had left."

Armstrong did not name the outlaws in his report, but Jennings later listed their names as John Martin, alias

"One-eyed John," Jim Roberts, and George Mullen. The wounded man Jennings referred to only as McAlister.

The Rangers recovered about fifty stolen horses and the weapons the thieves had carried. Armstrong's report concluded with a casual reference to the prisoner who had guided the officers to the outlaw camp:

> "We were informed by the guard [Rangers
> Devine and Evans] that while we were fighting,
> the horses became excited, calling their attention
> from the prisoner, who took this opportunity to
> attempt to escape, was ordered to halt three times
> but kept running and was fired upon and killed."

Returning to the clump of trees after the fight, the Rangers found Key lying on his stomach, a bullet hole in his back.

Jennings later wrote that he felt badly about Key, but the Ranger managed to keep the man's death in perspective, at least the perspective of the Nueces River country in the 1870s: "He was not an important loss to the community, however, for he was a well-known horse thief."

King Fisher, though he missed the Lake Espantosa fight, had only five years to live. Fisher was shot to death on March 11, 1884, at the Variety Theater in San Antonio, along with Austin city marshal Ben Thompson.

Six years later, when Jennings was in San Antonio for the first time in years to do research for the book he planned on his Ranger experiences, McAlister—the horse thief who survived the Lake Espantosa fight—got wind of it.

"I've been camping on his trail for sixteen years," he told someone in an Alamo City bar, "and now I'm going to kill him for shooting my jaw off that night."

Jennings picked up on the threat, and though he no longer had a commission to carry one legally, he bought a six-shooter.

"Then I went on a hunt for McAlister," he wrote. "I thought I would know him, with his disfigured face, a good deal quicker than he would know me."

But the two men never met. McAlister apparently heard that Jennings was aware of his threat and was looking for him to discuss the matter. A survivor of one gunfight with Rangers, McAlister opted not to try for two out of two and disappeared.

······ ★ ······

Sources

O'Neal, Bill. *Encyclopedia of Western Gunfighters*. Norman: University of Oklahoma Press, 1979, pp. 107-109.

Jennings, N.A., Ben Proctor, ed. *A Texas Ranger*. Chicago: The Lakeside Press, 1992, (Reprint of 1899 ed.) pp. 255-266.

Smith, Diane Solether. *The Armstrong Chronicle: A Ranching History*. San Antonio: Corona Publishing Co., 1986, pp. 94-96.

Webb, Walter Prescott. *The Texas Rangers*. Austin: University of Texas Press, 1965, (Reprint of 1935 ed.) p. 296.

Corporal Wilson's Ride

Major John B. Jones sat in the Adjutant General's office on the first floor of the limestone Texas Capitol and read the hastily scribbled note one more time: "We are on our way to Round Rock to rob the bank ... for God's sake be there to prevent it."

The envelope containing the note, postmarked in Georgetown, had come that afternoon in the day's final mail delivery. It was mid-July 1878.

Jones weighed the situation and pondered his options: Round Rock was seventeen miles north of Austin in Williamson County, a distance that could be covered by horse in half a day or by train in less than an hour.

But Jones had only four Rangers in Austin, a small detachment camped outside on the Capitol grounds. The closest full Ranger company, Lieutenant N.O. Reynolds' Company E, was camped near San Saba, some 100 miles northwest of the capital city. Jones needed those men in Round Rock, but there was no telegraph line from Austin to San Saba, a remote county seat town on the western edge of settled Texas.

In the small office with Jones was Corporal Vernon Coke Wilson. The nephew of former Governor Richard Coke, Wilson—born May 1, 1857—was an educated young Virginian who Jones employed as his clerk. Wilson's relation to Coke, however, did not afford the young man any soft treatment. He spent each night in a tent with the Ranger privates and ate with them around their cook fire.

Turning to the corporal, Jones explained the situation. The notorious train robber Sam Bass and his gang were headed into Central Texas. An informant traveling with him, Jim Murphy, had written to warn Jones of Bass' next target.

"I want you to leave at once to carry an order to Lieutenant Reynolds," Jones said. "Save neither yourself nor your horse, but get these orders to Lieutenant Reynolds as quickly as possible."

Jones told Wilson to ride to Lampasas and catch the morning stage to San Saba. From there he could lease a horse for the three-mile ride to the Ranger camp.

The order to Lieutenant Reynolds was simple: Get to Round Rock fast. Jones would meet him there.

Corporal Wilson left the capitol and headed south on Congress Avenue to the livery stable where he kept his horse. That horse, boarded at the expense of the state, had been living easier than the corporal. Regular feed and not having been ridden in several months had the mount fat and out of shape.

Wilson saddled his horse and headed out as the sun faded behind the cedar-covered hills to the west. The Ranger rode hard, pushing himself and his horse. Thirty miles a day was considered a normal pace for horse and rider. Corporal Wilson covered sixty-five miles overnight. Overheated, the soft horse laid down and died shortly after the exhausted pair reached Lampasas.

But Wilson had made it in time to catch the morning stage for San Saba. Pulled by only two horses, the stage took all day to reach San Saba. From there, Wilson hired another horse and galloped the three miles to Reynold's camp.

When Wilson dashed into the Ranger camp, the men knew immediately something important was afoot. Despite approaching darkness, it was still hot. The Rangers had fed and tied their horses for the night and were cleaning up from their evening meal.

Quickly reading Jones' brief orders, Reynolds turned to Sergeant C.N. Neville: "Bass is at Round Rock. We must be there as early as possible tomorrow. Make a detail of eight men and select those that have the horses best able to make a fast run."

Thirty minutes later the Rangers were mounted, armed and ready. Reynolds had been ill and did not feel up to a hard horseback ride. The Rangers under Neville rode out at a fast trot and the lieutenant followed in a hack pulled by two mules. Wilson, sleepless for thirty-six hours, settled down on some blankets in the back and tried to get some rest as the wagon bounced along.

By early Friday afternoon, July 19, the Company E Rangers were just west of Round Rock. Bass' plan was to rob the Round Rock bank on the next day. Had it worked out that way, the Rangers and Wilson would have been in the middle of the situation. But Bass, Seaborn Barnes, and Frank Jackson had come into town Friday afternoon to get some tobacco and look the place over.

A Williamson County sheriff's deputy, who may or may not have known who Bass was, saw he was carrying a pistol, attempted to disarm him, and the fight was on. When the smoke cleared, both the deputy and outlaw Barnes were dead, another deputy was wounded and Bass was mortally wounded. The Rangers found him the following day and he died a day later.

The all-night ride that killed a good horse and left a young Ranger dead tired had not been entirely in vain. Though the Company E Rangers missed the shootout by ten minutes or less, it was Sergeant Neville who found Bass the next day. And the large number of Rangers in town had a cooling effect on mob sentiment toward Bass, who had gunned down a popular local officer, himself a former Ranger.

Like many another Texan on one side or the other of the law, Wilson eventually drifted west. Based on his reputation as a Texas Ranger, the Virginian became a deputy U.S. marshal in 1885, serving in the New Mexico and Arizona territories.

The graves of two outlaws, Sam Bass and Seaborn Barnes, lie near each other in a corner of the Round Rock Cemetery. (Author's photos)

Five years later, working as a special officer for the Southern Pacific Railroad, Wilson was sent to California to track down whoever was responsible for a series of train robberies in the San Joaquin Valley. Starting in 1889 and continuing into 1892, there had been four holdups. The robberies caused much excitement, but no one knew who the robbers were until their final holdup, when Chris Evans and John Sontag were identified.

Wilson and other members of a posse caught up with Evans and Sontag's brother George at Sampson's Flat in Fresno County on September 13, 1892. The ex-Ranger and another officer died in a gunbattle with the robbers. Reinforcements soon arrived, and a standoff continued for eight hours. Both outlaws were seriously wounded and finally gave up. Sontag soon died, but Evans recovered and went to prison for life.

The railroad shipped Wilson's body back to Tucson, Arizona, where he was buried in the old Tucson Cemetery. Bodies from that cemetery later were reinterred at Evergreen Cemetery. The exact location of Wilson's grave is no longer known.

...... ✪ ......

Sources

Boessonecker, John. *Badge and Buckshot: Lawlessness in Old California*. Norman: University of Oklahoma Press, 1988, p. 200.

Browning, James A. *Violence Was No Stranger*. Stillwater, OK: Barbed Wire Press, 1993, p. 278.

Gillett, James B. *Six Years With The Texas Rangers*. Lincoln: University of Nebraska Press, 1976, (Reprint of 1925 ed.) pp. 63, 119-123.

_____. "Vernon Wilson Was A Texas Ranger," *Frontier Times*, Vol. 6, No. 7, April 1929, pp. 257-258.

O'Neal, Bill. *Encyclopedia of Western Gunfighters*. Norman: University of Oklahoma Press, 1979, p. 105.

The Killing of "Caige" Grimes

"**I**f I killed Grimes it was the first man I ever killed," Sam Bass said as he lay fading in and out of consciousness on a blood-soaked cot in a shed next to the Hart House in Round Rock.

Among those gathered around the dying outlaw were C.P. Cochran, a doctor who knew he could do nothing to save Bass' life, and Major John B. Jones, commander of the Frontier Battalion of Texas Rangers. At least one other Ranger was in the room at all times to write down anything Bass said.

Elsewhere in Round Rock, a twenty-four-year-old woman grieved the loss of her husband and the father of her three children—Williamson County sheriff's deputy and former Texas Ranger Ahijah W. "Caige" Grimes.

The young lawman was not the first Grimes to die in the service of Texas. His uncle, Albert Calvin Grimes, fell defending the Alamo. His grandfather, Jesse Grimes, was a signer of the Texas Declaration of Independence.

Born in Bastrop on July 5, 1855, Ahijah W. Grimes was named for his mother's father, Ahijah M. Highsmith.

A creased, time-splattered likeness of young Caige Grimes shows him as a solemn, good-looking youth—even featured and clean-shaven.

On March 2, 1874—Texas Independence Day as well as his bride-to-be's twentieth birthday—Caige married Lottie A. Lyman in Bastrop.

Like many Texas men of his time, Grimes was a Mason. He belonged to Gamble Lodge 244 in Bastrop. Although the original lodge records were destroyed in a fire in 1862, Grimes' father was a charter member of the lodge. Caige was initiated March 10, 1873, passed on April 26, and raised on May 14. He and his brother Masons met the fourth Sunday of each month on the second floor of a building at Chestnut and Pecan Streets.

A printer by trade, Grimes decided to give up ink and hot-lead type and strap on a gun in the name of the law. He came by his interest in law enforcement naturally enough. His grandfather was a well-known Indian fighter and his mother's younger brother was a Ranger who took part in the 1840 running battle with Comanches at Plum Creek.

In 1874 the twenty-three-year-old Grimes was serving as city marshal of Bastrop, earning $40 a month plus fees. For example, in April that year Bastrop city aldermen approved payment of fifty cents in addition to his monthly salary to Grimes for "removing dead hog." Later that month, the aldermen passed an ordinance declaring that city taxes were due by May 1. If taxes were not paid by that time, the amount owed would be doubled. "City Marshal Grimes will serve you in this line with pleasure," the Bastrop *Advertiser* reported.

If Grimes was involved in investigating any major criminal cases while serving as city marshal, the Bastrop newspaper was silent on the subject. All the action seems to have been taking place at the nearby Bastrop County community of McDade, where a murder and the hasty lynching of the alleged perpetrator were reported on May 9, 1874. The killing was the culmination of a small difficulty that started when a man tossed a dirty sock into the skillet of a railroad worker who was preparing his meal.

In Bastrop, meanwhile, the city aldermen were passing an ordinance delineating the borders of the "hog district," an area of the city in which swine no longer would be allowed to roam free. Grimes collected his usual salary in June, plus $3 in fees and $1.50 for stationery. In November 1874 he collected fines from six offenders totaling $26. That seems to have been an average month for fines.

Grimes ran for city assessor and collector against two other candidates in the municipal election of January 1875. He won office handily, receiving 131 votes. One opponent got 40 votes, the second only 23. "The municipal election of Monday last was the most exciting since the days when radicalism reigned supreme in our midst," the Bastrop paper opined.

The same month he won elective office, Grimes was installed as Steward of his lodge by Deputy Grand Master Joseph D. Sayers, a future governor of Texas.

Apparently holding elective office as city assessor-collector did not disqualify Grimes from being city marshal, an appointive position. He continued to draw his salary as marshal. In fact, in March his pay was raised to $50 a month.

Grimes decided to seek a county-wide office later that year. The January 1, 1876 issue of the Bastrop *Advertiser* reported: "We are authorized to announce A.W. Grimes as a Candidate for the office of Assessor of Taxes for Bastrop County." This time he must not have been successful in his campaign. No back issues of the *Advertiser* exist for the rest of 1876 to provide election results, but a list of Bastrop County officials shows that someone else held the office in 1876-77.

By then Caige and Lottie had two children: Elizabeth, born January 31, 1875, and Benjamin Lyman Grimes, born May 10, 1876.

On September 21, 1876, the Bastrop County Commissioner's Court appointed Grimes as Precinct 6 Constable. He put up his bond and was sworn in on October 25.

After working as a constable for a year, Grimes set out to join the Texas Rangers. When his enlistment papers were filled out, Grimes was described as being twenty-seven years old, five feet ten inches tall with dark hair, a dark complexion, and gray eyes. He was appointed as a Ranger private on September 20, 1877, joining Company A of the Frontier Battalion.

His captain was Neal Coldwell, a Ranger described by historian Walter Prescott Webb as "an active and zealous man who showed a disposition to discipline and control his men."

A contemporary of Coldwell, Ranger lieutenant (and later captain) Dan W. Roberts said, "He was more than any captain in ability, and one of the best officers in the service."

Grimes—whose younger brother, Albert, had joined the Rangers only nineteen days before he had—rode with Captain Coldwell and his men for two months and twenty-three days. At the time Company A was assigned to the lower Rio Grande border, from Eagle Pass on south. This was a period when the Rangers were preoccupied with a double threat to the citizens of Texas—hostile Indians and daring outlaws. No official records survive which relate any specific incidents in which Grimes was involved as a Ranger, but his service under a man like Captain Coldwell doubtless was not boring.

Neither do records indicate why Grimes chose to leave the Rangers so soon after enlisting, although short enlistments were not unusual. Perhaps he missed his wife and family. Maybe he did not like serving down along the border, where Texas Rangers were not exactly popular with all the local citizens. He mustered out in Starr County on the Rio Grande, where Sergeant G.W. Arrington completed paperwork showing Grimes was due $17.29 from the State of Texas for his services from December 1-13.

Following his honorable discharge from the Rangers late in 1877, Grimes, with his wife and two children, moved to Round Rock in Williamson County. Their third child, Mabel (Mae) was born in 1878.

Round Rock was enjoying a boom as a railroad town, and Grimes' cousin, Henry Albert Highsmith, operated a livery stable there. Since Grimes had gained experience handling money as an office holder in Bastrop, he went to work for Miller's Exchange Bank—the same bank that would lure the robber who would end his life.

Knowing of Grimes' previous experience as a city marshal and Ranger, Williamson County Sheriff Sam Strayhorn asked the young man to handle law enforcement duties in Round Rock as a deputy sheriff.

While Grimes seems to have been living a quiet life as a respectable family man, a man one year younger than he was building a different sort of reputation.

Sam Bass, orphaned as a young child, drifted into Texas from Indiana in 1870. For a while he did honest work around Denton in northeast Texas; he was even on the payroll of Sheriff W.F. "Dad" Eagan for a time—but only as a hired hand, not as a deputy sheriff as some writers have claimed. Bass was never a lawman.

He soon took up horse racing and gambling. He was a good judge of horseflesh and raced his Jenny—the famous Denton mare—at a number of small tracks until too many people realized wagering against her was a sucker's bet. He sold Jenny in San Antonio, did some cowboying, helped push a herd up the Chisholm Trail, lost a large part of his pay to Deadwood card sharps, tried his hand at running a freighting operation, and went bust after buying a mine in Dakota Territory. By 1876, as Bass was to say on his deathbed, he "went to robbing stages."

He was ludicrously unlucky.

On September 18, 1877—two days before Grimes joined the Rangers—Bass and the Joe Collins gang robbed a Union Pacific train in Big Springs, Nebraska. They netted $60,000 in freshly minted $20 double-eagle gold pieces. Bass was inclined toward generosity and quickly blew much of his $10,000 share of the loot.

By early 1878 Bass had returned to Texas. If he had quit after the Big Springs job he might have merited his description as a "Robin Hood." Many Americans believed the big railroad corporations were far too powerful and few Texans felt any greater love for the incumbent Republican President Rutherford B. Hayes than for his predecessor, U.S. Grant. Let the railroad and the government lose their gold, many thought.

Inside of two months, Bass and his gang pulled four train robberies in North Texas—at Allen, Hutchins, Eagle Ford, and Mesquite—all within a twenty-mile radius of the Dallas area. This was hitting too close to home. Not only did the brigands rip open registered mail for whatever greenbacks they might contain, but they robbed money and gold watches from male passengers and railroad workers.

The robberies gained the outlaws little in the way of hard cash but a lot of bad press. Hastily formed posses were enthusiastic but unsuccessful. Irate North Texas citizens demanded help from the Rangers.

Now Bass no longer felt safe hiding in the dense thickets around Denton. He and his companions started riding south, stopping in Waco to look over the three banks in that bustling cotton center on the Brazos River. They concluded the city was too big, too busy, had too many

This may be a previously unpublished photograph of the outlaw Sam Bass. It was found by the author stuck inside a privately published book in the mid-1980s. On the back it says, "Sam Bass Picture donated by Stephen Anderson."

armed men, and lacked a straight-away escape route. The streets were so dry and dusty that Bass knew lawmen would have no trouble tracking him if he hit a bank there.

Bass was pleased, however, that he was able to walk around the streets openly without being recognized. But he decided to take his bank business elsewhere.

He was well known in the Denton area where he had lived, worked, and raced his sorrel mare. But his face was not familiar to many people outside the North Texas area. Even after he had become a wanted man he had on occasion encountered posses and, identifying himself as a bounty hunter, had actually ridden along with them a short way in search of himself.

In Waco Bass tossed down his last $20 gold piece. He and his men mounted and rode on—through Belton and then Georgetown, heading south roughly along the route of the Chisholm Trail.

Meanwhile, Lieutenant (later Captain) Junius "June" Peak had been ordered by Governor R.B. Hubbard to form a company of Rangers whose specific assignment was to find Sam Bass. But as is often the case in law enforcement, more is involved in catching a criminal than simply following a set of hoofprints. It helps to have an informant.

On July 17, 1878, Major John B. Jones, commander of the Frontier Battalion of the Texas Rangers, received a hastily scrawled note from Jim Murphy, a young man accused of helping Bass hide out in Denton County who had been persuaded to provide information in exchange for immunity from prosecution or a lighter prison sentence. The note read: "We are at Georgetown on our way to Round Rock to rob the bank, the railroad or to get killed, so for God's sake be there to prevent it."

Jones had been expecting a message. He sent orders for Lieutenant N.O. Reynolds' Company E to head for Round Rock, but they were seventy-five miles away. The major also dispatched the only three Rangers he had in Austin —Richard C. "Dick" Ware, Chris Conner, and George Harrell—to ride to Round Rock.

The following day, with former Ranger Maurice B. Moore, then working as a Travis County sheriff's deputy, Major Jones took the train to Round Rock.

The major told his men to keep a low profile and await developments. Moore and Grimes were told to keep on the lookout for strangers. The deputies may or may not have been specifically warned about Bass, although author Wayne Gard wrote in his 1936 book *Sam Bass*: "He [Jones] took into his confidence several Round Rock citizens, including the banker, P.G. Peters . . . and A.W. Grimes, deputy sheriff."

Bass and his gang had been in and around Round Rock almost a week, camping outside town. The informant among them eagerly volunteered to hang around town, buy feed for the horses, and keep an eye out for anyone on their backtrail. Murphy must have been weak with relief when his pals consented.

On the afternoon of Friday, July 19, Bass, with Frank Jackson and Seaborn Barnes, rode into New Town, the portion of Round Rock that had developed near the recently laid railroad tracks, to look over the bank and assess the getaway route. This was to be the gang's first bank holdup and Bass did not want any mistakes. Seeing a store next door to the bank in question, the three men walked in. Bass wanted to buy some tobacco.

These were men who had actually ridden with posses looking for Bass and his gang without being recognized. Published purported likenesses of Bass show a broad open countenance, clean-shaven except for the handlebar moustache in vogue at the time.

On their long ride south from Denton the gang had stopped in towns along the way for visits to the barber shop and changes of clothing. They intended to pass themselves off as cattlemen while they hung around Round Rock. There is no evidence to suggest that Bass and his two associates behaved in a rowdy or suspicious manner. Nothing in their demeanor or attire identified them as would-be bank robbers.

Calling attention to themselves was the last thing they wanted to do.

Moore watched the three strangers ride into town, dismount in an alley, and walk around to Henry Koppel's two-year-old general store on East Main Street. As one of the men stepped down off his horse, Deputy Moore thought he detected the bulge of a pistol under his coat.

The Travis County deputy walked along the street to meet up with Grimes. After explaining to him that he believed one of the three men was armed, Moore said, "Down in Travis County I usually take them [guns] away."

"Well, in Williamson County I do the same," Grimes replied.

The two officers walked to the store and confronted the three men. Grimes patted Bass' coat and said, "Young man, give me your gun."

The lawman was simply doing his duty. Even in the turbulent 1870s, it was illegal in Texas to carry a pistol. The outlaws could have surrendered their guns quietly, paid a small fine if a complaint were filed, picked the weapons up again when they left town, and kept riding to the next town and the next bank.

Instead, Bass over-reacted and his two men went along with it.

"You can have both of them," Bass replied, pulling his two six-guns and firing instantly. Barnes and Jackson drew guns from their saddlebags and also opened fire at Grimes.

Hit five times, the former Ranger stumbled backward and went down. Most accounts of the shooting say that Grimes never had a chance to draw his gun. One version, though, holds that in his final instant of life he reflexively fired two shots before falling dead. If he did get off two rounds, he did not hit Bass or his cohorts.

In the same action that killed Grimes, Deputy Moore was shot in the upper part of his left lung. Thick gunsmoke obscuring his vision, the deputy fired toward the three men. The outlaws continued firing at him as they ran from the store. Moore hit Bass in his gun hand, blowing off two fingers.

Moore, operating on adrenaline, emptied his pistol and ran toward Highsmith's livery stable to fetch his saddle gun. A physician, Dr. A.F. Morris, seeing Moore's bloody chest wound, warned him he might die if he did not take it easy. Moore handed his rifle to a bystander and allowed the doctor to treat his wound.

A one-armed Round Rock citizen, J.F. Tubbs, ran to the scene, picked up Grimes' pistol, and blazed away at the fleeing bandits. Highsmith, Grimes' cousin, tried to get off a shot but a cartridge jammed in his rifle.

Hearing gunfire, the Rangers rushed to the scene, firing on Bass and his fellow outlaws as they tried to ride out of town. Major Jones ran over from the telegraph office at the railway station two blocks away and took aim at the outlaws. Dick Ware had been in a barbershop when he heard the shots and came running with lather still on his face.

A Ranger—Harrell or Ware—took careful aim at Seab Barnes and dropped him with a head shot. Bass, mortally wounded by a shot from another of the Rangers, made it into the brush outside of town only with Jackson's valiant help.

Jackson tended Bass' heavily bleeding wounds as best he could. Realizing he was done for, Bass urged his loyal friend to ride away and save himself.

Lieutenant Reynold's company of Rangers rode into Round Rock ten minutes after the shooting and joined in the search for Bass. They found the wounded outlaw the following day, Saturday, July 20—the day Bass had intended to rob the bank. He was taken to town, where he lingered a day and night on a cot near the Hart House. Dr. C.P. Cochran treated the outlaw's wounds.

According to legend, one of Grimes' brothers—Ranger Albert Grimes—reached Round Rock in time to keep vigil outside Bass' improvised hospital room as long as the outlaw clung to life, vowing that "he will never leave this building alive." A family letter written to Dallas newspaper columnist Frank X. Tolbert in 1969 supports this story.

The same letter also verifies a brief note in the Lampasas *Daily Times* for July 27, 1878:

"Sam Bass at least died game, and cheated the gallows. This thought must have been some consolation to him as he lay dying, looking at the carpenters who were making his coffin."

Bass died Sunday afternoon, July 21, on his twenty-seventh birthday.

Whether Caige Grimes knew what he was getting into when he confronted the three outlaws will never be known for sure.

In his account of the gunfight, Walter Prescott Webb wrote that Major Jones had "let Deputy Sheriff Grimes . . . and Albert Highsmith into the secret" that Bass and his gang were expected in Round Rock.

But in the summer of 1927, when he was eighty-four years old and probably the last surviving witness of the gunfight, Highsmith told a reporter for the Austin *American-Statesman*: "He [Grimes] had no idea they were notorious bandits, and was expecting no trouble whatever. Probably that was why he was so free in his approach of the desperadoes."

The Williamson County *Sun*, the closest newspaper to Round Rock at the time of the shoot-out, supports Highsmith's contention in its coverage of the shooting.

In a story beneath a one-column headline that said simply "The Tragedy in Round Rock," an anonymous reporter wrote that Grimes and Moore "without knowing who the strangers were, but having reason to believe that one of them at least was armed, followed them into a store . . . . "

It seems logical, however, that Major Jones, having ridden the train to Round Rock with Deputy Moore, would have confided in Moore and perhaps Grimes, whom he had personally enrolled into the Rangers less than a year earlier. Surely, if Moore had known what was afoot, he would have told Grimes even if Jones had not. After all, both of them were ex-Rangers.

No matter what he had known, Grimes died trying to uphold the law.

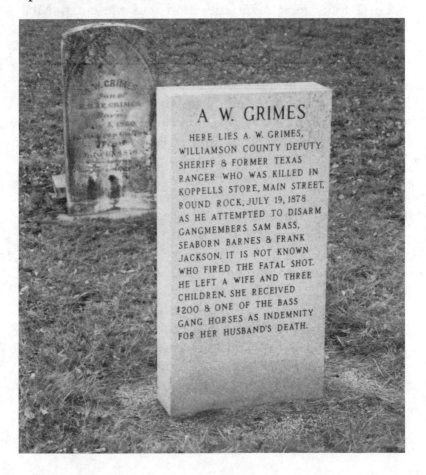

"He was an excellent officer and favorably known, as shown by the honors paid him at his funeral this evening," the Galveston *News* said of Grimes on July 21.

Less than a week after the shooting, the story in the Williamson County *Sun* said Grimes' family deserved part of any rewards that had been posted by the state and the railroads for the Bass gang.

"If these rewards can be obtained we hope that the family of Deputy Sheriff Grimes, and Deputy Sheriff Moore, one of whom lost his life . . . will be remembered liberally," the newspaper said.

Local folks took up a collection and presented Mrs. Grimes $200. Major Jones gave the young widow a horse that had belonged to one of the outlaws.

The day Bass died, Grimes was laid to rest with full Masonic honors in the Round Rock Cemetery. In a different part of the graveyard, Seaborn Barnes was buried without ceremony. Later, Bass was buried next to Barnes.

The young peace officer's simple tombstone is marked: "Gone But Not Forgotten." Unfortunately, for many years A.W. "Caige" Grimes *was* virtually forgotten. Dozens of books and magazine articles have been written about Bass, but the role of Grimes in the story gets a scant—and often inaccurate—paragraph or two at most in the various books on the outlaw.*

Sam Bass, whom numerous writers have glamorized as "the dashing Robin Hood of Texas," is the one who has not been forgotten.

The same writers who glorified Bass have vilified Murphy, calling him a coward, a betrayer, and a Judas for turning against the members of his own gang. Yet Murphy was never a member of the gang, never took part in the train robberies. His only crime—the one for which he had been arrested—was harboring a criminal. Murphy and his father had lived near Bass' thicket hideaway in Denton

County. They kept lookout and tipped the gang when lawmen got too close.

Jim Murphy would never have been riding with Bass, Barnes, and Jackson had he not been forced to do so in order to have his innocent father released from jail.

How Caige Grimes' life might have turned out if he had not confronted Sam Bass that hot July afternoon can be only a matter of speculation. He clearly was interested in holding elective office and eventually might have run in Williamson County. If Bass had meekly handed over his pistol when asked—and had he been recognized for who he was—Grimes might well have been able to win election as sheriff on the recognition it would have afforded him.

His brother, Albert Grimes, stayed with the Rangers for a decade and took part in several gunfights. He prevented a bank robbery in Wichita Falls in 1884 by killing one of the robbers. In 1887 Ranger Grimes and Ranger Walter Durbin killed an outlaw wanted for the murder of a South Texas sheriff.

Only when his company was disbanded did Albert Grimes leave the Rangers. He worked for a time as a federal river guard (precursor of the Border Patrol) on the Rio Grande and later moved to San Antonio, where he worked as a guard at Bexar County convict-labor camps. He died of typhus on August 4, 1908, at the age of 53.

Long after the death of Albert Grimes, one last aspect of the Sam Bass affair remained unresolved.

Frank Jackson, who had last been seen leaving the gravely wounded Bass outside Round Rock as the lead flew around them, was indicted for A.W. Grimes' murder.

In the late 1920s famed Texas Ranger Captain Frank Hamer got a lead on Jackson's location. Jackson had changed his name and was living a law-abiding life in another state, probably New Mexico. Hamer, who believed it was Bass who had killed Grimes, almost had it arranged for Jackson—then an old man in his eighties—to be brought back to Texas. Hamer expected the murder charge against Jackson would be dropped, but he wanted to prove that the Texas Rangers always get their man. Someone leaked the story to the press, however, and Jackson, fearing a trap, disappeared again. And forever.

Since the general sentiment was that Bass had killed Grimes, the murder indictment against Jackson was dropped in December 1936. Jackson—who surely would have hanged had he been caught any time soon after Grimes' murder—presumably died of old age.

Sources

"The Killing of 'Caige' Grimes" is largely based on the author's unpublished monograph of the same name.

Notes

*   On Jan. 14, 1993, the new city of Round Rock Police Headquarters at 615 East Palm Valley was dedicated in honor of "Caige" Grimes. A plaque on the building reads: "Dedicated to the memory of A.W. Grimes Jr. Deputy, Williamson County/Shot and killed in the line of duty by a common criminal/July 19, 1878."

Ranger, Texas

The Texas Rangers most likely are the only law enforcement body in the United States—probably the world—to have a city named in their honor.

Most communities are named after a local geographic feature, a person, an ethnic group, or animal. But southwest of Fort Worth, just off Interstate 20 in northeast Eastland County is Ranger, Texas, a town named for the Texas Rangers. And down in Cameron County, in the lower Rio Grande Valley, is a small community called Rangerville. Nowhere in Texas, though, has there ever been a community named Police, Sheriff, FBI, Royal Canadian Mounted Police, or Scotland Yard.

Indians—and not place names—were on the minds of the Rangers who made their camp in a valley on a branch of Palo Pinto Creek in what is now Eastland County, more than two decades before the area was settled.

The first Rangers to camp near the future site of the city that would one day commemorate their presence were men under James Buckner (Buck) Barry in 1859 and 1860.

This information came to light not in any official state records, which are sketchy for this period, but from the yellowing pulp pages of *Frontier Times* magazine. The October 1931 issue of the magazine carried a story on the eleventh annual Texas Ex-Rangers reunion, held the previous summer at Eastland.

An Eastland man, Barry Hargus, though not a former Ranger, went to the reunion and "exhibited an honorable discharge issued to his brother, James Hargus, by Colonel

Barry in 1860. James Hargus left the Texas Rangers to join Texas troops in the Confederate army and was killed in the war. His Texas Ranger discharge is one of the family's most treasured possessions."

The article gives the impression that the discharge might have been written at the Eastland County Ranger camp, although that is not clearly stated.

Barry, a noted Indian fighter who had been sheriff of Navarro County in East Texas before moving west, made numerous trips between Meridian, in Bosque County, and the Fort Belknap area in Young County. A map shows Eastland County is a fairly logical stopping place between those points. Yet Barry makes no mention in his memoirs of camping in what would become Eastland County.

E. James Pike, a Ranger who served in another Ranger company during the period the Rangers were camping near present-day Ranger, Texas, described the Rangers of this era in his book *Scout and Ranger*, first published in 1865:

> Imagine two hundred men dressed in every variety of costume, except the ordinary uniform, armed with double-barreled shotguns, squirrel rifles, and Colt's six shooters, mounted on small, wiry, half wild horses, with Spanish saddles and Mexican spurs; unshaven, unwashed, undisciplined, but brave and generous men, riding pellmell along roads, over the prairies, and through the woods, and you will be able to form a correct conception of a squad of Texan Rangers on the march. In such a band it is impossible to distinguish officers from privates, as the former have no distinct dress; and all act alike.

Pike went on to describe a typical Ranger camp of the time. The Ranger camp in Eastland County must have been much the same:

> Usually, we encamped in a hollow square, placing our tents at regular intervals around the outside. The horses were tied to stakes by a forty foot rope, and allowed to graze outside the camp until retreat, when they were led inside, and the rope shortened. Guards were posted outside the tents, and at some distance off; while the horse guards were inside the square.

Though he camped in Eastland County, Barry and his Rangers did their Indian fighting elsewhere. Eastland

A typical frontier Ranger camp. (Photo from author's collection)

County historian Edwin T. Cox mentions a local legend that Rangers and Indians had had a battle "in the canyon north of Ranger," but wrote that he had been "unable to find mention of such an event in any history of Texas or in the reminiscences of any individual."

Captain R.M. Whiteside had headed the Rangers whose campsite inspired the town's name, according to Ruth Terry Denny's 1941 master's thesis on the history of Ranger, Texas. Whiteside, who later settled at Cisco, was one of twenty people killed when a tornado struck the town on April 28, 1893.

Whiteside is not mentioned in *The New Handbook of Texas*, nor is Barry's antebellum camp, but the *Handbook* does note that Rangers camped in the valley in the 1870s. If so, it was prior to the creation of the Frontier Battalion in 1874, because there is no indication in the annual Adjutant General's reports of any Frontier Battalion camp in Eastland County. The Ranger camps of this era in this part of West Texas were in Brownwood, Coleman, and Colorado City.

Only eighty people were living in Eastland County in 1870 according to the U.S. census. But within a decade, the population had jumped to 4,800. Most of those people were law-abiding. The area "was fortunate in having a class of citizens which gave little trouble other than that which one would expect in a new county," Cox wrote in his *History of Eastland County*. The sheriff, constable, "and other peace officers ... were able to maintain law and order to the extent that the Rangers were not needed."

Well, not quite. Starting in the mid-1870s, the Adjutant General's Department began publishing a list of fugitives, the forerunner of modern computerized criminal information systems. The 1877-1878 book shows that eighteen persons were wanted for crimes in Eastland County, including three murderers, six wanted for assault with intent to murder, and four horse thieves—which was a hanging offense back then.

One of those horse thieves was David Ester, who also had been indicted on June 21, 1877, for two counts of assault with intent to murder. He was thirty years old, had "light thin hair, light whiskers, rather large grey eyes, about 5 feet 9 inches, talks hurriedly, is very familiar, a braggadocio, a villain of the first-class."

By 1879 a few settlers were living in tents near the old Ranger camp. The tent town, with a church, school, hotel, and general store all under canvas, was known as Ranger Camp, and the area around it was called Ranger Camp Valley.

When the Texas and Pacific Railroad reached Eastland County in 1880, the tracks were laid a couple of miles to the west. The residents and businessmen of the tent city pulled up stakes—literally—and moved to the railroad. In December a post office was established for Ranger, Texas, and permanent buildings began to go up.

The railroad brought prosperity as well as an assortment of other villains "of the first-class." A company of Rangers followed the railroad construction all across West Texas, offering protection to the railroad workers. These Rangers may have put up their tents for a time where the earlier Rangers had camped, but they moved on west as the tracks went down.

Once the railroad they had guarded began operation, the first significant law enforcement work that the Rangers did in the town named in their honor came on April 20, 1882.

Railroad officials had gotten information that a robbery of the T&P was planned somewhere in West Texas. At the request of Train Master R.J. Duncan, four Rangers were dispatched to ride the line in case the tip proved correct.

A group of robbers was indeed planning to hold up the train. The place they picked, whether by coincidence or for the fun of it, was Ranger, Texas. When the westbound T&P pulled into the Ranger station, the robbers rushed the express car at gunpoint, demanding all the money.

As historian Cox related it:

> While they [the robbers] were thus engaged, the porter, who had been instructed what to do, rushed to a coach and notified the Rangers of the attack. When the Rangers neared the express car, the shooting began. The robbers grabbed about four hundred dollars in silver, overlooking a large amount of currency, and made for their horses. They made their escape for the time being, but one of them was wounded in the arm and breast.

Four Rangers were on the train when it pulled into Ranger that spring day: Corporal John McNelly and Privates Gaines, Cartwright, and Stephens. Private Stephens was asleep when the robbers struck, according to Captain S.A. McMurry, and was "probably a little slow in getting out."

The gunmen confronted the porter and conductor the moment they stepped off the train at the Ranger depot, the captain reported. "The porter then returned to the ... car, [and] called to McNelly who was near the door saying the train was being robbed," McMurry wrote. McNelly called to the others & All got out instantly & opened fire on [the] robbers who soon began a hasty retreat to the brush. The one in the Exp [Express] Car took what papers were in reach & jumped out of [the] door on the opposite side."

One of the robbers, Charles Gullette, was wounded in the fight. He was captured near the Eastland County community of Merriman a few days later with the help of a concerned citizen who alerted the Rangers to his hiding place. From Gullette the Rangers apparently learned the names of the other three robbers: W.D. McDonald, J.T. Martin, and J.D. Brown. Brown, the captain said, "is supposed to have been killed by his 'pals' over the division of their small amt [amount] of money, or wounded in the fight & died in the brush—."

McMurry said he had a good description of McDonald and Martin and "their haunts etc. . . . " He added: "If I am not lucky enough to get hold of them myself, the information I have is certain to lead to their arrest."

The captain did not have time to get his report off to Adjutant General W.H. King in Austin until May 1. He had just arrived in another railroad town, Colorado City, after leaving Ranger on the theory that the two train robbers still at large "are likely to return as soon as they hear of our absence." The captain said there was "a reliable man near Ranger" (the same person who had tipped the Rangers off to Gullette's hiding place) who would let him know if the robbery suspects showed back up in the area. "The country [around Ranger] is so hilly, broken & brushy, it renders successful pursuit almost beyond question. The only way they can be caught is to not allow them to know that we are in the country."

The Ranger captain was not pleased with the Galveston *News*'s account of the train robbery, and defended his men against what he viewed as an unfair attack.

"The [Rangers] would have done more effective work had it not been through fear of killing some of the train men," he wrote in his report to General King. "I consider the guard did remarkably well. Never thought of any one saying anything to their detriment until my attention was called to the Galveston *News* a few days since."

Officials of the Texas and Pacific, he wrote, "speak in the highest terms of the courage & coolness of the four [Rangers] & I understand that Mr. Sands [one of those officials] has recommended that each be made a valuable present as a reward for their gallantry & prompt interference. I heard Gullette say had it not been for the Rangers, they would have gone through the entire train—had they have done so they would have got at least $25,000.00."

McDonald and Martin eventually were captured, tried, convicted, and sentenced to the state prison at Huntsville.

The Rangers kept riding the T&P for a while, but no one else tried to rob the train, at least not in the vicinity of Ranger.

History-minded Ranger residents know how their community got its name, but precisely where the Rangers made their camp has been open to discussion.

"The Rangers pitched their tents in the valley, 2 miles east of the present city of Ranger on land then known as the Watson Ranch," according to an article in the 1929 Tenth Anniversary edition of the Ranger *Times*. A later fact sheet prepared by the Ranger Chamber of Commerce said the Ranger camp was near Wyles Canyon. An unnamed old-timer, in a sketch published in an Eastland County history, said the Ranger camp was at Winsett Spring.

"There's always been some uncertainty about the exact location of the camp," said Charles Bonney, an Austin attorney who grew up in Ranger. He recalled listening when he was a youngster to Ranger's first mayor, M.H. Hagaman, spin tales about the old days.

"He said the ranger camp was in the valley, which was near his ranch," Bonney said. "I think the camp must have been near the head of the canyon. When the railroad was built, the tracks were laid through the canyon to the west."

Jeane Pruett, chairperson of the Ranger Historical Preservation Society, believes the camp was just south of Hagaman Lake, about two miles northeast of Ranger.

The society has tried to locate the Ranger camp site so it can put up a historical marker, but the precise location has remained a mystery. However, Pruett believes the approximate site has been determined.

"An old-timer told us he remembered seeing big nails in an oak tree where the Rangers supposedly tied their horses," Pruett said. "We had some archeologists with metal detectors check the tree, and though there is nothing visible, there is metal in it."

On two different visits by archeologists, Pruett said, an assortment of nineteenth century artifacts were found in the vicinity of the large oak, including ceramic fragments, an old spoon, and a portion of an unusual cork-lined metal container. Most intriguing, however, was a gold Masonic ring discovered fourteen inches beneath the ground.

Was the ring lost by a traveler, an early day settler, or was the unknown Mason one of the Rangers who camped beneath the tree?

Sources

Adjutant General's Report. Austin: 1884.

Cox, Edwin T. *A History of Eastland County*. San Antonio: The Naylor Co., 1950, pp. 16, 73.

Bonney, Charles. Interview with author, Nov. 25, 1996.

Denney, Ruth Terry. *A Short History of Ranger, Texas*. Ranger: Ranger Historical Preservation Society, 1996, p. 60.

McMurray, S.B. to Adjutant General W.H. King, letter dated May 1, 1882. Walter Prescott Webb Papers. Center for American History, University of Texas at Austin.

Pruett, Jeane. Interview with author, Nov. 27, 1996.

Smith, Roy. ed. *Gateway to the West: Eastland County History*. Eastland: Eastland County Book Committee, 1989, Vol. I, p. 635.

O. Henry and Lee Hall

On a burning August day in 1883, someone rode up on two skeletons in the brush near the Frio River in La Salle County. "Dead Men Tell No Tales," read the headline in the San Antonio *Express* a couple of days later, but bullet holes in the tattered clothing still clinging to the bones told their own story—one of double murder on a remote South Texas ranch.

Because someone recognized the hat that had been worn by one of the men, the remains were identified as those of two Mexican sheep herders who had disappeared the previous December. Until the skeletons were found, it had been assumed the pair had merely "run off."

Sheriff Charlie McKinney, a former Ranger, and Ranger Captain Joseph Shely had their suspicions as to who was responsible, but officially, the two murders were never solved. In a few years the crime would be far overshadowed by the unrelated slaying on December 26, 1886, of the sheriff who had looked into it.

But twenty years later, one person did remember the murder of the sheep herders. He took his memory of their bones, long since buried and forgotten, and added the flesh and blood of fiction to create a short story called "Jimmy Hayes and Muriel." The story, while in itself not much more memorable than the bleached bones which inspired it, was one of hundreds in the oeuvre of a man whose pen name will forever be linked with the American short story, especially those with a certain twist at the end: O. Henry.

Had William Sydney Porter ever moved on from the short story to booklength fiction, he could have gotten a novel out of all that he heard of or saw during the two years he spent on a ranch in La Salle County between San Antonio and Laredo in the early 1880s. Several of Porter's short stories clearly were inspired by his time in South Texas, and three of them, "The Caballero's Way," "An Afternoon Miracle," and "Jimmy Hayes and Muriel," have Texas Rangers as major characters. Two other stories, "The Lonesome Road" and "The Passing of Black Eagle," while not specifically about the Rangers, make mention of them.

Porter's Ranger stories, however, come at the end of this story. As O. Henry would write it, the beginning of this tale is in North Carolina.

In early 1882 Porter was nineteen years old and living in Greensboro, North Carolina. His mother had died of tuberculosis, or consumption as it was called back then, when Porter was only a young child. Now Porter, who worked in his uncle's drug store, had a cough and seemed sickly. Dr. James K. Hall, a family friend who had been a surgeon in the Confederate army, worried that the young man also was coming down with the dreaded lung disease that had killed his mother.

Four sons of Doctor Hall lived in Texas, including one whose fame had spread all the way back to North Carolina: Jesse Lee "Red" Hall. Lee Hall came to Texas in 1869. Within two years he metamorphosed from a schoolteacher to a peace officer. He served as city marshal in Sherman, was a Grayson County sheriff's deputy, and in 1876 became a Texas Ranger. Hall was a lieutenant under Captain Leander H. McNelly, succeeding him as captain after McNelly's death in 1877. He continued as a Ranger captain until 1880, establishing a well-deserved reputation as a lawman.

CAPT. J. L. (LEE) HALL.

Doctor Hall invited Porter to travel to Texas with him and his wife to visit a ranch Lee Hall had begun managing after leaving the Rangers. The dry climate would be good for his health, the physician told Porter.

The train trip from Greensboro took ninety-five hours. When Porter and the Halls stepped off the train at Cotulla, they alighted in a place where the West was still wild. The wide-open brush country, the *brasada*, made a strong impression on the young Southerner. Surely Porter was remembering the early spring day he arrived in South Texas when in "Madame Bo-Peep of the Ranches" he later wrote:

> They struck across a world carpeted with an endless reach of curly mesquite grass. The [wagon] wheels made no sound. The tireless ponies bounded ahead at an unbroken gallop. The temperate wind, made fragrant by thousands of acres of blue and yellow wild flowers, roared gloriously in their ears...

Porter lived on the 250,000-plus acre ranch, owned by the Dull brothers of Harrisburg, Pennsylvania, from March 1882 through March 1884. Though Porter spent more time with another of the doctor's sons, Dick Hall, the person whose influence was even more significant was Lee Hall.

It was Lee's personality, Porter's first biographer, Alphonso Smith, wrote, "and Lee's achievement that opened the doors of romance to him in Texas and contributed atmosphere and flavour to the nineteen stories that made up his *Heart of the West.*"

Not only did Lee Hall have a colorful background, he did not mind telling his stories. And he did so with a flair. Another former Ranger, Captain J.E. Lucy, later said his friend Lee Hall "was a rare entertainer."

Porter must have looked forward to Hall's storytelling sessions with great anticipation, but they probably did not happen as often as the newly transplanted North Carolinian would have liked. The name of the huge spread Hall managed may have been the Dull Ranch, but that did not describe the general state of affairs in La Salle County and elsewhere along the middle Texas border. As superintendent of the sprawling ranch, Hall had his hands full with cattle thieves and fence cutters. Throw in the known enemies he had on both sides of the border from his rangering days, and had Hall sought life insurance his life expectancy would not have appealed to actuaries.

"We lived a most unsettled exciting existence," the former Ranger's widow later recalled of those days along the border. "His life was threatened in many ways, and the mail was heavy with warnings, generally in the shape of crude sketches, portraying effigies with ropes around their necks, and bearing the unfailing inscription, 'Your Necktie.' We usually travelled at night, nearly always with cocked guns."

This "exciting existence" was one of the reasons Hall worked to get one of his former Rangers, Charles McKinney, elected as county sheriff. He succeeded, but it took Hall and some of his men standing around the ballot box with guns in hand to insure that democracy prevailed.

Porter soaked all of this in like a thirsty horse hock deep in a mudhole after a long ride through the brush. He did some chores around the ranch, cooking, tending sheep, and cowboying a little. He also rode fourteen miles to Fort Ewell for the mail, but as a friend of the Hall family, he was more guest than a hand. What he did most was take it easy and read, poring over any printed material he could get his hands on, from newspapers—the San Antonio *Express* and two of the Greensboro papers—to all the books Mrs. Dick Hall had in her private library, a collection she added to as often as she could.

"His thirst for knowledge of all kinds was unquenchable," she later recalled. "History, fiction, biography, science, and magazines of every description were devoured and were talked about with eager interest."

Porter liked to lay around on a cot in the shade of the mesquite and read *Webster's Unabridged Dictionary* as if it were a novel.

The young North Carolinian remembered what he read and saw and the stories he heard from Lee Hall and the other ex-Rangers Hall had working on the ranch, including Will Cavin, Netteville Devine, Frank and Will Hall (Lee Hall's other brothers), and Sam Platt. McKinney would have been a frequent visitor to the ranch, too.

Porter may have begun to experiment with writing while staying in La Salle County, and he did some drawings, but no examples of his early prose have survived other than some of his letters back to Greensboro. He poked fun at the South Texas climate in one letter to the Vesper Reading Club, pointing out that the weather was "very good, thermometer rarely rising above 2,500 degrees in the shade and hardly ever below 212."

Even as a young man, Porter's prose was evocative (though somewhat overwritten) and showed that despite his joking about the Texas heat, he liked the lonely border country:

> The moon is low and the wind is still. The lovely stars, the 'forget-me-nots of the angels,' which have blossomed all night in the infinite meadows of heaven, unheeded and unseen by us poor sleepy mortals for whom they spread their shining petals and silvery beams in vain, are twinkling above in all their beauty and mystery. The lonely cry of the coyote is heard mingling with the noise of a piece of strong Texas bacon trying to get out of the pantry.

Though Lee Hall was a dozen years older than Porter, their lives had some interesting parallels. Both were born and raised in the same southern state. Both would someday endure accusations of embezzlement (Hall was accused of graft after two years as an Indian agent in Anadarko, Indian Territory but was exonerated; Porter went to federal prison for allegedly embezzling an Austin bank) and both became heavy drinkers, which probably cut short each of their lives. They died within eight months of each other, Porter on June 5, 1910 in New York, Hall on March 17, 1911 in San Antonio. Both men had become legends in their own time.

Porter's reputation as a writer has lived on. His publisher, Doubleday, has kept his work in print, and when his material moved out of copyright into the public domain seventy-five years after original publication, other publishers brought out selected works, singly and in various anthologies.

The best known of O. Henry's Ranger stories is "The Caballero's Way," though it is not the title which anyone remembers, but one of its three characters: the Cisco Kid. First published in *Everybody's Magazine* in 1907, this tragic love story with a classic O. Henry twist at the end was the inspiration for twelve movies starring Duncan Renaldo as the Cisco Kid and Leo Carrillo as Pancho, his comedic sidekick. The two actors also starred in 156 half-hour television shows, the series ending in 1955.

Of course, the Hollywood version of the Cisco Kid is nothing like his portrayal in Porter's story, which begins:

> The Cisco Kid had killed six men in more or
> less fair scrimmages, had murdered twice as many
> (mostly Mexicans), and had winged a large
> number whom he modestly forebore to count.
> Therefore a woman loved him.

For the big and then the little screen, the story was turned into a Western version of *Don Quixote*, with the Cisco Kid and Pancho being on the side of law and order. They never killed anyone, except by tricking other outlaws to cause each other harm. The principal character's name is the only similarity between what Porter wrote and what Hollywood's scriptwriters did with the story. The Cisco Kid was transformed into an elaborately garbed Mexican *ranchero*.

The inspiration for the Kid may have been the real-life Texas outlaw John Wesley Hardin, variously credited with having killed somewhere between twenty and fifty men before being gunned down in an El Paso saloon in 1895. But O. Henry's outlaw probably was more a composite. From Hall, he doubtless heard of many bad men. And the

San Antonio *Express*, which Porter faithfully read, was full of stories concerning Texas outlaws.

The Lee Hall-inspired Ranger in "The Caballero's Way" is Lieutenant Sandridge, whom Porter described as "six feet two, blond as a Viking, quiet as a deacon, dangerous as a machine gun." Nevertheless, the Ranger lieutenant is outsmarted in the story by the Cisco Kid, tricked into killing his own girlfriend, Tonia Perez, instead of the Kid. The girl also had been the Kid's sweetheart, or so he had thought until he found she had eyes for the handsome Ranger.

Lee Hall is clearly the model for Ranger Bob Buckley in "An Afternoon Miracle." Porter wrote:

> "I've heard of fellows," grumbled [Ranger]
> Broncho Leathers, "what was wedded to danger,
> but if Bob Buckley ain't committed bigamy with
> trouble, I'm a son of a gun."

This story, though not published until 1902, was written when Porter was serving time in the federal prison in Columbus, Ohio.

A reading of the story suggests its author had some familiarity with the border city of Laredo, in addition to the Texas Rangers. Since the International and Great Northern Railroad passed through the La Salle County seat of Cotulla on its way to Laredo, it seems likely that Porter visited Laredo a time or two during his ranch interlude.

The unsolved murders of two sheep herders in La Salle County—though it has nothing to do with the plot of the story—is plainly visible as one of the inspiring factors behind Porter's "Jimmy Hayes and Muriel." The short story also shows Porter was familiar with McNelly's June 12, 1875, Laguna Madre fight, in which seventeen Rangers killed fifteen bandits. The only Ranger lost in the fight was sixteen-year-old L.B. Smith, a likable teenager whom

Porter probably had in mind when he came up with the protagonist for his story.

First published in the July 1903 issue of *Munsey's Magazine* under the byline of Sydney Porter, "Jimmy Hayes and Muriel" is the story of a young Frontier Battalion Ranger named Jimmy Hayes. The name of the protagonist suggests Porter also was familiar with the legendary Captain Jack Hays. Porter merely kept the same first initial and added an "e" to come up with a name for his Ranger.

As the story begins, a "half-troop" of Rangers are sitting around the campfire after supper, rolling their cornhusk cigarettes, when they hear a horse moving through the chaparral. Soon the rider's voice reaches the Ranger camp, and it sounds like he is talking to a girl!

"Brace up, Muriel, old girl, we're 'most there now! Been a long ride ... Hey, now, quit a tryin' to kiss me! Don't hold on to my neck so tight —this here paoint [paint] hoss ain't any too shore-footed ... He's liable to dump us both off if we don't watch out."

The rider is twenty-year-old Jimmy Hayes, newly transferred to this particular Ranger company. His companion
is not a girl, but a horned toad with a "bright red ribbon . . . tied jauntily around his spiky neck."

Muriel, Hayes explains, is his faithful traveling companion, a toad of many qualities: "She never talks back, she
always stays at home, and she's satisfied with one red dress
for every day and Sundays, too."

The other Rangers take to the likeable young Hayes, but
they are uncertain how he will stand up in a fight:

> They loved him for his simplicity and drollness,
> but there hung above him a great sword of sus-
> pended judgment. To make merry in camp is not
> all of a ranger's life. There are horsethieves to
> trail, desperate criminals to run down, bravos to
> battle with, bandits to rout out of the chaparral,
> peace and order to be compelled at the muzzle of
> a six-shooter. Jimmy had been "most generally a
> cowpuncher," he said: he was inexperienced in
> ranger methods of warfare.

Two months of inactivity slowly crawled by until a Mexican desperado and cattle thief crossed into Texas. He and

his gang caught the Rangers by surprise one evening as they were preparing supper. The Rangers rallied and gave chase. Plenty of gunpowder got burned, but the Rangers could not keep up with the fleeing raiders.

Hayes is missing, one of the Rangers in Porter's story realizes at this point. He had been seen running for his horse when the fight began, but no one had seen him since. A search proved fruitless. To their keen disappointment, the Rangers concluded that Hayes must have panicked at the first sound of gunfire and run. Afterward, they speculated, he had been too ashamed to face his fellow Rangers and left for other parts with Muriel the horned toad.

Meanwhile, the Rangers scoured the brush country for the Mexican outlaw and his band, but they could not even find his trail. He had disappeared.

Nearly a year went by. While on a routine scout, only a few miles from the scene of the surprise attack and the desertion of Hayes, the Rangers rode through thick mesquite, suddenly breaking into "a patch of open hog-wallow prairie." Before them lay three skeletons.

Here Porter must have relied on his memory of that earlier newspaper account of the double murder in the brush in La Salle County. Maybe with Hall he had viewed the scene of the crime, because his description closely agrees with the report in the San Antonio newspaper. In his short story, Porter's Rangers realize the human remains were those of the bandit leader and the two members of his gang they had fought the year before. The Rangers identified the remains by their clothing and the leader's bullet-pierced *sombrero*.

The lawmen thought it was most curious that the dead outlaws' rusting Winchesters all pointed in the same direction.

Riding that way for about fifty yards, the Rangers came up on another skeleton. The weapon on the ground beside the pile of bones pointed back toward the other three skeletons.

The battle, the Rangers concluded, had been one of total extermination. Some lone cowboy, they figured, caught in the brush by three bandits. He had managed to kill his three attackers, but in the process, he himself was mortally wounded.

"And then," Porter wrote, "from beneath the weather-beaten rags of the dead man, there wriggled out a horned frog with a faded red ribbon around its neck, and sat upon the shoulder of its long quiet master."

Jimmy Hayes had not been a coward after all. The Ranger had died fighting, mortally wounding three outlaws while he was at it.

This O. Henry ending has a second O. Henry-style ending.

Boyce House, a young man from Arkansas on his way to Laredo by train in 1920, had lunch at the Traveler's Hotel when the train stopped in Cotulla. After lunch, House continued to Laredo, but the bookish traveler decided he liked Cotulla better. He returned on the San Antonio-bound train a few days later. He ended up staying at the Traveler's Hotel for about five months, paying $10 a week for room and board.

House had not been in Cotulla long before he remarked to Owen Widener, the son of the hotel owner, that the place seemed strangely familiar to him. He had never been there before the train stopped there for lunch, but he had the feeling that he had.

"Did you ever hear of O. Henry?" Widener asked the hotel guest.

Indeed, House was a big fan of Porter and had read many of his stories.

Widener explained that Porter had lived in the county in the early 1880s, and House realized the short story writer's descriptions of the area were so good they had given him that eerie feeling of having been there before. While in Cotulla, House read more O. Henry stories, along with the works of Mark Twain.

Like Porter, House had come to Texas for his health. When he arrived at Cotulla, he later wrote, he had weighed only 102 pounds. By the time he left, having consumed a gallon of sweet milk a day, he had added twenty-five pounds to his five feet, ten-and-a-half-inch frame.

House eventually became editor of the newspaper at Eastland during the oil boom. The 1897-vintage Eastland County courthouse was razed in 1928 to make room for a larger structure. When the thirty-year-old cornerstone of the original building was opened, according to legend, a long-entombed horned toad emerged.

The man who reported this story—which resulted in tremendous favorable publicity for his city and garnered nation-wide attention for its author and his newspaper as well—was Boyce House. Old-timers used to swear the story was true, not some Chamber of Commerce publicity stunt, but then maybe House had an idea for a story of his own when he remembered reading O. Henry's tale of a young Texas Ranger and a beribboned horned toad named Muriel.

Sources

The Complete Works of O. Henry. New York: Doubleday, Page & Company, 1927, pp. 669-672.

Gallegly, Joseph. *From Alamo Plaza To Jack Harris's Saloon: O. Henry and the Southwest He Knew*. The Hague: Mouton, 1970, pp. 134-165.

Horwitz, James. *They Went Thataway*. New York: 1976, pp. 249-262.

Langford, Gerald. *Alias O. Henry*. New York: The MacMillan Company, 1957, pp. 19-21.

Ludeman, Annette Martin. *La Salle County: South Texas Brush Country*. Quanah, Texas: Nortex Press, 1975, pp. 129-131.

"Murdered Men Tell No Tales," San Antonio *Express*, Aug. 5, 1883.

Smith, C. Alphonso. *O. Henry Biography*. New York: Doubleday, Page & Co., 1916, pp. 106-108.

Ranger Oden's Diary

*N*ot every Texas Ranger becomes famous. Many simply follow orders and do their job effectively.

That pretty much describes the career of Ranger Alonzo V. Oden, who served in the Trans-Pecos in the 1890s. Oden certainly fit in with the stereotypical image of a Ranger. He stood six feet one inch tall and was described as "straight as an Indian, a fine marksman with both pistol and rifle, a skillful horseman, and with his bold physique and pleasant features an attractive appearance, and the testimony of Corporal [John R.] Hughes (later Captain) goes to show that not only is he a good Ranger and popular with the men, but he is also by no means indifferent to the ladies."

But Oden did do something that set him apart from most Rangers: He kept a diary. Though hundreds of men served Texas as frontier Rangers, Oden is the only one known to have had a bent toward written introspection. He was well read in the classics, liked poetry, had an appreciation of opera, and was capable of using words with the same skill as his six-shooter.

Born and raised in the South Texas community of Tilden in McMullen County, Oden joined Company D, Frontier Battalion, on March 1, 1891, at the age of 27. His grand-father and father both had served as Rangers and both may have died in the line of duty. Payroll records in the state archives show that Oden's salary was $30 a month, paid quarterly.

When Oden went on scout in the Trans Pecos, he carried a marbleboard-covered account book in his saddlebag. When time allowed, the Ranger wrote in the book in a neat, Spencerian hand. The diary was a mixture of undated journal entries, poems in his handwriting—some of which may have been original, others copied from other sources—and poems and essays clipped from newspapers and glued onto the pages.

The diary started out inauspiciously: "I'm 27, and have just joined the ranger service. I am 27, and have just started a diary—I wonder why? . . . This book is large, and the leaves are blank."

Alonzo V. Oden

Oden's rangering career did not get off to a very exciting start, either. In his second diary entry, he wrote that he had borrowed some books from his preacher. He discussed an article he had read which criticized "society ladies" who went to church in their finest array just to be seen by the men. The author of the article also took a shot at the men for ogling the girls, but, as Oden wrote, "I think he forgets that we're all just humans."

If the early days of Oden's Ranger career were dull, they certainly were not easy. In his fourth entry, Oden wrote with obvious excitement that he was going to El Paso, where he could take a bath in a long tub. Then he wrote something for posterity:

> Maybe, for future reference, I should go into a little detail as to the way a proud and hand-some—not to mention brave—Ranger takes a bath. We beg, borrow, or buy a galvanized wash tub, and put it in the middle of someone's kitchen and heat several kettles and pans of water. Then we nail blankets over the windows and prop chairs against the doors; next, we fill the tub with equal parts of hot and cold water; then, we get in the round wash tub (in the nude, natu-rally), and use our Lava or Colgate's lavishly— with many groans and some splashing.

In El Paso, the metropolis of West Texas, Ranger Oden got his bath, bought a new shirt, and picked up a suit he had ordered from a tailor the last time he was in town. By the time he had ordered a new pair of boots, as he put it, he had "spent my monthly salary, and then some." He ended the entry, his fifth, with the information that he was headed out to "see what I can find to do."

He ended up, evidently in the company of another Ranger, at 307 South Utah Street, the location of Tillie Howard's Sporting House. The term "sporting house" back then had nothing to do with baseball or boxing. In her mid-twenties, Tillie came to El Paso in 1890 after being dumped by Willie Sells, owner of the famous Sells Circus. Soon she was El Paso's premier madam.

Oden wrote:

> I've been anxious to visit Tillie. She is the talk of the border... She is tall, and I imagine she doesn't need these artificial bosoms the ladies are using now; hers look natural enough—I'll ask her when I know her better. She seems to take a shine to me. She has the blackest hair, and she is one of the most beautiful women I've ever seen. I'll be seeing more of Tillie...

The bagnio itself, Oden wrote, was just "a regular saloon, and sort of hotel and dance hall combined, but Tillie makes the place different."

Though he thought Tillie was beautiful, and despite weeks of lonely border vigil, apparently all Oden and Tillie engaged in was conversation. At least, that is the only activity he recorded in his diary.

In his next diary entry, Ranger Oden said Tillie had given him a tour of her establishment, where no loud talk or vulgarity was allowed, and had thanked him for treating her "as a human with brains."

Soon after his visit to Tillie's place, Oden left the refinements of El Paso for the silver mining town of Shafter down in the mountains of the Big Bend. A short time later, while on a scout, the Rangers rode up on a saddled, riderless pinto pony. Nearby lay the skeleton of a man. In those days, in that country, no one thought of an autopsy. The

Rangers examined the remains, deciding the cowboy had been thrown from his horse and suffered two broken legs. The Rangers further concluded that after several days of suffering, the cowboy shot himself with his Colt. If he had been bushwhacked, his pony and pistol would not still be in the vicinity, the lawmen reasoned.

"We buried him, said the Lord's Prayer...then brought the pinto back into camp with us," the Ranger wrote.

As remarkable as Oden's diary was, it is a shame he did not record more of his day-to-day activities as a Ranger. Oden realized this himself, and commented on it in his twenty-seventh entry. "Suppose it is another case of an old maid telling a mother of eight how the children should be reared," he wrote. But what Oden did leave for the sake of history provides a good feel for what it was like to be a Texas Ranger on the border in the 1890s:

> Sometimes, there are . . . weeks when we crawl through underbrush, until our bodies are cut and bleeding; nights when we freeze, sitting so quietly waiting for a raid to take place; hours in the broiling sun, slowly walking our horses down mountainous incline[s]; days of living in Mexican huts, eating enchiladas, frijoles and supapios [sopapillas] prepared by Mexican cooks. Chili and more chili, keeps the backbone of a Ranger from growing flabby.

Ranger duty on the border sometimes got as spicy as the food. But when Oden described a gunfight, it was in a matter-of-fact way that belied the seriousness of the situation he had faced.

One of those shootouts came after Oden and two other Rangers, including Hughes, had picked up a prisoner and stopped at a border trading post for supplies. They noticed four men, and after making discreet inquiries, were told that one of the men was wanted for everything from horse theft to murder. In the Trans-Pecos, where setting a man afoot could cost him his life, horse theft almost was a more serious crime than murder. Murder could have been a little difficulty that just got out of hand.

Oden tells the story like this:

> Well, Hughes and I got on our horses and started toward them. They quickly mounted and started firing on us, running as they fired, all except Carrasco [the wanted man]. He was mounted, but got down and deliberately set about getting his rifle out of his scabbard. One of us killed him. My horse was shot and killed by the fleeing bandits. When we got back to the store, considerable excitement was aroused.

Though the Rangers sometimes drew criticism for a lack of sensitivity to minorities and a predisposition, as the old saying goes, to shoot first and ask questions later, there is not even a hint of that kind of attitude in the writings left by Oden.

"I feel so inadequate," he wrote, "when we've finished a battle and I look on the bodies of dead men—men who were bad as the world . . . but men who had been born into this world for a purpose—who are we to end that purpose?"

For a young man, Ranger Oden's philosophical insight was impressive. In one diary entry, he recorded what he labeled as only a partial list of the bad men wanted in Presidio County, down river from El Paso. He named six men, half of them wanted for murder.

They were men, Oden wrote, "who lie and steal and cheat—men who murder—men who are so weak—men we hunt—men we shoot. Seems like this world is made up of two sets of men—each fighting the other. Can the weak ever grow strong, or the strong ever reach an understanding of weakness?"

In another diary entry, Oden waxed philosophically on the arrest of a bad cowboy wanted for killing a man in Ozona, in Crockett County. The outlaw used the alias of "Pecos Bill," a cowboy folk character already popular around the camp fire and destined for future fame in books and in a Walt Disney feature film. But this "Pecos Bill" was no cartoon character. Since his arrest, he had been sitting, staring into space. He was not eating much and talking even less.

"Bill may be staring into space," the Ranger wrote, "but the space is full of meaning for Bill, and Bill, at last, is seeing himself. I can not explain how I know this, but I do know it; and when a man sees himself, he has found himself—and he is no longer afraid."

When Captain Frank Jones, Oden's boss, was killed in a gunfight below El Paso on June 30, 1893, John Hughes was promoted to captain of Company D. Oden was transferred from the Big Bend country to Ysleta, the Ranger headquarters near El Paso.

Oden's writing was not confined to his diary entries. Oden had been corresponding with a sweetheart back home in South Texas. One day he got a letter from her containing a newspaper clipping—she had married a lawyer, which to some Ranger's thinking was only a step better than hitching up with an outlaw.

"Just as I was prepared to break down and cry, or shoot myself, a girl came pounding on my door, crying that a man was beating his wife to death," Oden wrote. "I grabbed my gun, and told her to get the sheriff; and I rushed off on my mission of mercy. The Ranger never deserts his duties—no matter if he is heart-broken."

But Oden's heart did not stay broken long. He made the acquaintance of the postmistress at Ysleta, a young widow with three children. The Ranger mentioned that development in his thirty-fifth diary entry. He did not date his entries, but three entries later, Oden's thirty-eighth, he wrote: "I'm not going to have time to write much more in this book. I'm getting married in the morning—to my widow—the one with the three children."

Oden was honorably discharged from the Rangers on May 18, 1894.

After marrying Laura Carr Hay, Oden enjoyed a peaceful and successful life, but not a long one. He made some money as a merchant in Sierra Blanca, a railroad town east of El Paso, and later ran a ranch near Marfa. He died of lung disease, with symptoms suggestive of cancer, in an El Paso hospital on August 11, 1910, at the age of 47.

In 1936 one of his children, Ann Jenson, published Oden's diary, saving her father's account of his rangering days for posterity.

······ ⭐ ······

Sources

DeArment, Robert K. *George Scarborough: The Life and Death of a Lawman on the Closing of the Frontier.* Norman: University of Oklahoma Press, 1992, pp. 71-72.

Gossett, Col. Leo. Speech to the Former Texas Ranger Association, San Antonio, Texas, May 4, 1986. Author's collection.

Jenson, Ann. *A Texas Ranger's Scrapbook and Diary.* Dallas: 1936.

Stephens, Robert W. *Texas Ranger Sketches.* Dallas: 1972, pp. 105, 107-108.

Did a Ranger Kill A.J. Royal?

An old rolltop desk sits just inside the main entrance of the Annie Riggs Museum in Fort Stockton. On the bottom of the upper right-hand drawer are two dark stains.

Are those indelible blotches on the wood bloodstains? Local lore has it that they are the only tangible evidence in the murder of former Pecos County Sheriff A.J. Royal, shot to death on November 21, 1894, as he sat at that desk in the courthouse.

The desk of former Pecos County Sheriff A.J. Royal at the Annie Riggs Museum, Fort Stockton. (Author's photo)

101

Some say these spots are bloodstains. (Author's photo)

The two spots are only ink stains, others maintain.

The origin of the stains is only a minor aspect of a much larger mystery: Who shot Royal?

The question remains unanswered after more than a century. The Texas Rangers made a diligent effort to bring the former sheriff's killer to justice, judging from the paperwork they generated. On the other hand, some believed the fact that no arrest was ever made in the case pointed to a Texas Ranger as the former sheriff's killer.

That was only one of several theories. Certainly plenty of people had motives, including the forebears of some of Fort Stockton's most prominent citizens today.

Fort Stockton, as the final decade of the nineteenth century began was the seat of Pecos County, but it had little else going for it. In 1886 the army had abandoned the cavalry post that gave the town its name. When they left, they had even taken down the telegraph line.

Five years earlier, the two trans-continental rail lines that spanned West Texas bypassed Fort Stockton. Not only that, the railroads had made obsolete the previously well-traveled wagon roads that crossed at Fort Stockton because of what was then one of Texas's largest natural water sources, Comanche Springs.* The town was left with fewer than 250 residents, a Catholic church, a courthouse, two stores, and two saloons.

The departure of the soldiers did not affect Comanche Springs, but it had a definite impact on Fort Stockton's other watering holes, places where beverages somewhat stronger than spring water were served. Maybe it was this downturn in the local economy and the prospect of real estate available at rock-bottom prices that attracted to the Fort Stockton area a saloon keeper from Junction named Andrew Jackson Royal.

Or maybe Royal came because of legal difficulties resulting from the shooting of a man outside a saloon which Royal owned in Junction. Royal had not pulled the trigger, but he was tried for murder anyway, then acquitted. Or maybe it was getting slashed in a knife fight that helped him decide to move on farther west.

Royal hit Fort Stockton in 1889. Trading 265 head of cattle, Royal got title to 1,800 acres of irrigated land at

Leon Springs, seven miles west of town. He also bought the former post trader's building at the abandoned fort.

Fort Stockton's new citizen—being male, white, at least twenty-one years of age, and owning real property—qualified for political office in those days. With the population of Fort Stockton considerably diminished, attaining a political position was not difficult. On August 25, 1890, Royal was appointed to the county commissioner's court, filling a vacancy created by the resignation of the previous commissioner. Whether Royal sought the appointment or it simply came to him is not known, but it seems to have given him a taste for holding office.

Royal served as a county commissioner until the fall, when he was elected county tax assessor. Despite his public service, he clearly was not above the law—nor above breaking the law. Seven days after his election as tax assessor, he was tried and acquitted for disturbing the peace. He was indicted in March 1891 on the more serious offense of assault and for unlawfully carrying a pistol. This time he also was acquitted.

Royal was in trouble with the law again by May 1892. He was charged with assault, disturbing the peace, and carrying a pistol. This case was continued and later dismissed for lack of witnesses willing to testify against him.

Four days after Royal appeared in court on these three misdemeanor charges, he found himself facing a possible felony charge in the shooting death of Apollinar Mendoza. Mendoza, who had worked on Royal's farm, was gunned down with a load of buckshot in the back outside of Herman Koehler's store on May 20, 1892. That Mendoza was dead proved to be the only uncontroverted fact regarding the matter.

When Royal appeared before Justice of the Peace Fell Sanders with a shotgun in his hands and a pistol on his hip, the assorted witnesses in the Mendoza shooting had trouble recalling the specific details. No two people seemed to remember the same thing, and much of the testimony was circumstantial or amounted to hearsay.

During the inquest, a concerned citizen pointed out that Royal flagrantly violated the law by wearing a pistol in court. Royal overruled this informal objection, threatening to kill the man if he did not shut up. The scattergun was perfectly legal—if somewhat of a distraction in court—and the JP evidently chose not to take judicial notice of Royal's six-shooter.

This point of law resolved, Royal testified that Mendoza and two other men had been planning to kill him. When he went to Koehler's store to pay Mendoza for some work, Mendoza "reached his hand to his side like he was pulling his shirt up—and about that time I let him have it . . . " The judge concluded the proceeding by setting a $1,000 bond for Royal and binding the case over for grand jury consideration.

In September the grand jury no-billed Royal, ostensibly buying his self-defense claim. The grand jury foreman, O.W. Williams, learned much later it was more than Royal's self-defense testimony that had affected the grand jury's lack of action. Royal had threatened some of the jury members and two key witnesses. His faith in the criminal justice system bolstered by the grand jury's inaction, Royal decided to run for sheriff of Pecos County.

He was elected to office on November 8, 1892, by a margin of fifty-six votes. The commissioner's court swore him in on November 17. Now he could carry a pistol legally. Williams—foreman of the grand jury that declined to indict Royal in the Mendoza shooting—was sworn in on the same day as county judge.

Wearing a badge did not shield Royal from trouble with the law. He pistol whipped "an unarmed, unresisting private citizen," on September 4, 1893, nearly fracturing his skull. The attack must have indeed been unprovoked. Though the term "police brutality" had not yet been coined, a Pecos Country grand jury indicted the sheriff for assault.

About the same time, one Jose Juarez was arrested for stealing a watermelon from a tenant farmer who worked on Royal's land. As Royal rolled up outside the county jail with the prisoner in his buggy, the accused watermelon thief tried to escape. Recaptured after Royal emptied his pistol at him in a series of warning shots—or misses—Juarez was recaptured and remained in custody until November. When Juarez had completed his jail time, Royal put the man in his buggy and headed south from town toward Twelve Mile Mesa.

Juarez was never seen again. "Royal claimed that he gave him a thrashing with a horse whip and told him never to show up again in Pecos County." In William's hearing, Royal added significantly, "He never will."

Royal, still under indictment for treating a Pecos County resident's head like a papershell pecan, failed to post bond or show up for trial in the case.

A pistol whipping was a minor matter compared to what happened next. In addition to his law enforcement duties, in February 1894 Royal decided to go back into the saloon business. Royal and a partner opened the Grey Mule Saloon. This put Royal in competition with Fort Stockton's other drinking establishment, the combination store and saloon owned by Herman Koehler. The sheriff did not bother with waging a price war. Royal took a more aggressive business stance, threatening Koehler and then thrashing him with a walking cane. In retaliation, some of Koehler's friends stopped patronizing the Grey Mule. That summer, Koehler died of natural causes. His saloon, however, lived on.

In August, Royal beat up a drunk who had mouthed off about the sheriff's still-pending legal difficulties stemming from the pistol whipping. He also cursed and threatened several members of the grand jury that had indicted him in the case and made noises about paying a none-too-social call on the late Mr. Koehler's liquid emporium.

The sheriff walked into the saloon on the afternoon of August 6, drew his pistol, and went into the adjoining store. Finding no one there, Royal turned back toward the bar. He came face to face with Jimmy Rooney, and Rooney had a shotgun in his hands. When Royal threw down on Rooney, Rooney let loose with the room sweeper. Incredibly, none of the lead managed to hit its target. Royal returned the fire, also missing. Somehow, Royal managed to get out of the gunsmoke-filled bar alive. Details are sketchy, but alcohol may have saved both men's lives.

Royal got a barrel of coal oil, gathered a few willing men, and surrounded the store. He threatened to burn it down and shoot the occupants as they came out. Rooney and a friend surrendered and were taken to the courthouse, where Sheriff Royal filed on them for assault with intent to murder.

"The row commenced," Judge Williams later wrote, while he was out of town. When a messenger brought news of what had happened, the judge rushed to Monahans and wired the adjutant general in Austin, pleading for "rangers at once to Fort Stockton. Serious trouble yesterday. Sheriff involved in the trouble."

By now of course some townfolks had figured out that the sheriff was more than just involved in the trouble. He *was* the trouble. Freed on bond pending grand jury consideration of the charges, Rooney and his brother, who also had been arrested, went to their farm north of town. When Williams reached there after sending his telegram to Austin, the judge found the place to be an armed camp.

The Rooneys and their allies expected that Royal would not be content to let the difficulty play out in the judicial system.

On sober reflection, Royal, too, realized the gravity of the situation at the county seat. He wired the governor, seeking "four rangers at once. I want them to help enforce the law as I am powerless as sheriff."

The adjutant general had already taken action on Judge Williams' request. Sergeant Carl Kirchner and four Ranger privates arrived at Haymond, the nearest railroad station, on the train from El Paso before dawn on August 9. Soon they were crowded into a stagecoach and jouncing toward Fort Stockton.

The next day the Ranger sergeant got off a letter to headquarters reporting that the town was still stirred up, that Royal and the Rooney brothers had been on the outs since the last election, and that the sheriff was "a very overbearing & dangerous man when under the influence of liquor." The sergeant summed up the situation: "Almost the entire County seems to be against the Sheriff & I think he will realize that he has no strength & behave for the present at least."

Sheriff Royal, however, did not share the Ranger's opinion on the mood of the electorate. He was running for re-election.

And less than a month before the election, an opportunity to virtually assure his return to office appeared before Royal as unexpectedly as a maverick tumbleweed rolling out of nowhere.

For almost a year, the El Paso and San Antonio newspapers—brought into the Fort Stockton area via train and then stagecoach—had devoted considerable space to stories dealing with one Victor L. Ochoa. Ochoa, an American citizen, published several Spanish-language newspapers in the New Mexico Territory, where he also held office. But

Ochoa's political interests extended across the Rio Grande. The Mexican government believed he was fomenting rebellion against President Porfirio Diaz and appealed to the U.S. Consul for help.

On November 30, 1893, Ochoa was named in a federal warrant alleging his violation of U.S. neutrality laws. Deputy U.S. Marshal George Scarborough arrested the newspaper editor, but the U.S. Commissioner in El Paso concluded the government did not have sufficient evidence for prosecution and Ochoa was released.

But the political mudslinging escalated into bloodletting in early 1894. The Mexican army attacked Ochoa and a group of his followers in Mexico, killing all but four of them. One of the survivors was Ochoa, who fled back to the United States wearing the uniform of a Mexican soldier he had killed. His violation of the neutrality laws was now obvious, and a new arrest warrant was issued.

Meanwhile, Ochoa had disappeared into the desolate landscape of Brewster County in the Big Bend of Texas. He teamed up with someone else on the dodge, a Mexican outlaw wanted for murder in San Angelo. When the outlaw killed a cowboy in Alpine, the search for both men intensified. Now the Rangers as well as the U.S. Marshal Service were on his trail. But Ochoa was popular with the Hispanics in the area and managed to stay on the lam for ten months.

None of this had anything to do with Sheriff Royal or Pecos County, but the sheriff was well aware of Ochoa, having followed the case in the press. And Ochoa's wanted poster hung on the wall in the sheriff's office. Unknown to Royal, however, Ochoa had ridden into his county.

Royal and Ranger J.W. Fulgham arrested a suspected horse thief on October 11, 1894, in Fort Stockton. The man said his name was W.C. Blade (another source spells it "Blode"), but when the officers went through the man's effects, they found documents proving he was in fact Victor Ochoa.

News of Ochoa's arrest did not reach the U.S. marshal's office in El Paso for two days. During that time, the Pecos County sheriff had been doing some thinking. It had occurred to Royal, or perhaps one of his key supporters, that as popular as Ochoa was with Hispanics in the Trans-Pecos, and as important as the Hispanic vote was to Royal's re-election, and as important as that re-election was to Royal and his supporters, perhaps an arrangement could be made. A politician himself, Ochoa agreed.

When Deputy Marshal Scarborough arrived on October 21 to pick up Ochoa and return him to El Paso, Royal refused to release the prisoner, saying he believed the Mexican government might have offered a reward for Ochoa's arrest. Texas law made it clear that a sheriff had almost dictatorial control over his jail, but even the sheriff could not ignore a federal warrant. Royal finally assented to the release of Ochoa the following day.

Royal's supporters held a campaign rally that Saturday afternoon at the courthouse. Ochoa, it developed, had been invited to say a few words in Sheriff Royal's behalf and had accepted with pleasure. Once every Hispanic of voting age in Fort Stockton had been assembled, Ochoa delivered an impassioned address, in Spanish. Royal and his fellow slate of candidates beamed as the crowd responded enthusiastically to Ochoa's oratory. Only later—and too late—did Royal discover that Ochoa had not been endorsing the sheriff's candidacy. He had been rousing his audience with a firebrand cry for revolution in Mexico.

Beer and whiskey flowed in Fort Stockton that night as abundantly as the crystal-clear water bubbling from Comanche Springs. Royal emptied his six-shooter into the sky in an ebullient celebration of the democratic process. Ochoa was an honored guest during the festivities, drinking heartily along with Royal and his supporters. Not until well after midnight did the sheriff return the orator-fugitive to the Pecos County jail.

A few hours later, the jail was stormed by a party of masked men armed with rifles and leading a saddled horse. Swinging into the empty saddle, Victor Ochoa galloped off into the cool desert night. Rangers Fulgham and William Schmidt picked up Ochoa's trail the next morning and tracked him to Toyah, in Reeves County. Arrested without incident, Ochoa was booked into the Reeves County jail in Pecos and held there until Scarborough came out by train and returned him to El Paso.

Scarborough and the Rangers knew Ochoa's escape had not been a spur of the moment occurrence. The federal magistrate in El Paso issued arrest warrants for Royal and several of his followers, charging that they aided in the fugitive's escape. The deputy marshal returned to Fort Stockton on November 1, a week before the election, to serve the warrants. They found that Royal still had some doubt about his chances of being returned to office. Despite the support he believed he had gained from Ochoa's speech, the sheriff had adopted another campaign strategy: threatening to kill his political opponents.

One of Royal's deputies, Barney Riggs—a man considered even more dangerous than the sheriff—was first to be arrested. A convicted killer, Riggs had been released from the notorious Yuma, Arizona, prison after helping to foil a mass escape attempt by killing two inmates. After Riggs was safely in custody, the Rangers then rounded up Royal and the other two defendants in the federal escape case.

Royal claimed his arrest was merely dirty politics on the part of his opponents. From his jail cell Royal swore out complaints alleging livestock theft on the part of Judge Williams and three others from the political opposition. A

111

warrant being a warrant, the Rangers arrested three of these four men. The fourth was out of town at the time.

All seven defendants—opponents on both sides of a growing feud—were transported to Del Rio where a justice of the peace released everyone on bond.

The results of the election a few days later disappointed the sheriff. Although he carried Fort Stockton, the rest of the county's voters turned Royal out of office. The badge would go to R.B. Neighbors, the candidate supported by the Judge Williams faction. Royal was no more gracious in defeat than he had been in victory. Judge Williams and others expected more trouble from the vanquished sheriff. In fact, Williams feared for his life.

Williams, however, went on to live to old age. It was Royal who would die young. In 1939, probably realizing time was finally running down for him, Williams wrote a nine-page, single-spaced statement concerning the Royal case. That description remains the best account of Royal's demise.

Even though he was no longer sheriff, cases in which he was either a witness or a defendant made it necessary for Royal to be at the courthouse when county court convened. On November 21, 1894, after the day's last case was heard about four o'clock in the afternoon, Williams went into the clerk's office and opened a copy of the state statutes "to examine into a point of law." As he studied the law book, he heard someone yell "Royal," followed in a few seconds by "the muffled sound of a gun shot."

Williams's first thought was that Royal had shot someone. Then he pondered what to do. If Royal was outside with a smoking gun in his hand, Williams thought, the ex-sheriff's next shot might be at him. Finally, Williams left the clerk's office to see what had happened. Emerging into the hall, he saw others who also had been a little slow in leaving their offices after hearing the shot.

"I was looking closely for Royal as I knew he would shoot me on any chance like this might offer," he wrote. "Not seeing him . . . I looked towards the sheriff's office and saw a haze of smoke, out of which a moment or two afterwards came Mr. Crosby calling out 'Where's the sheriff' [referring to the newly elected officer, not Royal]."

As Williams moved cautiously toward the sheriff's office, he heard Crosby say "Royal is dead."

Two Rangers, Sergeant Kirchner and Private Schmidt, came running in the east door of the courthouse along with the newly elected Sheriff Neighbors.

Williams looked inside the small sheriff's office. Royal

> was sitting in a chair with his head bent for-
> ward and down over it with blood coming from
> his mouth. The left arm hung loosely down at
> [the] side of [the] chair and blood was streaming
> from it to the floor. The right arm rested on the
> desk on an elbow with a pen . . . loose in his
> hand. . . . The shot wound was apparently of buck-
> shot, 5 or 6 round bullet holes close together,
> being at the lower part of the left shoulder. The
> shot ranged toward the neck.

In his statement, Williams listed nine men he remembered seeing in or near the sheriff's office shortly after the shooting. "Yet I might be mistaken as to one or two of them, and there may have been one or two there that I do not now recall," he wrote.

With the blackpowder smoke still hanging in the air, these men were walking around like "cattle milling," saying, "I wonder who did it?" and "How did it happen?" Williams saw no one, however, who seemed unduly excited and "there was nothing in the appearance of anyone of them to lead me to suspect that he was the party who did the killing."

Neither of the two witnesses to the shooting were able to tell the Rangers and Sheriff Neighbors much of value. Crosby, an old man with bad eyesight, said he had been sitting in the sheriff's office reading a newspaper when he heard someone—in a voice he did not recognize—call out Royal's name. Then he saw the end of what sure looked like a Winchester shotgun sticking through the door and pointing at Royal. After the gun went off, Crosby said, he caught a momentary glimpse of someone wearing black clothing. But in the 1890s black was the most common color.

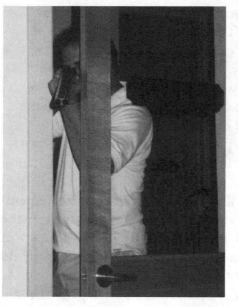

The killer stood in this doorway and blasted Royal with a shotgun. Brad Newton of Fort Stockton demonstrates the likely angle of fire. (Author's photo)

The Rangers had little physical evidence to work with. The killer took the murder weapon and the unejected spent shell with him. A doctor could have removed the lead from Royal's body, but all that would prove was the obvious: Royal had been killed with a load of buckshot. The ability of law enforcement to analyze projectiles and link them to a specific weapon by microscopic comparison was decades in the future. Though the killing happened in broad daylight in the middle of a small town, no one saw anyone running from the courthouse with a shotgun in his hand.

Coincidentally, Williams said in his statement that he had taken his shotgun to the courthouse that day because he feared for his life. But at the time of the shooting, he wrote, the gun was in a vault in the clerk's office. When he examined it later, he said, it was still loaded though one barrel did appear to have been fired a few days before. Since it was his shotgun, one would think he would remember whether he had shot it recently. Whether anyone was curious enough to sniff the barrel to determine if it had been fired was not recorded.

Williams and several others who were in the courthouse that afternoon were definitely suspects in the murder. No one ever disputed that Royal was roundly feared and hated and that the town's civic leaders had decided they'd had enough. The electorate had spoken, but removal from office had only made Royal a mean, drunken ex-sheriff. Buckshot, however, offered a permanent solution to the county's problem—at least from the standpoint of those who were not among Royal's family and friends.

In fairness to Royal, he did have his supporters. While he clearly had a drinking problem, he also sang in the church choir. His children adored him, and judging by the touching message inscribed on his tombstone, his widow had truly loved her husband. The power of the feelings generated by the Royal case, which boiled down to an old-fashioned feud between his faction and Judge Williams and his crowd, is clearly evident in an article by Royal's granddaughter published in a two-volume Pecos County history ninety years after Royal's death:

When told they were bringing him home [after the shooting], my mother [one of Royal's daughters] ran around the house to hide—and ran into a large group of his friends carrying him home on a stretcher—and she stood very still, seeing the blood dripping from his boot!

There could never be any justification for his death . . . a grieving, loving wife—frightened small children—deprived forever of the warmth, the goodness, the protection, the tender guidance and love of this good husband and father.

(Author's photo)

"Who shot Royal?" remains a popular parlor game of sorts among the historically minded residents of Pecos County.

The prime theory is that a group of Fort Stockton men, including Williams, either fearful for their own lives or in the interest of what they felt was a civic improvement project, agreed that Royal should be killed and drew straws to determine who would have the honor. In one version of the story, the "winner" of the draw declared he could not go through with it and another of the conspirators stepped forward to do the job.

Another theory is that one of the many men with a grudge against Royal acted alone and managed to escape without being seen.

A third theory is that a Texas Ranger was paid $500 by some unknown party or parties to kill Royal. Though Royal constituted no serious threat to any of the Rangers, at least not in a fair fight, the Ochoa affair had definitely strained relations between the state officers and Royal. Of the trio of Rangers in Fort Stockton at the time of Royal's murder, the one whose name came up in this connection was Private Schmidt.

But Sergeant Kirchner said in his report of the shooting that Schmidt had been with him on a routine walk-through of local saloons when the shot was fired, which means both Rangers would have had to have been involved in the murder plot. That two Rangers would go bad for an assumed 50-50 split of the blood money, only a few month's pay each, seems highly unlikely. Besides, the Rangers generally only carried .45 revolvers and .30-30 rifles, not shotguns.

Still, stories circulated about Schmidt. One was that as an old man, some time in the 1950s or perhaps even earlier, he had written a Fort Stockton judge that he had killed Royal for $500 while serving as a Ranger and wanted to get it off his chest before he died. But when West Texas historian Clayton W. Williams—the son of Judge O.W. Williams—checked the story with the son of the man who

117

supposedly received the letter of confession, the son knew nothing of it.

Fort Stockton historian Lee Harris tells the other story: "In the late 1970s, Ross McSwain of the San Angelo *Standard-Times* was to be the speaker at the Pecos County Historical Commission's annual meeting. He told me he was going to interview an old man in his nineties who had been a Texas Ranger around Fort Stockton and asked me if there was anything he should ask him. I told Ross to ask him who killed A.J. Royal."

Later, Harris said, McSwain talked with the former Ranger, who was hospitalized and not expected to live much longer. When McSwain asked the question Harris had suggested, she said, the old-timer "nearly fell out of his bed."

After composing himself, Harris said, the man replied, "Why do you ask?"

The old man would not talk about the case, she said.

Interestingly enough, a Texas Ranger also was mentioned as a possible suspect in another mysterious shooting death not too long before Royal's murder. This case was in Langtry, only 125 miles southwest of Fort Stockton, and involved the shooting of Charlie Small, a well-known border character who had spent time in a Mexican prison. Someone shot Small in the back as he walked past the water tank in Langtry.

The case was never officially solved, but as historian Jack Skiles wrote, "It was believed generally that a ranger, who Langtry folks later said wanted to make a name for himself, had been hiding near the water tank and ambushed Small as he walked by."

Was a killer angel with a silver star working the Trans-Pecos country in the mid-1890s? No one will ever know, unless the alleged written confession by Schmidt—if indeed it was Schmidt—ever comes to light and could be authenticated. One thing about the case is fairly certain: The people around Fort Stockton are not likely to stop speculating about who shot A.J. Royal.

...... ✪ ......

Sources

Daggett, Marsha Lea. ed. *Pecos County History*. Fort Stockton: Pecos County Historical Commission, 1984, Vol. II, pp. 420-421.

DeArment, Robert K. *George Scarborough: The Life and Death of a Lawman on the Closing Frontier*. Norman: University of Oklahoma Press, 1992, pp. 53-57.

Harris, Lee. Interview with the author, July 29, 1996.

James. Bill C. and Mary Kay Shannon. *Sheriff A.J. Royal: Fort Stockton, Texas,* n.p., 1984, pp. 21-31.

Skiles, Jack. *Judge Roy Bean Country*. Lubbock: Texas Tech University Press, 1996, p. 181.

Williams, Clayton W. Ernest Wallace. ed. *Texas' Last Frontier: Fort Stockton and the Trans-Pecos, 1861-1895*. College Station: Texas A&M University Press, 1982, pp. 339-388.

Williams, O.W. "Statement." Photocopy of 1939 typescript. A.J. Royal file. Annie Riggs Museum, Fort Stockton, Texas.

Notes

* Comanche Springs dried up in the 1950s drought and now flows only intermittently and in low volume.

Zane Grey and the Texas Rangers

To the accompaniment of a tinny piano, the jerky action unfolded on the theater screen in flickering black and white. Cowboys in high-crowned white hats blazed away at villains in black hats in the silent Tom Mix film *The Taming of Texas Pete*. Ladies in the audience already had removed *their* hats, so as not to block someone's view of the moving picture. Everyone wanted his ten cents' worth.

In 1913 a growing audience was enjoying the nascent motion picture industry's romanticized vision of the Wild West, a time that even then seemed long ago. After all, the second decade of the twentieth century was one of ragtime music, fast cars, and airplanes. War was brewing in Europe, and in New York City, 40,000 women marched in a suffragette parade. The world was changing rapidly.

But down along the Texas-Mexican border, life was different. This was readily apparent to the Western writer Zane Grey, who had grown up in the comparative refinement of Ohio and now lived in an area generally known to Texans as "back East." When Grey stepped off the Southern Pacific train at El Paso's Union Station on San Francisco Street, newsboys hawked papers full of stories of border violence from Texas to Arizona. Soldiers from Fort Bliss, soldiers of fortune, and temporarily displaced Mexican revolutionaries crowded the bars, brothels, and gaming houses in the city's well-known red-light district. Horse-drawn hacks competed for space with Hupmobiles,

Hudsons, Chalmers, and Fords on the city's busy streets. Soldiers who still fought on horseback could hire a ride in a new automobile to Tillie's Parlor House for a nickel. Services available inside Tillie's were somewhat more expensive.

Grey had come to West Texas to do research for a novel on the Texas Rangers. After spending some time in mid-April with Ranger Captain John R. Hughes and his men of Company A, Grey would write in his dedication in *The Lone Star Ranger*:

> To Captain John Hughes and his Texas Rang-
> ers... Gentlemen,—I have the honor to dedicate
> this book to you, and the hope that it shall fall to
> my lot to tell the world the truth about a strange,
> unique, and misunderstood body of men—the
> Texas Rangers—who made the great Lone Star
> State habitable, who never know peaceful rest
> and sleep... who will surely not be forgotten and
> will some day come into their own.

Grey also wrote that in the North and East, "there is a popular idea that the frontier of the West is a thing long past, and remembered now only in stories." But the dentist-turned-writer had quickly learned, as one seasoned Ranger told him, that the border in 1913 "Shore is 'most as bad an' wild as ever!"

Maybe that Ranger had a premonition. Only a few months after Grey's novel was published, the lawman would be dead, gunned down by outlaws in a classic Old West ambush. Even before the book came out, time had already run out for two of the Rangers Grey met that spring.

★

In 1913 El Paso was a city of 48,604, the largest community between San Antonio, Texas, and San Diego, California. At the McCoy, facing the downtown Pioneer Plaza, rooms were $1.50 and up. Since the hotel was brand new, Grey might have stayed there, but the larger Hotel Paso del Norte, with 300 rooms, advertised "accommodations equal to the best that can be obtained anywhere." Fifty of its rooms even had baths.

Hotel Orndorff and Plaza. El Paso. Texas

El Paso in the early 1900s.

Grey's novel *Riders of the Purple Sage* had earned him national recognition as a writer, but with El Paso's sister city Juarez teeming with revolutionary intrigue just across the river, Grey's arrival in El Paso apparently did not stir up much local interest. His name does not show up in indexes of El Paso newspapers published that year.

The papers were, however, full of stories related to Captain Hughes and his Rangers, who had their camp downriver from El Paso at the old Spanish settlement of Ysleta, the original county seat. With the unrest in Mexico, and its spillover effect in West Texas, the captain and his men had their hands full. On top of that, labor trouble had hit the American Smelting and Refining Company, El Paso's largest employer. In fact, it is a wonder that Hughes had any time at all to spend with Grey.

The border in 1913 was "as bad an' wild as ever!"

But Captain Hughes, while feared by the lawless element, was a kindly man, ever the gentleman. He did not drink, smoke, or use rough language, and did not tolerate such behavior in his men. He would have welcomed Grey into his camp. That was the Code of the West.

Grey profited from his time with the Rangers. He learned how real Rangers looked, thought, made their camp, and risked their lives for the State of Texas. Years later a full-page magazine ad taken out by the Zane Grey Library in Roslyn, New York, touted: "Zane Grey actually lived and rode with the Rangers. He even chased down desperadoes with them. And finally he weaved everything he'd experienced first-hand into fiction that blazes with realism."

That advertising copy was stretching the blanket a bit, but Grey heard plenty of good stories from Hughes and his men. Whatever Grey's experiences with the Rangers were, other than what he wrote in his four-paragraph dedication, he left no known account of his dealings with Hughes and his men. Though a prolific correspondent and diarist, Grey apparently preferred to filter his Ranger experiences through the prism of his fiction.

Official records of the activities of Company A for 1913 are scant, though revealing. Ranger captains were required to submit a monthly scouting report, but only the report for December 1913 survives in the State Archives. That month the company consisted of Hughes and four privates, five horses, and four mules. State property on hand included: one wagon, one hack, three sets of harnesses, three pack saddles, six iron bedsteads, two pairs of handcuffs, two pairs of leg irons, one old cook stove, two tables, and one "pack pocket." Though the Rangers furnished their own horses and weapons, the State of Texas magnanimously supplied ammunition. Company A had 1,000 rounds in its inventory. The Rangers traveled 5,316 miles that December and made four arrests—one for burglary, two for disturbing the peace, and one for unlawfully carrying a pistol.

······ ✪ ······

Grey's dedication, though effusive, raises many more questions than it answers about his time with the Rangers. Aside from Hughes, five other Rangers are mentioned— "Ranger Coffee," "Joe Sitters," "the giant Vaughan," and "Russell and Moore." For some reason, Grey did not offer the first names of Coffee, Vaughan, Russell, or Moore. Who were these men who helped inspire a Western classic? Whatever happened to them?

"Ranger Coffee"

"Ranger Coffee" remains a mystery man. No one named Coffee shows up on the muster rolls of Captain Hughes' company.

An A.B. Coffee served in the Frontier Battalion starting in 1879, eight years before Hughes first joined the force. Hughes may have known Coffee and suggested that Grey talk with him about the Rangers.

Coffee later became commander of the Ex-Rangers Association and was active in Ranger reunions, which is good circumstantial evidence that he was something of a raconteur, the sort of person Grey would have sought out for stories of Ranger lore.

When W.W. Sterling became adjutant general in 1931, he put Coffee on the state payroll. His principal duty was to help old Rangers in getting pensions for their frontier service. When Sterling stepped down as adjutant general after Miriam "Ma" Ferguson was elected governor, Coffee followed suit on January 16, 1933.

While A.B. Coffee is the most likely suspect, there is one other: Robert William Coffee. Born in Paint Rock,

Texas, on Halloween in 1883, he was appointed as a Texas Ranger on New Year's Day, 1945. Coffee was stationed in Captain Hughes' old stomping grounds—Sierra Blanca in Hudspeth County—until his retirement on August 31, 1953. But Texas Department of Public Safety records show no indication of previous Ranger service by Coffee, which would auger against his being the one mentioned in Grey's dedication, since Grey specifically referred to his source as "Ranger Coffee." Still, the old records are not perfect, and Coffee would have been thirty years old in 1913 when Grey was in West Texas. But Robert Coffee would not have had as many stories to tell as A.B. Coffee. As they say on the border, *Quien sabe?*

"The Giant Vaughan"

When Grey met Jefferson Eagle Vaughan, the Ranger's head was still bandaged from a gunfight only a few days earlier.

Captain Hughes had written the Adjutant General on April 1, 1913, quoting a telegram he had just received from the sheriff of Presidio County: "Vaughan captured one cow thief on river. Returning from river with prisoner was ambushed. Killed one Mexican in fight."

Vaughan had been in the Rangers only a short time before Grey's visit. His first enlistment form is not in the State Archives, but subsequent enlistments are documented. When he reupped in the Rangers on September 15, 1917, he showed his age as 35 and place of birth as Kendalia in Kendall County, Texas. He was six feet one-and-a-half inches tall, had blue eyes, brown hair. He listed his occupation as ranchman and said he was single.

Two years later, when Vaughan again reenlisted, he showed his prior experience as one year as a U.S. Mounted Customs Inspector and three years as a deputy sheriff. This was probably in Presidio County, though it is not noted on the form.

Vaughan, like most of the Rangers on the border, saw plenty of action. A fellow Ranger, Robert Lee Burdett, was killed on June 8, 1915, by Mexican bandits near Fabens, in El Paso County. Riding with Ranger Ivey Findley, Vaughan splashed across the river into Mexico to hunt down the two killers. Vaughan had been on the border long enough to develop something of a friendship with Pancho Villa, who had not yet fallen out of favor with Americans by raiding Columbus, New Mexico. Villa agreed to help the two Rangers and found the two murderers first. He held the men for Vaughan and Findley to identify. The cooperative revolutionary then obligingly saved the State of Texas the cost of a trial and stood the two Ranger killers up before a firing squad as Vaughan and the other Ranger looked on with approval. The two Rangers then rode back to Texas and reported the case closed.

Vaughan stayed in the Rangers until 1919, when he resigned to run for sheriff of Presidio County. He was elected and served until 1927, when he was defeated in the July 24, 1926 election. The former Ranger returned to ranching full time. In the fall of 1929 he was selected as the only judge from the United States for the fourth annual World Series of Rodeo at Madison Square Garden in New York. Vaughan was quite a hit in the Big Apple. He rode his horse, Jack O'Diamonds, up to City Hall, where he was greeted by the city's dapper mayor, Jimmy Walker.

Returning to the Rangers in January 1933, Vaughan went back as a captain. A year later a Presidio County newspaper noted that Vaughan was the "last surviving member of a little group of four Texas Rangers to whom Zane Grey dedicated ... *The Lone Star Ranger*. (The newspaper reporter apparently had not realized Captain Hughes was still very much alive and well in El Paso at the time.)

Vaughn left the Rangers for the last time after a couple of years service.

He moved to Stephenville, in Erath County, Texas, in 1949. On a business trip back to Marfa in 1958, he suffered a heart attack and died on October 1 in an Alpine hospital.

"Russell"

Grey must have been particularly impressed with a young man who had been one of Captain Hughes' Rangers less than a year, Scott Russell. The writer even used Russell's last name for one of the Rangers in his novel, the only real name he used.

Twenty-four years old, Russell enlisted in the Rangers on October 1, 1912. He was five feet, ten inches tall, had brown eyes, black hair, and was single.

Russell would have an active but short career as a Ranger. Barely two months after Grey spent time with Company A, Captain Hughes wired the adjutant general in Austin:

"Ranger Russell killed in action here today."

The message came to the Postal Telegraph-Cable Company office in Austin's Driskill Hotel at 10:22 on the night of June 23, 1913. An operator telephoned the adjutant general with the news eight minutes later.

General Henry Hutchings got more detail on Russell's death in the next day's Austin *Statesman*, which had a banner story on the tense situation in El Paso. Pancho Villa's army was moving on Juarez. Ranger Russell's death, since it was not directly related to the ongoing revolution across the river, did not get mentioned until the fourth paragraph of the newspaper story.

Captain Hughes typed a letter to the general on June 24 with additional details: Russell and El Paso sheriff's deputy W.H. Garlick had a warrant for one Manuel Guadarama for cattle theft. They went to a store run by

Juan Guadarama, hoping to find Manuel. Not wanting to immediately tip their hand, they went into the store and asked for ten cents' worth of tobacco.

At that point, the captain wrote, "Mrs. Guadarama, mother of Juan, struck Russell in the back of the head with an axe handle and stunned him, and Juan shot Russell as he fell—then shot Deputy Sheriff Garlick, killing both. Then he pulled down the window curtains and beat them both with a hatchet.... We have plenty of evidence that the killing was planned several days ahead, and that they were prepared for the first opportunity."

Hughes did not mention it in his letter, but Mrs. Guadarama had caught a stray round during the shooting and died later that night.

The body of the young Ranger was sent by train back to Central Texas, escorted by a Ranger comrade. Russell was buried in East End Memorial Cemetery in Stephenville.

Nine arrests were made in the murder of the two lawmen, but the El Paso County Grand Jury indicted only Juan and two brothers, David and Jesus. The case was tried twice. On June 18, 1915, at the conclusion of the second trial, the El Paso *Herald* reported that Juan had been found guilty of second degree murder in the slaying of the Ranger. Jesus was acquitted. His brother David was released on an instructed verdict of not guilty. A week later, Juan's attorney withdrew a motion for a new trial, his client settling for a five-year prison sentence. Given the sentiments of the day, the Guadarama boys must have had a very competent lawyer working in their behalf. Many had died on the border for much less than killing a Texas Ranger.

"Moore"

C.R. Moore was not a tall man, only five feet six-and-a-half inches, but he had what it took to be a Ranger.

Born in Indianola, a once-flourishing seaport on the middle Texas coast, Moore enlisted in the Rangers on February 23, 1909. By 1913 he was a sergeant under Captain Hughes.

The year before Grey's visit to El Paso, the situation along the border was particularly tense. Captain Hughes was writing the governor almost daily, and his men were keeping a close watch on the movements of revolutionary forces on the other side of the Rio Grande. The captain had information that the revolutionaries were thinking about crossing into Texas to appropriate food and supplies.

In August 1912 Sergeant Moore and Private C.H. Webster were shadowing a rebel force maneuvering parallel to the river. The two Rangers walked their horses in cadence with the opposing Mexican army. This show of force ended without incident, but when another rebel group seemed likely to raid into Texas, Captain Hughes once again sent Moore and Webster to hold themselves forth as a reception committee.

The two Rangers found the revolutionaries and camped across from them. Two days later six rebel soldiers started across the river. When Moore told them to turn back, the Mexicans took one look at the Rangers' leveled rifles and reined their horses.

The Mexicans moved upriver, followed by the two Rangers, who had a sheriff's deputy riding along with them. The rebels must have been giving the odds some thought, finally concluding there were more of them than there were Texans. This time the whole party splashed into the water, headed for Texas.

Moore, Webster, and the deputy quickly took position behind some rocks. Moore yelled for the riders to halt. The rebels did what they were told, but only so they could shoot better. But when three rebel horses suddenly found themselves without riders, the surviving rebels ignored their orders and wheeled their horses for the safety of the Mexican side. The Texas officers settled in for another attack, but it was not forthcoming. When they got tired of waiting, they rode back to El Paso to report the incident.

Only a couple of months prior to Grey's arrival in El Paso, Texas Governor O.B. Colquitt wrote Captain Hughes on February 3, 1913:

> I think the time has come when the State should not hesitate to deal with these marauding bands of rebels in a way which they will understand. I approve the course of Sergeant Moore and Private Webster in this incident, and I instruct you and your men to keep them off of Texas territory if possible, and if they invade the State let them understand they do so at the risk of their lives.

For standing off small armies, the State of Texas paid Sergeant Moore $50 a month. Webster and the other Ranger privates earned $40 a month. About the time of Grey's visit, Moore resigned from the Rangers and took an appointment as a deputy U.S. marshal.

Moore's career as a lawman was cut short, not by a bullet from a Mexican rebel, but by a medical problem. On April 7, 1914, three days after undergoing intestinal surgery, Moore died at Hotel Dieu, El Paso's Catholic Hospital. The official cause of death was listed as "intestinal obstruction." Though a brief article in the El Paso *Herald* noted that Moore saw "intense action on the border as a deputy sheriff, Ranger and a federal officer," it made no mention of any act of violence that preceded his hospitalization. The former Ranger had not died with his boots on, though submitting to surgery in the days before antibiotics was in itself a brave thing to do.

"I have never lost a battle..."

In 1913 Captain Hughes was the oldest Ranger still in active service. He had worn a Ranger badge since 1887 and had known many of the legendary characters of the Old West, including outlaw-turned-lawyer John Wesley Hardin, gunned down in El Paso's Acme Saloon on August 19, 1895.

Two years after Grey met the captain, a newspaper proclaimed: "Captain Hughes has made for himself a name that was a terror to evildoers, particularly those who inhabited the Big Bend region of the state and made a business of 'cattle rustling.'"

By accident of birth, John Reynolds Hughes was a Yankee. Hughes was born in Cambridge, Illinois, in 1855. When he was a child, his parents moved to Mound City, Kansas. In 1869 Hughes' father gave the lad a pony and a saddle and the fourteen-year-old began cowboying on neighboring ranches. A year later Hughes rode off to Indian Territory (Oklahoma) and hired on with an outfit that provided beef to reservation Indians. Hughes' first gunfight came when a half-breed rustler made the mistake of trying to cut out some stock the young cowboy had been herding. The outcome was a funeral for the rustler and a bullet in Hughes' right arm. After that, he never had full use of the limb. Before long, however, he was as quick with his left hand as he had been with his right, leading most folks to believe he had been born left-handed.

When the beef contracting job played out, Hughes threw in with a herd headed from Indian Territory back to Kansas. In Ellis, Kansas, he met a Texas cattleman who hired him to make a trail drive from Texas to the railhead in Kansas. In Texas for the first time, Hughes liked what he saw. Returning to the Lone Star State in 1878 with his wages from the cattle drive, he bought a seventy-six-acre ranch in Central Texas with his brother.

Now thirty, Hughes had been in some of the wildest spots in the wildest years of the Old West and already had prevailed in one shoot-out. But he was a peaceable man, one who preferred poetry and the quiet contemplation of a passage from his Bible to any of the vices so easily available on the frontier. His pistol stayed in its holster, hanging on the ranch house wall. Unlike many men of his time, Hughes considered the weapon a tool to be used when needed, not an item of ornamental apparel.

Hughes specialized in horses, building his stock from the herds of wild mustangs still roaming West Texas and New Mexico. He was a contented man until one morning in 1886, when he awoke to find that someone had had the poor judgment to ride off with sixteen of his best animals, including Moscow, his favorite stallion. Another fifty-four horses were missing from neighboring Williamson County ranches.

As Hughes later related it, "I followed them to New Mexico, got all my horses back and a lot of my neighbor's horses. The band of [horse thieves] was all broken up. Two of them were . . . sent to the New Mexico penitentiary. I just lacked 15 days of being gone a year on that trip." Hughes forgot to mention that he had killed three of the horse thieves, leaving two survivors to stand trial.

Back in Texas, Hughes returned his six-shooter to its place on his ranch house wall and "went about attending to my stock."

Things were quiet until a loyal friend of the jailed horse thieves came to Texas to settle accounts. The man intended to kill Hughes, but when he showed up at Hughes' ranch, Hughes happened not to be there. Hughes did not know someone was gunning for him, nor did he know that a Texas Ranger already was on the outlaw's trail with a murder warrant. Ranger Ira Aten, who would become Hughes' lifelong friend, met up with the gunman at Hughes' ranch.

"They exchanged shots," Hughes recalled. "The ranger shot the pistol out of his hand, but the man got away. The man was wanted for murder, and some other offense. The ranger asked me to help catch the man."

Three weeks later, Hughes and Aten found the outlaw.

"Unfortunately," Hughes put it years later, "he would not surrender and was killed. His friends then were so annoying to me that I could not go without arms, so the ranger persuaded me to enlist in the company with him."

On August 10, 1887, in Georgetown, Texas, Hughes began a Ranger career he expected to last no more than six to eight months. But rangering agreed with Hughes and months turned into years. By the spring of 1890 he had made sergeant. Three years later, when Captain Frank Jones died in a gunbattle with Mexican outlaws, Hughes was named as his replacement. If he needed any other reason to stay in the Rangers, the young woman Hughes intended to marry became ill and died. Each year after that, the captain made a pilgrimage to visit her grave on the Texas coast. The rest of the time, he trailed badmen.

When he retired with twenty-seven years' service to the state, Hughes modestly summarized his career as a Ranger: "Unfortunately, I have been in several engagements where desperate criminals were killed. I have never lost a battle that I was in personally, and never let a prisoner escape."

Despite his success as a Ranger, Hughes had never figured on reaching his golden years. "For several years," he said, "I did not expect to live to the age that I am now. I expected to be killed." In retirement, he returned to ranching and eventually became a bank president.

Hughes was ninety-two years old before a bullet finally did end his long and rich life—a bullet fired by his own hand. On June 3, 1947, the old Ranger's body, his .45 nearby, was found in a garage behind a relative's home in Austin, where he had been staying. The captain's health had been failing, and he did not want to be a burden to his family. He was buried in the State Cemetery with other heroes of Texas.

Sources

Cox, Mike. "Zane Gray and the Texas Rangers," *The Zane Grey Reporter*, Vol. 5, No. 3, Summer 1990, pp. 1, 4-8.

Zane Grey and the
Rangers II: Joe Sitters

*I*f the size and quality of a grave marker are a legitimate indication of the caliber of the person buried beneath it, Joe Sitters has been cheated.

One of the toughest and most efficient Rangers ever to ride the river lies in a lonely cemetery at Valentine, Texas. His marker is a piece of metal welded to an iron rod. Crudely cut in the metal are the words "Joe Gitters." Whoever did the work did not even get his name spelled right.

Had *The Lone Star Ranger* been published in the second half of 1915 rather than January, Zane Grey undoubtedly would have wanted to rewrite his introduction so he could let the world know about what had happened to Sitters, the Ranger who told him in 1913 that the Texas-Mexican border was "'most as bad an' wild as ever!"

Few on the border were any more qualified to make that pronouncement than Ranger Sitters, who had been on the river almost as long as the Border Boss himself, Captain John Hughes.

Born in Medina County, Texas, Sitters was a descendant of a pioneer family that settled near Castroville, a community largely made up of immigrants from Alsace-Loraine who came to Texas in the 1840s. Sitters stood five feet eight inches and had reddish-brown hair and light blue eyes. "His eyes saw everything," his daughter later recalled, "and he was quick with a gun." He had worked as a cowboy before turning to law enforcement.

Sitters joined Company D, Frontier Battalion, on August 1, 1893, shortly before his thirtieth birthday. He stayed with the Rangers until October 25, 1896. On December 7 he was appointed a Special Ranger. Special Rangers were not paid by the state, though they generally were on someone else's payroll, often as inspectors for the Texas and Southwestern Cattle Raisers Association. On paper the authority of a Special Ranger was somewhat limited in comparison with members of the Frontier Battalion, but the qualifier "Special" did not get much attention. Along the border the word people paid attention to was "Ranger."

Grey was in El Paso in 1913 doing his Texas research when he met Joe Sitters. The mustachioed former Ranger was not on the state payroll, but in that era, most folks figured once a Ranger, always a Ranger.

Before he had signed on under Captain Hughes back in 1893, Sitters had been working as a U.S. Mounted Customs Inspector along the river below El Paso. "Joe could hardly spell his name," one Western writer later put it, "but he could read a cold trail like a book. [He was] a first class fighting man, with the low forehead and big, bony eyebrows of a close observer."

Despite Sitters' excellent reputation as a tracker of cattle thieves, the federal government decided its inspectors all had to take a civil service examination. A wave of "Eastern dudes" handier with fountain pens than six-shooters took over as Customs Inspectors, and old pros like Sitters were out of a job. Before long, however, smugglers and cattle rustlers along the border were having a field day. Pickings were easy under the watch of the green Customs Inspectors new to the border.

When local cattlemen began complaining to the government, Sitters was rehired—temporarily—to recover missing stock. In one rustling investigation, Sitters followed sixty head of cattle and their outlaw appropriators, crossed the river into Mexico and back into Texas, and pursued his quarry a hundred miles north of the river, up into the Davis Mountains. It took a while, but Sitters finally returned to El Paso with the stolen livestock and the thieves. The feat attracted Captain Hughes' attention and led him to hire Sitters away from federal service.

One time Hughes was hurrying to meet a man at the train station in Ysleta. During the bumpy wagon ride to the depot, the captain's gun jarred out of its holster. When he realized the gun was gone, Hughes instructed one of his men to retrieve the pistol on his way back to camp.

The Ranger dispatched on this errand, no slouch at cutting sign, could not find the weapon. He came back and told Sitters, who rode out of camp, saying nothing. On Ysleta's dusty main street, Sitters found a mark made in the dirt by Hughes' falling .45. Then he saw the sandal tracks of the man who had picked it up. That explained why the first Ranger had not found the captain's pistol. Sitters followed the tracks to the Rio Grande, where he found a Tiqua Indian sitting in his camp, weaving a basket.

"Did you see a pistol uptown?" Sitters asked.

"No," the Indian replied.

Sitters' blue eyes, shaded by his high brows, studied the Indian and his surroundings for a moment. The Ranger's gaze settled on a blanket spread on the ground near the Indian. He walked over and pulled it up, exposing the captain's pistol.

The Ranger's skills as a tracker eventually won him another federal job. Sitters went back to work as a Customs Inspector, this time somehow getting around the required civil service test.

As Grey mentioned in his dedication, at the time he was with Sitters, the veteran lawman "grimly stroked an un-healed bullet wound" while making his pronouncement that the border still was wild. Grey was not taking poetic license. When they met, Sitters was recovering from a head wound suffered in a gun battle on February 10, 1913. Two years later, he would face gunfire again.

Sitting around the camp fire with the Rangers in the cool mountain air, Grey doubtless heard plenty of stories from Sitters and the other men about a Mexican outlaw named Chico Cano. Cano never enjoyed the national recognition afforded various other border outlaws, but he was a thief who would steal the canteen from a man dying of thirst and a vicious killer. He had vowed to kill Sitters, and the Ranger warmly returned the sentiment.

Cano and two brothers, Jose and Manuel, operated across from two small settlements in the Big Bend, El Pourvenir and Pilares. Though on the Texas side of the river, these two communities were isolated by a rugged mountain range. In reality, they were much more accessible to Mexico than Texas, and most of their residents were Mexican. Cano had many friends—not to mention relatives—on both sides of the river. Though revolution was raging in Mexico, the Cano brothers adroitly sided themselves with whomever happened to be prevailing at the time. They were outlaws, not patriots.

The gang, through friends and relatives, generally heard about it when Rangers or federal officers were in the vicinity. But during the second week of February in 1913, their grapevine must have failed them.

John Simpson Howard, a Customs Inspector in Presidio County since 1902, along with Sitters and J.S. "Ad" Harvick, an inspector for the Texas and Southwestern Cattle Raisers Association, found out that Cano and his brothers were on the Texas side of the river to attend a wake. Since Cano was wanted for cattle theft, Sitters suggested that they pay their respects to the departed and arrest Cano while they were at it.

The officers quietly surrounded the house where the wake was in progress and shouted to Cano and his men to surrender. In Spanish the outlaws answered back, asking that the ladies in the crowd—in consideration of their safety—be allowed to leave. Then the men—hastily appropriating suitable gowns from the female mourners—left the house and quickly disappeared into the night.

The outlaws had correctly read the officers. The chivalrous lawmen fell for the ruse. Cano's brothers soon shed their skirts and safely crossed the river into Mexico. Chico Cano, however, was too tall to pass himself off as a *senorita*. He was arrested. The officers were disgusted with themselves, but at least they had Cano, the outlaw they wanted most.

Back on their side of the Rio Grande, the Cano brothers got together a group of sympathetic *pistoleros* and splashed back across the river to free their arrested *hermano*.

Meanwhile, the officers and their prisoner had camped near Pilares for the night. In the morning, the men started back to civilization with the wanted outlaw.

During the night, Cano's friends and relatives had positioned themselves at each of the three passes on the trails leading out of Pilares. The officers would have to take one of the three.

On the morning of February 10, the three officers and their prisoner got about a mile and a half from their camping place near Pilares when the bandits opened fire on them from both sides of the pass. Howard tumbled from his horse, dead. Harvick also took a bullet, suffering a serious wound. Another slug glanced off Sitters' skull, knocking him off his horse, unconscious. When he came to, Cano and the other ambushers were gone.

After a convalescence at Hotel Dieu, the Catholic hospital in El Paso, Sitters went back on the job. He was still wearing a bandage when Grey met him a few months later.

The slow-talking lawman immortalized in Grey's dedication began his final scout on May 21, 1915. Sitters and
four other officers rode out of Valentine in Jeff Davis
County and headed south toward the river. The following
day they camped at a water hole about seven miles from
Pilares. The officers had heard from some of Pancho Villa's
men that a group of Mexican bandits were hiding in the
mountains on the Texas side of the Rio Grande.

On May 23, with Sitters in command, the officers moved
into the mountains in search of the bandits. Sitters, of
course, was hoping Cano would be with them. Sitters and
Ranger Eugene Hulen—the brother of former Adjutant
General John A. Hulen—worked their way up a peak to
take a look-see with field glasses while the other three men
rode into a canyon, cutting for sign.

Sitters, expert tracker that he was, had nevertheless
fallen into another trap. Suddenly, from the high rocks on
either side of the canyon, lead started raining down on the
officers. Seeking cover in the rocks, the lawmen began
returning fire. The three officers could see Sitters and
Hulen, trapped in their observation spot by gunfire.

Five times the men tried to fight their way to Sitters
and Hulen. Each time they were pushed back by the
bandits' fire. Four hours later, still under heavy fire, the
lawmen made it to the place Sitters and Hulen had been,
only to find that the two officers had moved their position.
Apparently, Sitters and the Ranger had made it farther up
the canyon, where shooting still could be heard.

Outnumbered, afoot—their mounts had run away or
been killed—and facing heat exhaustion from lack of water,
the three officers had to pull back out of the canyon. When
they were out of rifle range, the distant gunfire stopped.
The officers had no way of knowing if the silence meant
their colleagues had escaped, or been captured or killed.

The trio walked five miles back to the water hole where they had camped. Fortunately, their pack animals were still there. The officers unstrapped the pack saddles and rode the mules another five miles to the Bill McGee Ranch. From there, the exhausted officers hastily scrawled a note and sent it with a rider to another ranch, six miles distant. After reading the note, rancher Joe Pool telephoned news of the ambush to Marfa, the Presidio County seat. As word spread, men quickly formed a posse. Eleven armed men rushed to the Pool Ranch by automobile, reaching it that night. Pool provided saddle horses for the men, who mounted up and rode to the McGee Ranch to meet up with the three officers who had escaped the ambush.

The posse's departure was reported in the May 25 El Paso *Herald*. The location of the ambush was fixed as six miles from the Mexican border. The article noted that "Sitters is said to have killed several Mexican outlaws on the border."

By 3 o'clock in the afternoon on May 25, the posse reached the mountain pass where bandits had trapped the lawmen. A short time later they found the bodies of Sitters and Hulen.

Only one empty shell casing was found near the dead Hulen, leading posse members to surmise that the young Ranger had been gravely wounded at the outset of the fight. But they found sixty shells scattered around Sitters. He had put up a tough fight, but by that point, it was one man against an estimated thirty-five bandits.

One of the posse members, R.M. Wadsworth, later described the scene during a Congressional investigation of border violence. He testified that Sitters "was lying on his back in a sort of cramped position; looked like he died in great agony, his knees drawn up, cramped up, his hands and fingers . . . drawn up over his face; you could see where his flesh had been knocked off his knuckles by rocks; his left eye . . . had been caved in . . . He had eleven bullet holes in his body."

A bloody twenty-pound rock was found near the bodies, Wadsworth said, indicating both men had been pummeled with the stone. The bandits had taken the officers' clothes, boots, watches, money, and weapons.

The bodies had been lying in the desert heat for a day and a half. Grimly, the posse members loaded the two dead lawmen onto skittish pack mules. On the way back to the Pool Ranch, the mule burdened with Sitters' body became sick and vomited.

The murder of the two officers—a well-known former Ranger and a young man still on the Rangers' rolls—outraged the state.

Captain John Hughes, Sitters' old boss, had retired five months before. But he was so angered by his old friend's death that he considered saddling up and personally tracking down Cano and his band. From the west, fifty volunteers took the train from El Paso to Marfa. Many of the men were friends of Sitters. From the east, Ranger Captain Monroe Fox arrived from Austin with every man in his company.

The Texas House of Representatives passed a resolution demanding more federal protection along the border. A short time later—reacting not to the Texas Legislature but to the reality of the situation—the military command at Fort Bliss in El Paso began moving additional cavalry to the Big Bend Country.

Ten soldiers of the 15th Cavalry captured three Mexicans near Valentine believed to have been involved in the killing of the two officers. The khaki-clad soldiers, having no civil law enforcement authority, turned the trio over to the Texas Rangers. The Rangers agreed to take the prisoners to Valentine. When the lawmen arrived in Valentine, however, they had no prisoners.

A rocky, unpaved road leads to the ranch where Ranger Joe Sitters was gunned down and beaten to death by outlaws. (Author's photo)

Cano was indicted for the murder of Sitters and Hulen. But despite the best efforts of the Rangers, federal authorities, and enraged possemen, the bandit eluded capture.

No one knows for sure what happened to Cano. Hearsay had it that he was later killed by a horse and buried in Ojinaga, across from Presidio.

Hallie Stillwell was teaching school in Marathon when Sitters was killed.

"I was taking meals with Mrs. Craighead," Mrs. Stillwell recalled years later. "Her husband (Customs officer Charles Craighead, a former Ranger) was with Sitters [before] he got killed. He came in and told us all about it before it got in the papers."

In the late 1980s Mrs. Stillwell visited the place where the two lawmen died. "It's below Marfa, in a canyon," she said. "It's a very beautiful place, with a lot of cottonwood trees. There's no marker."

Sitters was buried at Valentine, near his ranch. In the distance is the mountain range where he had his last fight. According to his daughter, Mattie Baca, a report reached the family shortly after her father's death that Cano still did not consider the score settled. Unless the family left the area immediately, the word was, Cano would kill them all.

"My mother was afraid for our lives, so we left," she recalled years later. "At the time my father was ambushed I was only seven. I did not understand what it meant then. I only knew that he never again came home to us!"

Sources

Cox, Mike. "Zane Grey and the Texas Rangers," *The Zane Grey Reporter*, Vol. 5, No. 4, December 1990, pp. 9-12.

Iron Gray's Last Ride

Around campfires and in *cantinas* from Brownsville to El Paso, Iron Gray was celebrated in story and song on both sides of the Rio Grande.

The powerful stallion was *mucho caballo*. He was both Pancho Patino's means of making his living and of staying alive while he was at it.

Patino had raised Iron Gray* from a colt. If he had a name for his horse, it was not known on the Texas side of the river. The Texans called him Iron Gray because that described his color, dark skinned with a mixture of white and black hair. Tall, deep-chested, the horse always was well groomed and cared for.

Not only was Iron Gray strong, fast, surefooted, and smart, he could catch the scent of *los rinches* (the Rangers) or U.S. Mounted Customs Inspectors and avoid them like coiled rattlesnakes.

All horses have a sense of smell, of course, but just as some mammals—human, equine, or whatever—have one sensory ability stronger than another, Iron Gray's olfactory senses were extraordinary. On a dark night, downwind, Iron Gray could smell a human being from a mile or more away. Somehow, the horse seemed to be able to distinguish whether that human was wearing a gun and a badge. Working his way through the mesquite, nostrils flaring and ears alert, Iron Gray at the first whiff of potential trouble would snort and adjust his direction of travel with no urging from his rider, alerting Patino that he was moving him out of the path of approaching officers. Experienced riders knew Iron Gray had been well trained, but his knack with his nose was more an inborn talent.

On the Mexican side of the river, they boasted of the horse's exploits in their *corridos*, or border ballads. In Texas, they shook their heads at Patino's luck and pluck and speculated with idle envy about what it would be like to own Iron Gray. The horse, of course, was not for sale at any price. Iron Gray could only change hands if his owner were dead.

The man who rode Iron Gray was no less impressive than his coveted mount. Tall and strong, with dark eyes and a long black mustache, at forty-five *anos* Pancho Patino showed no signs of slowing down. He had fought in the name of freedom in Mexico's bloody revolutionary period, and since the *norteamericanos* had begun the profitable venture they called Prohibition in 1919, he had been a *tequilero*, a smuggler of liquor. Though middle-aged, Patino had only grown wiser in the ways of the river with the accumulating years. He knew the middle border country from Villa Acuna to Piedras Negras very well and he knew his horse-flesh.

Pancho Patino also knew how to shoot, as testified to by his having survived several gunfights. The Texans prided themselves on being better shots than anyone who lived south of the river, but Patino was as comfortable with the .45 he carried low-slung on his hip and the .30-30 in the mesquite-scarred scabbard tied to Iron Gray's saddle as he was astride that saddle. Poor marksmen in certain high-risk occupations did not live long on the border, but by 1925 Patino had been fighting and surviving for fifteen years.

It took a while before the Rangers began to pay Patino particular attention—plenty of outlaws rode the river. For about the first three years of his outlaw career, the Rangers learned, Patino had ridden with a gang. But he stood out from the other bandits, becoming known as "the *hombre* that rides the gray streak of lightning," and eventually moved off from the outlaw herd to begin solitary operations.

"His horse . . . is responsible for the particular notice paid him," a newspaper reporter wrote. "During the years that followed in which Patino made many miraculous escapes on . . . Iron Gray he was not only noticed by officers but wanted badly."

Texas officers wanted Iron Gray as much as they did Patino—maybe more so—but Patino was the one they had an arrest warrant for.

The warrant was for one of Patino's more notable capers, an escape from the Kinney County Jail in Brackettville. He had been awaiting sentencing on a horse stealing conviction when he broke out of the lockup in 1916. If arrested, he would go straight to prison. Without Iron Gray.

"He had the reputation of being a thoroughly bad man and a leader of rumrunners and smugglers," the San Antonio *Express* said of Patino.

Actually, Patino's livelihood centered on two enterprises: smuggling *tequila* and stealing horses. Trusting Iron Gray to get him across the river and back quickly, Patino would splash into Texas, collect a few head of choice Texas horses off some border ranch, and herd them back to Mexico. Even in 1925, long after the passing of the Old West, stealing a horse in Texas was a felony crime. During the early settlement of Texas, it had been a hanging offense. The short story writer William Sydney Porter, better known as O. Henry, put it this way: "On the Rio Grande border if you take a man's life you sometimes take trash; but if you take his horse, you take a thing the loss of which renders him poor, indeed, and which enriches you not—if you are caught." But reform-minded lawmakers eventually changed horse stealing from a capital offense to one punishable by incarceration. Assuming, of course, that the defendant made it to the courthouse. Old traditions died hard in Texas and often, so did horse thieves.

As for smuggling, that had been going on since the Rio Grande became an international boundary. Mexico always seemed to have something the *norteamericanos* wanted, even if their government forbade its importation. Since 1920, with the beginning of enforcement of the Eighteenth Amendment to the Constitution, the principal contraband had been liquor. Demand was high, and so was the return on investment for those willing to undertake getting the liquor across the river to the land of gin-joints and speakeasies. A bottle of *tequila* in Mexico cost 60 cents. In San Antonio, Texas, that bottle was worth $15. Considering a single pack mule could carry up to eighty bottles, enormous profits awaited the successful smuggler.

Years after Prohibition ended with the realization that the so-called "noble experiment" had been a singular failure, longtime Ranger W.W. "Bill" Sterling, who had served as Texas' adjutant general from 1931 to 1933, put liquor smuggling into perspective in *Trails and Trials of a Texas Ranger*, the memoir he published shortly before his death:

> Apprehending violators of the eighteenth amendment was always a distasteful duty to the Rangers. They were never interested in the cargoes of pack trains, as such. Other serious factors were involved in the movement of this illicit liquor. Too often they escaped the notice of an uninformed and thirsty public.

First of all, Sterling said, the *tequila*-laden pack trains were protected by rifle-carrying escorts and "constituted an armed invasion of the United States." These *tequileros* would kill anyone who "crossed their trail," be they law enforcement officers (the San Antonio newspaper reported that Patino had boasted "he would shoot any officer he encountered on sight"), ranchers, oil geologists, or "innocent tourists."

Secondly, though the smugglers were deliberately carrying one illegal commodity into Texas, they also were bringing ticks across the river. This played havoc with the hard work going on to eradicate the dangerous parasites from Texas ranchland, an effort that required the dipping of livestock every fourteen days. When Mexican horses and pack mules cut across some rancher's land on their way north, the property was reinfested. The smugglers were further compounding the problem by cutting fences, which brought the possibility of cattle from an infested pasture mixing with stock in a tick-free pasture. Fence-cutting had been a felony crime in Texas since shortly after the invention of barbed wire and was not tolerated much more than horse stealing.

The Rangers, in cutting sign for rumrunners and *tequileros* along the border, simply were doing what they had been expected to do since their inception: Protecting life and property.

As Sterling wrote, "They were not scouting to deprive some thirsty toper of his firewater."

The Mexicans, as reflected in their border ballads, saw it differently. As border folklorist Americo Paredes would write:

> The attitude of the Border people [on the Mexican side] toward smugglers was a far from negative one. Smuggling occupied a much higher position than other kinds of activities proscribed by law because, in the traditional scale of values, the smuggler was seen as an extension of the hero of intercultural conflict.

Smuggling across an international boundary was not a capital offense, but it was a risky undertaking, celebrated in song and legend. Everyone knew the Rangers, as the old saying went, tended to shoot first and ask questions later. One verse of the song, *"Los tequileros,"* goes *"Los rinches seran muy hombres, no se les puede negar, nos cazan como venados para podernos matar."* ("The rangers are very brave, there is no doubt of that; the only way they can kill us is by hunting us like deer.")

Sterling gave an accurate description of how the state and federal officers worked:

> The method used by the Rangers and the
> United States Mounted Inspectors of Customs,
> practically all of whom were ex-Rangers, was to
> ride a course roughly paralleling the Rio Grande
> until they cut the sign of a pack train. . . . After
> picking up a trail, the Texans followed it until the
> pack train was overtaken, and then a battle,
> usually a running one, would take place.

In their efforts to capture Patino and Iron Gray, however, this technique had not proven very effective. Either by managing to avoid the Rangers outright, or outrunning them if discovered, Patino had been able to stay in business.

Along the border, however, change was in the air—literally. As men on horseback rode the river looking for Patino and other smugglers, the U.S. Army Air Corps had begun an aerial photography project along the Rio Grande. Army biplanes had recently criss-crossed a fifty-square-mile section around the old cavalry post of Fort Clark at Brackettville, photographing the terrain. The well-worn smuggler's trails snaking north from the river showed up clearly on the images, which would be used to update maps based on traditional cartographic surveys.

The new method of mapmaking, the San Antonio *Express* noted, "may revolutionize survey work. If successful, [it] will mean about two men with a plane can accurately map as much ground in a day as would require months for numerous engineer field groups to complete."

Left unsaid in the newspaper article was the effect airplanes would have on the government's efforts to protect the nation's border. In only a few years, except for their use in ranching or for recreation, horses would no longer be necessary along the Rio Grande. But the downfall of Iron Gray and Pancho Patino would not come from any new technology or any failing on the part of the horse or undue carelessness on the part of his master. Iron Gray was loyal to his owner, but someone who knew of Patino and his operations was not. Whether for cash or because of a competitor's professional jealousy, U.S. Customs got a tip that Patino would be leading a liquor pack train across the Rio Grande on the night of Thursday, February 12, 1925. The bandit intended to move north through the Fort Clark military reservation in Kinney County.

A look at the calendar told the officers the tip was probably legitimate. The moon had been full on Sunday, February 8. On Thursday night, it would rise at 9:13 p.m., providing plenty enough light for a night crossing. But another possibility occurred to the officers after receiving the tip: Patino had about as much use for them as they did him. The river riders were bad for business. It could be a setup.

Two Customs Inspectors, Harrison L. Hamer and S.P. Witt, planned the operation. Hamer, along with Customs Captain W.L. Barler (a former Ranger), Kinney County Sheriff R.S. Salmon, and several immigration officers, would watch the well-known smuggler's trail at a point several miles inland from the river. Witt and other immigration officers would ride the river bottom.

Like Patino, Hamer knew the brush country. Born in the Wilson County community of Fairview on August 15, 1888, Harrison's older brother was Francis Augustus Hamer, better known as Frank, a man who would gain more fame than he ever wanted with his role in tracking down and killing the outlaws Clyde Barrow and Bonnie Parker.

Harrison Hamer, following in his brother's footsteps, joined the Rangers on October 20, 1918, serving in Captain W.W. Taylor's Company F. By the time he was sworn in as a Ranger, Harrison already had been with his brother in two gunfights. In the first, he did not have a chance to shoot in his older brother's defense. In the second, a wounded Frank Hamer prevented Harrison from killing the man who had just shot him. Re-enlisting on June 20, 1919, Harrison was assigned to Captain Will Wright's Company D. In 1920 Hamer—as had many other Rangers —joined the better paying U.S. Mounted Customs Service and was stationed at Del Rio.

On July 4, 1924, Hamer arrested one of the most wanted men in America, Jess Newton. A Texas boy, Jess and his brothers—Doc, Joe, and Willis—had pulled a $3 million mail train robbery near Chicago on June 12. Jess returned to Texas, then crossed into Mexico where he spent most of his time and much of his money drinking. Spotting the wanted outlaw at an Independence Day rodeo in Del Rio, Hamer waited until Newton started to leave the grandstands.

"Don't make a move," Hamer said as he grabbed Newton by the right arm. "You're under arrest."

"I ain't going to do nothing," Newton replied.

Not all of Hamer's arrests went as peacefully. As he later recalled, "Every time you went to the river in those days, you would get shot at."

That would certainly be the case on the night of February 12, 1925. Harrison, eight years younger than Patino, was as tough and straight-shooting as his brother Frank.

Patino and the smugglers he led managed to slip past the first group of officers. Perhaps Iron Gray had sniffed the lawmen and guided Patino around the danger. But now the wind was blowing out of the south, depriving the horse of his ability to smell what was ahead. Iron Gray became nervous, but Patino knew that was because he could not smell anything. The horse acted similarly when it was rainy, which also interfered with being able to pick up scents.

Around 10 o'clock, Hamer saw riders approaching, plainly visible in the bright moonlight. The former Rangers and the other officers kept still, letting the smugglers get well into range. Too late, Iron Gray smelled the danger, snorted in alarm, and swung around to run.

Rifles spat orange flame as lead started flying. Bullets from Patino and his *tequileros* cut harmlessly through the thick brush around the well-concealed officers, but the mounted outlaws made better targets silhouetted in the moonlight.

With a scream, Iron Gray went down, carrying his rider with him. Kicking his legs wildly, the horse reflexively struggled to regain his feet as he lay dying. Before Pancho Patino could scramble behind his dead mount for cover, he, too, was dead.

The smugglers—racing for the river with Hamer and the officers right behind them—ran head on into Witt and his men. Another outlaw went down before the smugglers managed to make it back across to Mexico.

Hamer did not even mention Pancho Patino and Iron Gray in a newspaper interview more than a half-century later. From the vantage point of many years, the nighttime shoot-out along the Rio Grande was merely one of many during a long career in which Hamer always had prevailed.

The reporter wrote: "Hamer says there is no real means of estimating how many he has either arrested, shot at, or killed."**

Harrison Hamer stands near where he killed Iron Gray and his rider.

Even contemporary newspaper accounts of the gunbattle left questions unanswered. Nothing was said, for instance, about who shot first when Patino and Hamer confronted each other. One of the news stories did note that after the fight the officers did not find any liquor, leaving the presumption that the surviving smugglers made it back across the river with their supply.

Word of Patino's death "was received by mounted customs inspectors and rangers attending Federal court here with much joy," a San Antonio paper reported. "John H. DeWees joined by Rangers John Gillon, Buck Taylor and others [who] have seen border service, sang the praises of Inspectors S.P. Witt and Hamer for their work in killing one of the most notorious bandits the border has known in the last decade. All told of gun fights with Patino."

The officers brought the two smugglers' bodies to the Kinney County Jail. They turned Patino's body over to his brother, Simon, of Brackettville, who made the funeral arrangements. The outlaw was buried in the Brackettville City Cemetery on February 14. His fellow smuggler, never identified, was buried in a pauper's grave at county expense. "Patino's buddy had been seen here once or twice before," the San Antonio *Express* said in a brief report from Brackettville, "but no one knows his name."

Kinney County Jail in Brackettville, where Pancho's body was brought after he was killed. (Photo from author's collection)

The sketchy newspaper accounts of the border incident never said what was done with the carcass of Patino's Iron Gray. Despite the admiration the Texas officers had for the legendary horse, it may have been left to the buzzards and coyotes. Sometimes, the bodies of *tequileros* did not fare much better. Looking back on the wild Prohibition days along the border, Ranger Sterling later wrote that there were "a considerable number of shallow and unhallowed graves along the old *tequila* trail..." While serving as a justice of the peace in South Texas, he recalled, "I was called upon to hold inquests over several of these permanent residents. One of the boys, as an impromptu epitaph, wrote on the headboard this self-explanatory couplet: 'Here lies the body of a rumrunning stranger. He tried to kill a Texas Ranger.'"

Sources

Gilliland, Maude T. *Wilson County Texas Rangers*. Floresville: 1977, pp. 58-59.

"Inspectors Trap Rum Runners On River," undated newspaper clipping, ca. Feb. 1925, author's collection.

Johnson, Franklin. "Bandit And Iron Grey [sic] Die In Fight," undated newspaper clipping, ca. Feb. 1925, author's collection.

Newton, Willis and Joe, as told to Claude Stanush and David Middleton. *The Newton Boys: Portrait of an Outlaw Gang*. Austin: State House Press, 1994, pp. 267, 289-290.

Paredes, Americo. *A Texas-Mexican Cancionero*. Urbana: University of Illinois Press, 1976, pp. 43-44, 100-102.

"Patino, Bad Man Of Border, Slain," San Antonio *Express*, Feb. 14, 1925.

Powell, Cleve. "Oldest Ranger fought outlaws border to border." Austin *American-Statesman*, undated clipping, ca. 1976, author's collection.

"Rio Grande Delta Being Air-Mapped," San Antonio *Express*, Feb. 15, 1925.

San Antonio *Express*, Feb. 17, 1925.

Sterling, William Warren. *Trails and Trials of a Texas Ranger*. Norman: University of Oklahoma Press, 1968, pp. 83-85.

Yelvington, Henry. "When Tequila or Mescal Costing 60 Cents Brought $15 in San Antonio, Smugglers Had Toughest Scrapes With River Guards," Austin *Statesman*, Feb. 21, 1941.

Notes

* Contemporary accounts have the horse's name Iron "Grey" or Iron "Gray." The accepted modern American spelling of "Gray" is used here.

** Harrison Hamer went back into the Rangers on April 1, 1932, serving in Company D again and stationed in Falfurrias. He resigned effective January 1, 1933, when Governor Miriam "Ma" Ferguson began her second (nonconsecutive) term in office. After his ranger service, he worked for the Texas Sheep and Goat Raisers Association, the Sutton County Livestock Association, and later became head of security for Magnolia Petroleum Company until retiring in 1953. He died in Houston in the 1980s and was buried in Del Rio, Texas.

The Readin' Ranger

The two tall men boarding the train in Wichita Falls could have been oil company executives going back East to take care of some lease business. Wearing dark suits, Stetsons, bow ties, and fashionable tie shoes, they had three black suitcases between them.

As they settled into their seats in the Pullman car, no one paid these men any particular attention, which was exactly what they wanted and a good thing. Protected from view by their coats, each man packed a .45.

Texas Ranger Captain Roy W. Aldrich and Ranger J.B. Wheatley were on their way to St. Louis. If anyone had known these two were Rangers, they would have assumed they were on their way to pick up a prisoner arrested out of state. But that was not the case.

Divided between the three bags carried by the Rangers were $4.5 million in negotiable bonds issued by the City of Wichita Falls to pay for municipal waterworks improvements. City officials had contacted an express company about the job and were quoted a cost of $2,500 for delivery of the bonds to St. Louis. Not wanting to pay that much money, and knowing that mail and express robberies were not uncommon, the City of Wichita Falls turned to the Texas Rangers for help.

Aldrich later summed up the unusual escort duty in three short sentences: "We just loaded the bonds into three suitcases and rode to St. Louis with them in a Pullman drawing-room. One of us slept while the other kept guard.

I believe the whole expense of the job was something less than three hundred dollars."

The bonds were delivered to St. Louis without incident and booming Wichita Falls got the needed upgrade of its water system.

Aldrich kept one of the bags as a souvenir of the trip. He and Wheatley had safely delivered enough bonds, as someone later estimated, to "buy the whole train, fifty miles of the road, and two villages for terminals." Probably with considerable funding left over.

Despite the brevity of his remarks on this case, Aldrich was not a stereotypical Texas Ranger. He was tall, with a sternly angular face and blue eyes. That part fit. He wore a badge and a gun and enforced the law, but he also was something else: a bibliophile. Many of his contemporaries did not even know what the word meant, but Aldrich was a reading Ranger who built one of the largest private collections of Texas books of his time.

Aldrich was more even than a booklover. When he joined the Rangers in 1915 at age 45, he was a seasoned soldier of fortune who had traveled the world before coming to Texas.

Born September 17, 1869, in Quincy, Illinois, Aldrich was an Illinoisian only by circumstance. His family lived in Barton County, Missouri, on the west side of the Mississippi, but his mother had been visiting in Illinois when she went into labor. He grew up in Missouri and stayed there until 1888, when he went to the Pacific Northwest as a lumberjack. From there he went to Oklahoma Territory as a horsetrader, then to Mexico to run a coffee plantation. Back on the north side of the Rio Grande, he was a miner and stagecoach driver in Arizona Territory before returning to Missouri to volunteer for military service at the outbreak of the Spanish-American War. After service in the Philippines, he went to South Africa with a shipment of horses for the British army during the Boer War.

Aldrich came to Texas in 1907 with his brother Jules. Together they built and operated a bayfront resort in Corpus Christi, selling it at a profit after several years. The brothers moved to San Antonio and dealt in real estate there until 1915, when Aldrich joined Company A, Texas Rangers.

At an age when most men might be content to settle down, Aldrich spent time on the border in the Rio Grande Valley and in the Big Bend, guarding against raiding bandits from Mexico.

A decade later, Aldrich recalled:

> Back in 1916, when I was a private in Company A . . . on border duty, an urgent appeal came one day from a ranch district in the lower Rio Grande Valley. Our commander, Capt. John Sanders, sent another Ranger and me down there, and we found that the people were very uneasy on account of threatened raids. They [the bandits] would ride over the border in gangs of fifty or sixty, shoot up a ranch, burn the ranch house, take people from their work and shoot them down, fire bridges, and destroy other property. On one of these raids they wrecked a train . . . and killed several people, including the locomotive engineer. Our entire Ranger force then did not exceed one hundred men, and the border we had to patrol extends for eight hundred miles.

Aldrich never was specific about his personal experiences on the border. Whatever role he played, by 1917 conditions were beginning to improve. The Alice *Echo*, noting that Company A had been headquartered there for more than a year, said that any "feelings of uneasiness which might have been felt by reason of our nearness to the Mexican border, the Ranger force has eliminated. The Ranger boys are a stalwart type of Southern gentlemen and Alice folk are mighty glad to number them among her citizenship."

In 1918, with the border quiet, Aldrich was transferred to Austin where he took over as quartermaster for the Ranger force with the rank of captain. He was stationed in the capital city for the rest of his career, but he worked assignments in the field as they came up. In 1919 he and other Rangers calmed a race riot in Longview. A few years later, in booming Ranger, Texas, Aldrich and a handful of other Rangers shut down a gambling operation in the Commercial Hotel, arresting eighty-seven men, most of them armed. Asked a few years later how so few Rangers could disarm so many men without trouble, Aldrich replied: "Saw our guns cocked, I reckon."

Aldrich was among the contingent of Rangers and National Guard troops who held the East Texas oil town of Mexia under martial law for forty-seven days in 1922 to control lawlessness. Four years later he helped investigate one of the more sensational homicides of the decade, the 1926 murder of Mathis physician J.A. Ramsey. When the doctor's body was found in a shallow grave nearly four months after his disappearance, an examination showed he had been hit over the head and his throat had been slashed. Ramsey's hand was protruding from the grave, leading to speculation that he was still alive when his killer buried him. South Texas rancher Harry J. Leahy went to the electric chair for the robbery-murder.

In 1927 Aldrich was on the train for Borger, another wild town fueled by black gold. The twenties roared in Texas, with the Rangers called on to handle everything from catching bootleggers to breaking labor strikes.

Though not earning all that much as a Ranger, Aldrich must have set aside some of the money he had made in the real estate business. In the early 1920s Aldrich and his brother purchased an old plantation, 110 acres of land off Manor Road, three miles east of Austin. A two-story white frame house was the centerpiece of the tract, which was irrigated by a spring on the property. The place was known as Hillcrest.

Aldrich always had been a reader, but by 1919 he began seriously collecting books. By the late 1930s, he had acquired several thousand volumes: works of Texana, including books on the history of the Rangers, as well as books on ornithology, botany, and Africa. Most of the books published after 1900 had been inscribed by their authors, and many of them had been annotated by the reading Ranger.

The Ranger bought books, but he did not sell books.

"Several of his books are so rare that the giant University of Texas library has photostated them, so they would have a copy. Many of the books have huge values, but you might as well ask Capt. Aldrich to sell you his ranger badge—they just aren't for sale," one newspaper reporter wrote.

When Western writer William MacLeod Raine came to Austin in early 1938, he paid Aldrich a visit. Raine, an Austin newspaper reported, was "following in the wake or custom of all visiting writers of note" in looking up Aldrich. The writer admired the Ranger's 6,000-volume library, a collection which included Raine's 1910 novel, *A Texas Ranger*.

A more frequent visitor to Aldrich's farm over the years was University of Texas biologist Dr. Fred A. Barkley, who came to study the Ranger's extensive collection of native Texas flora, from trees to cactus. Shortly after World War II, Barkley and a colleague, Dr. B.C. Tharp, named a West Texas shrub in the old Ranger's honor: *Thamnosma Aldrichii*.

Not all of Aldrich's visitors came to see his books and plants. Over the years, he had gathered at least a hundred animals from all over Texas as well as some creatures not indigenous to the state. By the mid-1920s his farm was Austin's unofficial zoo, a home for armadillos, alligators, bear, deer, wolves, javelinas, raccoons, foxes, rattlesnakes, peafowl—even baboons and monkeys. On practically any Sunday, the cars of as many as a hundred visitors might be parked at his place.

Captain R.W. Aldrich and one of his javelinas, Austin, 1929.

(Photo from author's collection)

"One cold day mother, Auntie Ruth and I decided to see Capt. Aldridge's [Aldrich's] zoo," one sixth grade student wrote in a letter to the Austin newspaper in 1929. After describing the bears, a monkey that jumped at her younger cousin, the howling coyotes and a porcupine ("It was not true about the porcupine throwing spears," she reported), the Wooldridge Elementary pupil concluded, "That was one of the best zoos I have ever visited."

Aldrich ran his private zoo until the summer of 1939, when the feed bill and the time commitment became too much for him to handle anymore. "It's just a case of a man getting to the place where he can't afford to be riled up all the time," the Ranger told a reporter. "I'm tired and it costs money to keep a man to watch out for them."

For the past seventeen years, the reporter wrote, Aldrich's backyard zoo "had more visitors than a baseball hero with a broken leg."

Most of the Ranger's animals were donated to the San Antonio Zoo, though Aldrich kept his 150 love birds, his finches, and his squirrels. Also staying behind was his prairie dog town, with an estimated population of fifty.

Though advancing age had forced him to scale back his menagerie, Aldrich continued on the Ranger payroll well into his seventies. Finally, in the early fall of 1947, the seventy-eight-year-old Aldrich was one of ninety state employees who applied for Texas' first retirement plan, a pension available for persons age sixty or older with at least ten years' state service. Aldrich's last day at Camp Mabry as a Texas Ranger was October 31.

"Between my rose garden and straightening out the library I'll keep pretty busy," the old Ranger told Dallas *Morning News* reporter Wick Fowler as he filled out the necessary paperwork to wrap up his career.

Though Aldrich did his share of traditional rangering, as quartermaster of the Rangers when the force was still under the Adjutant General's Department Aldrich handled most of the paperwork for the service. He kept the payroll records, ordered supplies, answered correspondence, and clipped newspapers. He cut out any story relating to the Texas Rangers—old or new—and pasted them in a large scrapbook, one book for each year.

After creation of the Department of Public Safety, and the transfer of the Rangers from the Adjutant General's Department to the new state agency, Aldrich wrote a history of the Rangers that the department would send to school children and others who contacted the DPS for information on the Rangers.

When the old Ranger retired, DPS Director Colonel Homer Garrison pointed to Aldrich's institutional memory. "I'm afraid we'll have to break into his flower-tending occasionally for information," he said. "It has been a privilege to have had him with us for so long."

Aldrich certainly had seen a lot of change in the Rangers.

"Although I started out as a horseback Ranger, when it comes down to brass tacks a Ranger has to know a lot more nowadays about crime detection because science is playing such a large part," Aldrich told Fowler.

Breaking into a smile, he added, "But you couldn't beat the old-timers when it came down to the rough and tumble stuff."

Surrounded by his books, artifacts, and memories, Aldrich spent his last days on his acreage in East Austin, not far from the municipal airport that was becoming increasingly busy. Occasionally, a newspaper reporter would drop by Hillcrest for an old-timer interview.

Two years after Aldrich's retirement, a reporter for the Houston *Chronicle* came by for an interview. He found the veteran Ranger's library filling three rooms and spilling over into the landing leading downstairs. Most of the books were old and out of print, but the reporter found contemporary titles as well, including Texas writer Fred Gipson's newly published novel *Hound Dog Man* and a new book on big Texas cats, *Texas Lion Hunters*.

"Seems foolish for a man my age to be buying books when he will have to dispose of them before long," Aldrich said, "but I just can't help it."

By the early 1950s the old Ranger was hard of hearing and beginning to get a bit cranky. The reporter wrote: "Were you to visit him, you'd find him hospitable but you'd find traces of the inflexibility that made him a Ranger captain within eight years of his enlistment." A year later, Aldrich asked another reporter, "What have I done that people keep wanting to write me up?"

Not everyone admired the old Ranger, however. W.W. "Bill" Sterling, who had become adjutant general in 1931 and served until 1933 when he resigned after the re-election of Governor Miriam "Ma" Ferguson, had an entirely different view of Aldrich. But only other Rangers and Sterling's closest associates knew anything about the former adjutant general's true feelings until after Aldrich's death.

Shortly after taking office, Sterling had fired Aldrich, though Aldrich told the newspapers he had retired.

Not until Sterling's lengthy memoir, *Trails and Trials of a Texas Ranger*, was published in 1959 did he reveal why he had given Aldrich the boot. Letting loose with a verbal load of buckshot, Sterling referred to Aldrich at various points in his book as a "synthetic Texan," "a counterfeit Ranger," "a small time Machiavelli," "a schemer," and, by metaphor, a coyote.

Sterling devoted twenty-three substantial paragraphs to his brief against Aldrich, with accusations a lawyer could have argued before a jury as libel had Aldrich still been alive when the book came out. Sterling himself died of a heart attack within a year of his book's publication.

Sterling's major points:

☆ Aldrich as Ranger quartermaster had "been allowed to usurp the rank of senior captain." The statute organizing the Rangers clearly placed the senior captain in charge and had the quartermaster as a clerical position with no supervisory authority, Sterling argued.

☆ Aldrich "did not look like a Texan, talk like a Texan nor think like a Texan, for he was not a Texan."

☆ Not only was Aldrich not a real Texan, he was a drugstore cowboy who, when he first joined the Rangers, showed up in camp in "store bought boots" with his pale face shaded by a sheep herder's hat.

After Sterling left office in 1933, Aldrich went back to work for the Rangers, taking up where he had left off as quartermaster. When the Department of Public Safety was created in 1935, Aldrich continued as a state employee.

Sterling's multicount literary indictment aside, Aldrich's firing and subsequent reinstatement, as well as Sterling's resignation when the gubernatorial election did not come out the way he would have liked, merely underscore the highly political atmosphere of the Ranger service during the first third of the twentieth century. Despite what Sterling wrote, Aldrich left his mark on the Rangers and a considerable body of research material for scholars.

During his long tenure, he had become the spokesman for the Rangers long before the state ever hired someone specifically for that purpose. For any writer doing a story on the Rangers, or for any student assigned to write a paper on the force, Aldrich was the man to see. Stories based on these interviews generated considerable favorable publicity for the Rangers over the years, though the writers never failed to point out what a great Ranger Aldrich was. Though Aldrich's picture showed up periodically in the newspapers, his quotes always were modest.

"The world never will learn of Capt. Aldrich's most interesting exploits along the border, unless, indeed, it learns them from a friend who happened to be present. But he is not loath to speak of the achievements of other men," the Dallas *Morning News* said in a long Sunday feature on Aldrich in 1927.

Aldrich died at home off Manor Road in East Austin on Saturday afternoon, January 29, 1955. He had outlived most of his contemporaries. His only survivors were two cousins who lived out of state.

He was buried February 1 in Oakwood Cemetery in Austin. Newspapers noted he had served in the Texas Rangers more years than any other man. The old Ranger's obituaries were brief but praising. United Press noted that "Almost his entire life was punctuated by violence, but in leisure he became a scholar and was a recognized authority on natural history and botany."

Most of his library and papers went to Sul Ross University in Alpine in West Texas. His home, Hillcrest, was razed and the site covered up by the expansion of the capital city's Robert Mueller Municipal Airport.

Aldrich would have been surprised that others always viewed his life as divided and contrasting. In his own mind, he was just a reading Ranger.

• • • • • • ⭐ • • • • • •

Sources

Aldrich, Roy W. Letter to George W. Gray, Sparkill, N.Y., Oct. 6, 1925. Author's collection.

"Capt. Aldrich Funeral Rites Set Tuesday," Austin *American*, Feb. 1, 1955.

"Captain Sanders Gets Commission For Two More Years," Alice *Echo*, April 8, 1917.

Carley, W.T. "World Famous Writer Visits Capitol [sic] City." Austin *Dispatch*, Jan. 19, 1938.

Coyne, Brian. "Capt. Aldrich Will Play Role of Noah Sans Ark to Move His Animals Away." Austin *Statesman*, July 20, 1939.

"File Murder Charge in Mathis Case." San Antonio *Light*, Aug. 29, 1926.

Garrett, Eudora. "When a Ranger Keeps a Zoo." Austin *American-Statesman Sunday Magazine*, Sept. 23, 1928.

Richardson, Vivian. "Captain Aldrich of the Texas Rangers." Dallas *Morning News*, Jan. 16, 1927.

Skyhawk, W.F. "Capt. Roy Aldrich: Last of Texas Rangers." *The Pony Express*, Placerville, CA., Vol. XX, No. 11, April 1954.

Springfield, C.C. "Retired Texas Ranger Relives Past In Ranch Home Filled With Trophies." Houston *Chronicle*, Nov. 29, 1949.

Sterling, William Warren. *Trails and Trials of a Texas Ranger*. Norman: University of Oklahoma Press, 1959, 1968.

"Visited Zoo; Monkey Interesting Animal." Austin *Statesman*, March 16, 1929.

"The Days of Our Boyhood"

That summer of 1927, most of the highways in West Texas were still unpaved. The Pecos River and other streams, assuming they were running, had to be splashed across.

Three high-topped cars with spoke wheels clattered east on the Old Spanish Trail, between Fort Stockton and Ozona, a roadway improved from the days of the stagecoach only by mule-drawn graders. But times were changing. There was talk in Austin of big plans to connect Texas cities with wide ribbons of concrete and asphalt.

Inside the cars were men who had traveled this route many times, often on horseback. In one of the flivvers was J.D. Jackson of Alpine, cattleman and former Ranger. In the lead car ahead was Captain James B. Gillett, one hand on the wheel, the other hand busily pointing out familiar landmarks.

Riding with Jackson was a younger man, Eugene Cunningham, a journalist. Another former Ranger drove behind them. They were headed for the West Central Texas town of Menard for a reunion of old Rangers. At not even twenty miles an hour, there was plenty of time for talk before they got there.

"Ever run into Ben Thompson?" the reporter asked Jackson, hoping for a story about the English-born gambler, gunman, and one-time Austin city marshal gunned down in a San Antonio saloon in 1884.

"Knew him when he and his younger brother, Billy, drove a water wagon in Austin," Jackson said.

In 1882, he continued, he and the other Rangers of Company E were guarding the construction camps as the Texas and Pacific Railroad pushed across West Texas. The tracks were laid out as straight as the terrain permitted, but a lot of crooked men were following the rails.

One day a man came up to the captain's tent at the Ranger camp near Monahans and said a gambler had skinned him for $500 or $600 using loaded dice.

"The cap'n told me to go down into the construction camp—it was a rough place, full of tinhorn gamblers and tent saloons—and get this fellow's money back, then kick the gambler out of camp," Jackson said.

When the Ranger went to the camp, he recognized the gambler, but did not let on just yet that he knew him.

"Cap'n says you better give this fellow back his money," Jackson told the gambler.

"Like hell I will!" he said. "You Rangers may have the authority to arrest me, but you can't make me give back the money."

"Better give it back to him, Mr.... " the Ranger said, pausing significantly after the word "mister."

The gambler gave the Ranger a hard look and then asked what the lawman had started to call him.

"I told him I used to watch a couple brothers driving a water cart in Austin," Jackson recalled.

"You think I'm Bill Thompson, don't you? Well, I'm not! But if you're going to raise so much trouble over the money—here! Take it! But I'm not Bill Thompson."

Jackson took the money with his left hand, leaving his gun hand available for any sudden developments. The gambler was indeed Bill Thompson, a young man with two killings to his credit and wanted in connection with a third.

"Thanks for returning the money," Jackson said. "But you'll have to go to the cap'n with me."

Jackson walked Thompson to the Ranger camp and explained the situation to the captain. Responding to the news with a shrug, he said he had heard there were papers out on Thompson, but he did not have them.

"Go out and carry out the order I gave you," the captain snapped. "You've just executed half of it."

The old ranger smiled at the memory of what happened next.

"Well, it was funny. Mostly, a man feels downright indignant about being kicked out of a place, but Bill Thompson seemed to get a world of satisfaction about jumping down the trail ahead of a boot toe that morning."

(Thompson's luck held only a few more years. His dice came up snake eyes in a little difficulty south of Laredo in the early 1890s. The exact date is not known.)

The gathering of old Rangers that summer in Menard was the seventh annual reunion of the Ex-Texas Rangers Association, an organization started in 1920 by W.M. Green. The Colorado City businessman had served with the Frontier Battalion in Company A in 1874.

Green had begun by mailing invitations to every old-timer he knew of, with the request that the recipient notify anyone else he knew who had served in the Rangers. He also wrote to the *Semi-Weekly Farm News* in Dallas "calling on all ex-rangers to write me . . . " Publication of that letter netted more then seventy-five replies.

The Ranger veterans gathered in Weatherford and met in the Parker County courthouse. Enthusiastic over the idea of meeting annually, the thirty-two former Rangers on hand for the reunion called by Green formally organized the Ex-Texas Rangers Association. They picked Green as their first leader, his official title being "Major Commanding." Except for a secretary and chaplain, the other officers were based on the structure of the old Frontier Battalion—captain, first lieutenant, second lieutenant, adjutant, and orderly sergeant.

A few years later, Green wrote a letter to *Frontier Times* magazine explaining that the purposes of the association were "for social benefit, to meet once a year, to live over again as far as possible the days of our boyhood, and to get a line if possible on all the old boys so as to make it easier to get up proof in order to obtain pensions for those who are entitled to receive them."

Green's successful organization of an association of Ranger veterans was the first time such an effort had been made in the relatively new twentieth century. In the summer of 1897, a broadside was circulated in the state announcing "Formation and Meeting and Reunion and Organizational Meeting of Ex-Texas Rangers." First planned for July 12 that year, the meeting was rescheduled for October 4. Former Ranger Captain John S. "Rip" Ford likely was a prime mover in this effort, as he was in the creation of the Texas State Historical Association. But he died on November 3, 1897, from a stroke he had suffered on October 1.

The Ranger reunion movement apparently died with Ford, because no subsequent meetings are known prior to Green's gathering twenty years later.

In selecting a meeting site each year, the old Rangers favored places they had camped during the heyday of the Frontier Battalion. One of their favorite reunion locations was Menard, where Captain Dan W. Roberts and his Company D had camped in the 1870s. Following his visit to Menard, Cunningham wrote: "Under the supervision of that fine old ranger and ex-mayor of Menard, Bill Lewis, a new ranger camp rose swiftly, white tents gleaming against the dark green of pecan trees, just as stood thereabout, 50 years, other ranger tents ..."

In addition to Jackson and Gillett, sixty other old Rangers had shown up for the 1927 reunion, along with their wives, children, and grandchildren. Cunningham calculated that the former Rangers, with an average age of seventy, represented 4,300 years of Ranger service. Membership was limited to those who had been Rangers more than thirty years earlier.

"All Menard was one great, hospitable town," Cunningham wrote. "On the grounds meals were served to all who came. From 6 in the morning until late midnight the coffee pots were never cold."

The same independent spirit that had made these men good Rangers now made it difficult to corral them long enough for a business meeting. Talking about the old days, not the new business of the association, was what they wanted to do more than anything else.

"In vain Major Green pounds his gavel," Cunningham wrote. "Heads turn slowly; for a moment he has attention. But only for a moment. In twos and threes white heads draw together; from the depths of memory they draw pictures of places, faces of men a half century buried beneath the prairie grass..."

Captain Roberts and his wife made the 1924 reunion at Menard. A few years later, she wrote:

> We traveled from Austin to Menard in an auto in a few hours; a trip in the 'good old days' required four days. We arrived after dark... We were the guests of Mr. and Mrs. W.W. Lewis. He was a young man and a member of our company when we last saw him. He is now a grandfather...

Each year, as old age accomplished what Indians and outlaws had failed to do, the number of frontier era Rangers attending the reunions declined. But as the days of the frontier grew fainter in memory, and the surviving old Rangers more frail, the annual reunions became increasingly attractive to writers looking for a good newspaper or magazine story.

The 1936 reunion, held the year of Texas' Centennial observance, attracted considerable press attention. The old-timers had their picture taken outside the log headquarters of Company B Texas Rangers, a $45,000 Works Progress Administration project located on the State Fair grounds in Dallas. The Rangers now were part of the newly created Department of Public Safety, which some of the old lawmen feared meant the end of the venerable force. Thousands of fair goers took in an exhibit on Ranger history as old Indian fighters and that generation's Rangers talked shop at the Company B headquarters.

Just because they liked to swap stories among themselves did not mean the old Rangers were particularly chatty with the reporters. "Why, I don't think of anything I've done that's worth putting in the paper," an old Ranger would tell a reporter. "Why don't you talk to Tom over there? He's had some right interesting experiences." Tom, of course, could not recall anything extraordinary about his career, either. He suggested the scribe talk to old Bill. Maybe he had some stories.

One reporter who spent the first day of the Ranger reunion "sagashiatin'" around among tight-lipped old men tried a different tack the second day. When referred to someone else, he asked the referring Ranger to at least tell him what the party he was passing the buck to had done, so he would know what to ask about. When not asked to talk about themselves, the old-timers got a lot more conversational, the writer found.

Retired Captain Will Wright remembered a man who had the honor of being hanged by friends.

The "beneficiary" of the friendly hanging lived in South Texas, Wright said, "and had many admirable qualities, which endeared him to most of the people who knew him well. But he was an incorrigible cow thief, who always managed to escape conviction by some hook or crook. It was a great joke to him, which he made the most of, but the perennial vexation and expense of trials finally exhausted the patience of his friends, so they just strung him up to keep him out of further trouble."

R.G. Kimbell, who had been a Ranger corporal, learned that love could be an even stronger motivator than friendship. Drifting down to Texas from Tennessee in 1870, he ended up in Limestone County. There he met, as he later described her, a pink-cheeked girl he called his "Texas Rose."

Kimbell found himself agreeing with the verse of a popular Texas song, that "The Yellow Rose of Texas beats the Belle of Tennessee." It was love at first sight, but this particular Texas Rose was not going to be easy to pick. She would accept his suit, she said, with one condition. First he had to join the Texas Rangers.

No recruitment poster could have been more effective. On September 10, 1878, Kimbell was sworn in at Austin as a member of the Frontier Battalion. His first job seemed easy enough—guarding the state treasury vault at the capitol. No one tried to rob it, and he figured he was doing pretty good as a Ranger. The pace picked up when he and other Rangers were sent out west to Kimble County to deal with outlaws. Later, the pursuit of a party of Indians who had stolen some horses ended in a roisterous battle.

Kimbell made it through a three-year hitch in the Rangers with his scalp and hide intact. He went back to East Texas and found the romance that had blossomed three years earlier had not lost its bloom. He married his "Texas Rose."

Though the old lawmen spent a lot of time telling stories like Kimbell's, they also fished and square danced. In her memoir, Mrs. Roberts recalled the 1924 reunion:

> One of the entertainments given the old Rangers was a dance. Some of us had never seen modern dancing. An old Ranger who sat by Captain Roberts was very much shocked, and as the dance progressed kept remarking to the Captain, 'Now ain't that scandalous?' Music and songs and the old-time ballads, varied the program.

But mostly the old Rangers talked, remembering their youth and a frontier long gone. And sometimes they disagreed with one and another.

Even former comrades in arms could not be expected to get along all the time. These were tough, individualistic old men, with strong opinions. Those opinions did not always match. By early 1940 internal strife had broken out over the four-year-old $100,000 Pioneer Memorial Hall adjacent to the Witte Museum in San Antonio. Built with funding secured by then Vice President "Cactus Jack" Garner, the building at 3805 Broadway was intended as a memorial to the pioneers, trail drivers, and Rangers of Texas. But the membership of the Ex-Texas Rangers Association did not want to take on ownership—and maintenance—of the building. George B. Black, major in command of the association for six years running, resigned in protest.

Black headed a spinoff organization, the Texas Rangers Memorial Association, which was organized at Brady on March 14, 1940. A new organization was imperative, Black told a reporter in Brady, in order to "maintain right and title to the . . . memorial building erected several years ago in San Antonio by the U.S. Government." The new organization would have a president and vice-president, with a secretary to keep the membership informed of association activities and to handle collection of the one dollar annual dues.

The Ex-Texas Rangers Association met in Santa Anna, in Coleman County, in the summer 1941. Only seven old Rangers showed up. The youngest, S.O. Durst, was 59. Also attending were Jeff Wood of Brady, 92; Noah Armstrong, 89, of Coleman (he was elected as major); A.T. Mitchell, 88, of Lampasas; C.M. Grady, 87, of Brownwood; N.J. Jones, 86, of Archer City, and M.H. Roberts, 80, of Llano. A year before, Durst and Wood had been listed as charter members of the Texas Rangers Memorial Association.

Within a few years, the last of the old Frontier Battalion Rangers was dead. But with each generation, there is a new crop of old Rangers.

The Texas Rangers Memorial Association organized in Brady was short-lived. In 1949 five former Rangers formed a nonprofit corporation called the Texas State Association of Ex-Rangers. According to Article II of the charter the group filed with the Secretary of State's office in Austin, "The purpose of this association shall be to keep alive Texas History, to perpetuate traditions of the Rangers of Texas; to cultivate friendly relations between Texas Rangers, Ex-Texas Rangers and their descendants; . . . to establish land marks, memorial halls, historical museums and institutions calculated to carry out the educational and social purposes of this organization."

In 1965 the charter was amended to return the organization to its first name, the Ex-Former Texas Rangers Association. Six years later, the corporation was rechartered as the Former Texas Ranger Association. According to past President Jerome Preiss of Floresville, the name change came at the behest of his old boss, Captain A.Y. Allee. "Cap said, 'By golly, I don't want to be an ex-anything. I'm a former Ranger,'" Preiss recalled, imitating Allee's famous gruff voice.

The association eventually deeded the Memorial Hall to the City of San Antonio, which maintains the building and leases it to the association for one dollar a year. In 1973 the association opened a Ranger museum in one of the downstairs rooms in the building. The Pioneers of Texas and the Old Trail Drivers of Texas also have exhibits in the building.

The Former Texas Ranger Association, made of up re-tired Rangers and their descendants, still holds annual reunions every May in San Antonio and publishes a news-letter, *Straight Talk*. Retired Rangers also meet each year at the Texas Rangers Hall of Fame and Museum in Waco.

Before the museum ownership fight broke out in 1940, a perennial item of business at the meetings of the old Ex-Rangers Association was discussion of the possibility of a monument in honor of the Rangers.

"But these quiet old men refuse to become excited over a monument to commemorate their own deeds in that day when the foundations of a state were laid and cemented with human blood," Cunningham wrote of the frontier veterans of the 1920s.

The Rangers did not really need a monument of stone to remind the people of Texas of their accomplishments, Cunningham continued in the flowery newspaper prose of his era.

"For every line of fence lying thread-like toward the far western horizon," he concluded, "every chimney of farm and ranch house, crowned by lazy smoke; every road white across the Texas prairie—all these make a monument to the men who rode over ahead of the settler and homebuil-der—the Texas Rangers."

······ ✪ ······

Sources

Cunningham, Eugene. "Rangers Tell Of Old Days When Men Carried The Law In Their Holsters And Lives In Their Hands," Houston *Post-Dispatch*, Oct. 23, 1927.

O'Neal, Bill. *Encyclopedia of Western Gunfighters*. Norman: University of Oklahoma Press, 1979, pp. 321-323.

"Origin of The Ex-Texas Rangers Association," *Frontier Times*, Feb. 1924, p. 3.

Preiss, Jerome. Interview with author, Oct. 18, 1996.

Roberts, Mrs. Dan W. *A Woman's Reminiscences of Six Years in Camp With the Texas Rangers*. Austin: 1928, pp. 58-59.

"Texas Rangers Meet in Reunion," *Frontier Times*, Oct. 1930, pp. 6-8.

"Texas Rangers Memorial Association Would Perpetuate History and Ideals of Lone Star State's Mounted Patrol," Brady *Standard*, March 15, 1940.

Tyler, Paula Eyrich and Ron Tyler. *Texas Museums: A Guidebook*. Austin: University of Texas Press, 1983, pp. 218-219.

"Wrangling the Rangers," *Farm and Ranch*, April 1, 1937, pp. 6, 19-20.

Old Monk and Other Ranger Mules

*Y*ears after his rangering days were over, James B. Gillett devoted a few paragraphs to Ranger mules in his memoir, *Six Years With the Texas Rangers*.

"A number of little bronco mules were secured for packing," when the Frontier Battalion was organized in 1874, Gillett wrote.

Rangers on scout in West Texas with a faithful pack mule.
(Author's collection)

The Ranger mules learned quickly and followed the Rangers around as faithfully as dogs, Gillett recalled. He wrote:

> Carrying a weight of one hundred and fifty to two hundred pounds, they would follow a scout of Rangers on the dead run right into the midst of the hottest fight with Indians or desperadoes. They seemed to take as much interest in such an engagement as the Rangers themselves.

The mules were curious "as a child or a pet coon," the old Ranger wrote. When the Rangers were on a scout, the mules would clop up to greet any horses or campers encountered by the lawmen.

If the Rangers kept riding, the mules would wait until they had moved on a thousand yards or so, Gillett continued, and then "scamper up to us as fast as they could run."

When the Rangers had occasion to return to civilization for more ammunition, fresh supplies, and new arrest warrants to serve, "the mules with their packs would march up to strange horses and frighten them out of their wits."

In Austin one time, a mule loped up to rub noses with a city mule engaged in pulling a streetcar down Congress Avenue. The Ranger mule, displaying the steadfastness of his gun-toting handlers, refused to yield right-of-way to the streetcar mule.

The city mule shied and jerked the streetcar off its tracks, considerably surprising and annoying its driver.

"The tiny animals pulled off several stunts like this and caused so much complaint that Adjutant General Jones issued an order for all rangers to catch and lead their pack-mules when passing through a town," Gillett wrote.

Gillett had served in Company D, and his first captain was Dan W. Roberts. Roberts, too, thought highly of Ranger mules.

In the late summer of 1875, Lipan Apaches raided the Texas Hill Country, striking in Kimble, Mason, and Menard Counties. Roberts and his Rangers saddled up to hunt the Indians down. When a rattlesnake bit his horse, Roberts switched to one of the company pack mules.

"I knew the mule and knew she was a 'dandy,' and could run like a red fox," the captain later recalled.

The Rangers caught up with the Indians and engaged in a running fight with them for most of the day. The mule carrying Roberts kept up easily.

"'Don't talk to me about a mule,'" Roberts wrote, adding quotation marks for emphasis. "If he will run at all, and you give me a starter, you will never catch him."

During the chase, the company's other pack mule, laden with all their grub, was lost. The Rangers got so hungry they sampled some of the food abandoned by the Indians—lightly cooked horsemeat and some prickly pear fruit. They did not get a full meal until they rode up on a settler's camp seventy miles later, on their way back to camp.

Six weeks later Roberts detailed Sergeant Ed Seiker to guide a military detachment from Fort McKavett in Menard County to Fort Stockton, an outpost west of the Pecos at Comanche Springs. On the way, Seiker and the soldiers found a dead mule, its packsaddle and load near what was left of its coyote-gnawed body. The Ranger sergeant recognized it as the missing Ranger mule. If the other men of Company D had been with him, Seiker later told his captain, the pack mule would have been buried with full honors.

Another incident remembered by Roberts had a happier ending.

In December 1874 a detail of Roberts' Rangers tangled with Indians near Little Saline Creek in Mason County. During the fight, Roberts was told, the Rangers "were so busy looking after their own hair... the mule had to take care of itself." After the smoke cleared, the mule was missing.

The following day, Roberts and four men returned to the scene of the fight and began cutting the mule's trail. A clear set of tracks soon led the Rangers to a dead Indian. The tracks plainly told the story: The Indian, suffering from a mortal wound, had tried to catch the mule in the hope of escaping, but failed. The mule got away and the Indian, afoot, soon died. Roberts kept on the trail, which led him to one of his old camps in Menard, then called Menardville.

He later learned that when the mule showed up by itself in Menard, local residents thought the Rangers might have been wiped out by Indians, the mule being the only survivor. When Roberts rode into town, the uneasy townsfolk were greatly relieved when he explained that the mule had wandered off after an Indian fight which the Rangers had won. Roberts soon caught up to the missing mule. Finding that animal was more than merely recovering missing state property.

"Our pack mules in the service displayed almost human intelligence and were our faithful friends," the Ranger wrote years later in his memoir of his days on the frontier.

A couple of Ranger mules, and too much whiskey, led to a gunfight that claimed a Ranger's life in 1885, precipitating a sheriff's sudden removal from office in a hail of Ranger lead.

When the Texas and Pacific Railroad cut across West Texas in 1881, Pecos and Toyah, the next stop down the tracks from Pecos, became wild and wooly railroad boom towns. Adjutant General W.H. King moved seven men of Company E, Frontier Battalion, to Toyah to settle things down.

Until the Rangers set up camp near the spring southeast of town, local law enforcement had been in the not-overly-competent hands of J.T. Morris, Reeves County's first sheriff. Whether Morris felt his authority somewhat usurped by the arrival of state officers is not recorded, but the sheriff was sore at Captain J.T. Gillespie for not loaning him a pair of mules and a buggy when asked.

Morris, as later reported, had "abused the Ranger Captain and his men in public at every opportunity" since the mule incident.

At 6:40 on the evening of August 18, 1885, already well-liquored up, Sheriff Morris took the train from Pecos to Toyah. As he alighted from the passenger car, he was heard to say, "I run Pecos and damned if I don't run Toyah."

Though Morris' remarks "to and about the Rangers were very insulting," as Gillespie later wrote in his report, "I paid no attention...and went to camp."

But Morris kept drinking, getting drunker and drunker with each downed shot glass of whiskey. "He indulged freely in liquor, and became quite boisterous, abusive and dangerous, flourishing his pistol and threatening the lives of a number of citizens," the San Angelo *Standard* later reported. Alarmed townspeople reported the matter to Ranger Sergeant Cartwright. When the Ranger approached the belligerent sheriff, the drunken lawman pointed his pistol in Cartwright's direction. But not wanting to escalate the situation, Cartwright let him be, figuring Morris would get his comeuppance the next morning when he sobered up and his head felt as big as one of the mules he'd wanted to borrow.

Concerned townsfolk must have sent word to Captain Gillespie that the situation was getting out of hand and that professional courtesy between state and county officer was no longer in order. The captain sent Ranger F.W. DeJarnette back to town with orders for Sergeant Cartwright to arrest the sheriff and hold him until he sobered up.

Cartwright and Corporal Hughes, along with Privates DeJarnette and T.P. Nigh found Morris in The Favorite Saloon, six-shooter in hand and mean drunk. When the Rangers walked in, all occupants of The Favorite scattered like a covey of startled quail. Only proprietor Sam Lane stayed behind to witness what happened next.

As a statement signed by seven local citizens acting as a coroner's jury later attested, when Cartwright told Morris he was under arrest and the place cleared out, "a general shooting followed, in which Morris killed Ranger T.P. Nigh and was himself killed by the other Rangers."

In the final analysis, the chain of events leading to the loss of two lives had begun with a dispute over mules, aggravated by one of the Old West's perennial trouble-makers, John Barleycorn.

One of the last Ranger mules to see service was Old Monk. The Rangers thought so highly of the mule they posed him for a photograph in November 1909 at a Ranger camp in Alpine. The mule is packing a rifle in a scabbard—maybe the same gun some Ranger used to collect the big set of mule deer antlers tied to the top of Monk's pack. The picture later became part of the famous Noah H. Rose Collection at the University of Oklahoma.

With Company C and later, Company D, the faithful mule saw duty from Amarillo to the Mexican border. One longtime Ranger said of Old Monk: "A better pack mule never followed a Texas Ranger."

Mules continued to be important to the Rangers well into the twentieth century, particularly during Prohibition, when the Rangers were almost constantly scouting the border in search of liquor smugglers coming across the Rio Grande from Mexico.

When Will L. Wright resigned as sheriff of Wilson County in 1917 to take over as captain of Company D in South Texas, the state furnished him three mules: Lizzie,

Polly, and the veteran, Old Monk. In 1921, after a gun-battle with smugglers on a ranch in Zapata County, Wright added two more mules to his company's remuda, two Mexican mules renamed Rat and Spider.

The captain bought Spider, so named because of her long legs, for twelve dollars of his own money when she was auctioned off by the U.S. Customs Service. Rat, who had a rat-like face and was mouse colored, had been wounded in the gunfight. She was given to Wright by the Collector of Customs at Laredo after she recovered.

Both mules, well trained by their previous owners, made excellent additions to Company D. The smugglers, however, had not treated their mules very well. Both animals bore scars and still-healing wounds on their backs, a clear indication of heavy loads poorly packed.

Mule packing was an art.

An unnamed old Ranger from the horse and mule era later told Maude T. Gilliland of Cotulla:

> We used a regular pack-saddle for carrying our
> bed-rolls. The blankets were folded just so wide
> and long and five feet wide. After folding the
> 'tarp' over the blankets the bed-roll was put on
> the pack mule and then the Dutch oven was
> turned upside-down and placed on top of the
> pack and all were drawn down with the soft pack
> ropes and securely tied. This way it would ride for
> many miles over the roughest kind of country
> without ever coming loose.

The pack mules also carried groceries, other cooking utensils, and a couple of pieces of equipment the old Rangers of the Frontier Battalion probably never dreamed of—two state-issued Thompson submachine guns.

Rangers admired pack mules for their endurance, intelligence, and personality.

The same Company D Ranger who told Gilliland how the mules were packed marveled at their endurance and intelligence: "These mules could trot all day long carrying their packs and never seem to tire. When they came to a limb too low to go under with their packs, they would go right up to it as if measuring the height, then suddenly stop, and back up and go around it. They also kept a safe distance from tree trunks to keep from scraping their packs on them."

Captain Wright commanded Company D until 1925, when he left the Ranger service after the election of Governor Miriam "Ma" Ferguson. At Laredo he turned Lizzie, Polly, and Old Monk over to his successor, since they were state property, then saddled up and rode back to his native

Wilson County, southeast of San Antonio. Trailing behind him were the captured Mexican mules, Rat and Spider.

At Pleasanton, Wright's last stopover before reaching Wilson County, he sold the mules. For the next decade, under two owners, Rat and Spider pulled cultivators on farms in Atascosa County. In 1935 their peanut-farmer owner traded them in on a new tractor. Rat and Spider, two Ranger mules, were last seen on a truck headed for Gurinsky's Mule Barn in San Antonio.

Mules continued to be used by the Rangers into the 1940s, when Rangers scouted the border during World War II.

A.Y. Allee, who joined the Rangers in 1931, used mules on scouts in the Big Bend. Years later he looked back fondly on the long-eared animals who packed many a load in the service of the state.

"We never led them or paid any attention to them, because we knew they would follow us like dogs," he said. "Finally, when they would look up and see us so far away, here they would come in a run, braying and rattling packs, and when they caught up, they were perfectly happy."

······ ⭐ ······

Sources

Fenley, Florence. *Heart Full of Horses*. San Antonio: The Naylor Co., 1975, p. 154.

Gillette, James B. *Six Years With the Texas Rangers*. Lincoln: University of Nebraska Press, 1925, 1976, pp. 55-56.

Gilliland, Maude T. *Horsebackers of the Brush Country: A Story of the Texas Rangers and Mexican Liquor Smugglers*. Cotulla: Privately published, 1968, pp. 51-52, 54-57.

Hughes, Alton. "First Reeves Sheriff killed in fight," *Pecos Enterprise*, Jan. 10, 1978.

Roberts, Dan W. *Rangers And Sovereignty*. Austin: State House Press, 1987, pp. 59-60, 68-74, 78.

Sherman, Jean Dale. "Texas Rangers Riding Highways and Byways: Century-Old Force Is Conducting Intensified Campaign to Prevent Livestock Theft." *The Cattleman*, Nov. 1941, Vol. 28, No. 6, p. 31.

"Texas Ranger, Sheriff Killed in Gun Fight." San Angelo *Standard-Times*, Aug. 28, 1954.

Three Hours in the Rangers

Oscar Warnke spent more than half a century in law enforcement, but his career as a Texas Ranger lasted only three hours.

Warnke was driving a bread wagon in 1925 for Richter's Bakery in San Antonio.* The wagon actually was a Model T Ford, but it had not been all that much earlier that horses pulled bread delivery vehicles in the Alamo City, and most folks still referred to the conveyance as the "bread wagon."

Warnke's route included all the downtown cafes and hotels. One of his stops was the Southland Hotel at 105½ South Flores Street. The Texas Rangers had their San Antonio office in the building.

On his afternoon run, Warnke stopped at the Southland to replace bread sold earlier in the day and collect the bakery's money.

Inside the hotel, Warnke ran into Ranger Sergeant Dan Coleman. The Ranger had known Warnke since he was a boy growing up in Karnes City, where everyone called him "Punkin."

More than fifty years later, Warnke recalled what Coleman said that afternoon:

"Say, Punkin, we've got a vacancy on the Rangers. Wouldn't you like to join?"

That struck the young man as a tremendous career advancement over driving a bread truck.

"I couldn't say 'Yes' quick enough," he recalled. "Coleman took me over to Captain Will Wright and told him all about me. Wright called Austin, got me accepted, and I signed up. By that time it was between 4 and 5 o'clock."

The veteran Ranger captain told Warnke they were leaving San Antonio that night for a scout along the Rio Grande at Laredo.

"I didn't have a pistol so they took me down to a pawnshop and I bought a single-action Colt .45, the gun all Rangers carried," Warnke said.

Then he drove the Model T bread wagon back to the bakery, turned in the day's receipts, and announced his resignation as a truck driver, effective immediately.

From the bakery, Warnke rushed home to tell his wife Clara the good news: She was no longer married to a bread wagon driver. Her husband was now a Texas Ranger and proud of it!

Mrs. Warnke broke into tears. Warnke quickly realized they were not tears of joy.

"She thought my joining the Rangers meant that I was signing my death warrant," Warnke remembered from the vantage point of five decades. "Her mother was there and joined in the protests."

Warnke's wife and mother-in-law would not listen to his assurances that he would be safe with the other Rangers. Finally, Mrs. Warnke put the situation in perspective: If he left for Laredo that night, she would not be home when he came back—*if* he came back.

"She insisted that I resign at once," he said. "I told her how embarrassed I would be to have to face the Rangers and resign and asked her if she wouldn't go to town and tell them I was quitting."

If Warnke were man enough to be a Ranger, she said, he was tough enough to tell them thanks, but no thanks.

"So I headed back to the hotel, turned in my still un-loaded pistol and quit the Rangers," he said.

By then it was about 7 o'clock in the evening. He had been a Ranger for roughly three hours.

Early the next morning, "Punkin" was back at the bakery to explain that he had had a sudden change of mind and really preferred bread delivery to rangering. He got his job back and went to load up the wagon.

Warnke never got to wear a Ranger badge, but he did go on to a long law enforcement career in Bexar County, starting with a job under one of the county's constables. He spent eight years as a motorcycle patrolman, later serving as a vice officer with the San Antonio Police Department and then as a deputy with the Bexar County Sheriff's Department. For many years, he was chief jailer. After retiring from the county in 1969, he worked as head of security for the San Antonio Livestock Show and Rodeo.

Clara Warnke clearly adjusted to the idea of her husband carrying a badge and gun. When the veteran officer died at the age of ninety-one in 1989, the couple had been married for sixty-five years.

······ ⭐ ······

Sources

Carmack, George. "'Twilight Ranger' served 3-hour term." San Antonio *Express-News*, April 28, 1979.

"Veteran lawman Warnke was county's chief jailer." San Antonio *Express-News*, Aug. 1, 1989.

Notes

* When interviewed by a newspaper writer in 1979, Warnke said his three-hour Ranger career was in 1926. However, Captain Wright had resigned from the Rangers in early 1925 with the election of Governor Miriam "Ma" Ferguson to her first term. Wright went back into the Rangers two years later when she went out of office. The old Southern Hotel was razed in the first quarter of 1925, so Warnke's Ranger service must have been in early 1925, not 1926.

The Battle of Borger

The Santa Fe passenger train from Fort Worth rolled toward the Texas Panhandle, lurching and rocking along the rails.

The motion lulled twenty-nine-year-old L.A. Wilke to sleep.

City editor of the scrapy Scripps-Howard-owned paper in Fort Worth, *The Press*, Wilke was on his way with a contingent of Rangers to the Hutchinson County boom town of Borger, where life was considerably cheaper than a barrel of oil.

As Wilke snored away, leaning back against his seat, a tall man in a black suit slipped up to him and deftly fished something out of the newspaperman's vest. The big man was Captain Frank Hamer of the Rangers.

When Wilke woke up, he immediately realized something was missing: his gun, a .25 caliber semiautomatic. He had a commission from the Fort Worth police chief to carry it.

Hamer and the other Rangers on the train had a round of laughs before the lawman finally returned the small weapon to the newspaper editor. The way things were in Borger, he might need it, though Hamer had his doubts whether it would do Wilke any good.

"You know," Hamer said, "if I ever got shot with that thing and found out about it, I'd be mad."

The Ranger captain disdained small-caliber pistols, .22s, .25s, and .38s. "When I go to hub a little Hell," he told Wilke, "I want a .45!"

Plenty of hell was there for the hubbin' in Borger, where trouble was as easy to find as the black gold fueling the boom. Oil was first discovered in the Panhandle in 1921, but for four years production was modest. At the end of 1925 the whole Panhandle had only fifty-three operating wells. But on January 11, 1926, a well in the rugged Canadian River breaks of Hutchinson County, about sixty miles northeast of Amarillo, came in with production in excess of 5,000 barrels a day. When another gusher blew in on March 6, 1926, the oil companies realized they had discovered a major field. By the end of the year, 813 wells were producing a staggering 167,597 barrels a day.

The rich field lured thousands of people to one of the most remote parts of Texas, a land rush comparable to the opening of Oklahoma's Cherokee Strip in 1889. Some came to do honest work. Others came looking for easy money. An economy fueled by supply and demand over-heated to the point of mutation, triggering malignancy. A city of 40,000 or more materialized inside ninety days just a few miles away from the spot where only fifty-two years earlier—well within the memory of old-timers still living in the Panhandle—Billy Dixon and other buffalo hunters stood off a party of warring Comanches at a trading post called Adobe Walls.

"Since the finding of oil in this section 18 months ago," the Associated Press reported on April 8, 1927, "Borger and nearby towns have been running wide open. Many persons have been killed including several officers and two or three women. Daylight robberies, hold-ups, explosions, bootlegging and vices attendant to the wide-open dance halls have continued practically unabated."

Now Hamer and the Rangers were on their way to clean it up. Again.

In September 1926 two Rangers had been in Borger but were ordered out of the county when Governor Miriam

"Ma" Ferguson received a petition "bearing many names" requesting that she do so. Among the signatories was the county sheriff and the president of the Borger Chamber of Commerce. This was a reversal of the way things normally happened. When a situation got out of hand in a particular city or county, a governor usually received pleading letters and telegrams requesting Rangers to come and help—not that they get out of town.

Not quite a month later, lame duck Governor Ferguson ordered Rangers back to the boisterous boom town—this time four of them—after a sixteen-year-old girl was shot to death on the night of October 12 during a robbery just outside town.

"A company of tall and grim Texas rangers strode down the streets of Amarillo," the Associated Press reported two days later. "They called at the police station, left word to forward mail and rode off in the darkness for Borger to rid the famous oil boom town of the alleged vice and lawlessness which a citizens' committee and a subsequent investigation by federal and state officials declared existed there."

Despite the murder of the teenaged girl, the sheriff and the local newspaper editor, G.C. Allbright, both told the Associated Press that the Rangers had not been requested and were not needed.

"This town has no more lawlessness than the average town," chimed in Sheriff Joe Ownsby. "The whole situation is due to wild stories from the outside."

Actually, when it came to lawlessness, Borger had not yet hit its stride. The stories would get wilder, and most of them would be true. Two weeks after the teenager's murder, Borger was incorporated as a city. The newly elected mayor, John R. Miller, an attorney and crony of town founder A.P. "Ace" Borger, was a crook. So was the man hired as Borger's first police chief, a convicted killer paroled from Oklahoma called "Two Gun" Dick Herwig.

Learning that Captain Roy Nichols and three Rangers from Company C at Marshall would be going to Borger, the Fort Worth *Record* ran an editorial labeled "Borger's Troubles." The anonymous editorial writer said Borger was going through a cycle all boom towns did, comparing it with the gold mining boom towns of earlier days. The "inevitable result," the writer continued, was "a cleanup of the riffraff and criminal element which always reaches a new gusher before the shock of surprise is over." The writer went on to make a lame comparison of Borger to another city in the midst of a well-publicized crime wave, Chicago. "Maybe that sorely beset city could be as progressive as Borger if it could get four Texas Rangers for the asking," the editorial continued. Whoever wrote that editorial might have been to Chicago, but it was clear he did not know anything at all about what was really going on in Borger.

John P. "Slim" Jones, a driller who had seen his share of boom towns, described one of the events that helped Borger earn its reputation:

> Earl Ridgley was an oil field law from Oklahoma. Toughey Williamson was a bootlegger, gambler, hijacker and business manager for several women on Dickson [Dixon] St. at Borger. Williamson came into a barber shop where I was waiting for a shave. Told the barber that he wanted to get a shave. Williamson was about half drunk and said that he was going to kill a law. I asked him what for. He said for double crossing him also for pistol-whipping him . . .
>
> I told Williamson if he was in a hurry he could shave ahead of me. He thanked me, got his shave

and walked out. I didn't notice any six-shooter on him if he had one. He went off singing "When I Meet You Face to Face." I got my shave and drove down town. I soon heard two smoke-wagons [pistols] banging. I thought about what he said and walked over to where the trouble was. There they lay both shot and dying. Ridgley soon passed away. I heard Williamson say, "I got him" and he had. He talked freely before he died, didn't seem to mind dying and bade some of his friends farewell.

The newspapers made much of the Ranger presence at Borger, but four state officers were not enough to handle a crime situation fostered by corrupt local officials. Still, working with deputy United States marshals and federal prohibition agents, the Rangers quickly arrested twenty men and women, destroyed 300 gallons of liquor and seized 5,000 bottles of beer. More than twenty Borger businesses, including "confectioneries, domino parlors, rooming houses, and soft drink stands" were padlocked with federal injunction notices nailed to their doors. Despite this tough Prohibition action, no mention was made in the newspaper accounts that any gambling establishments or brothels had been shut down.

In early 1927 some of Borger's honest citizens asked the state's former attorney general and newly inaugurated governor, thirty-three-year-old Dan Moody, to declare martial law and occupy the town with state troops. Not wanting to take such a drastic step unless he had to, Moody sent Captain Hamer from Austin to Borger to take a look at the situation. Hamer reported back that something had to be done.

By the time the train carrying the Rangers and the young Fort Worth newsman rolled into Borger on April 4, 1927, another eleven homicides had occurred in or near Borger since the murder of the teenage girl the previous October. Two of the victims were police officers shot to death in the line of duty one mile north of Borger only three days before the Rangers arrived.

Once in Borger, Wilke met up with Dudley Davis, a reporter for the Houston *Press*, a sister Scripps-Howard sheet, and checked into the newly opened Black Hotel at Main and Grand. They had the biggest room in the three-story, $250,000 hotel, the young city's most imposing building. The shoebox-shaped brick building had gone up in less than three months. From the window in their room, the two journalists could look out on a sea of tents, tar-paper shacks, trucks, cars, wagons, and wooden oil derricks.

The city of Borger at the height of the boom. (Photo from author's collection

At night, gas flares lit up the sky. Through their hotel window as they tried to get some sleep came the sounds of the boom. This is how Borger attorney John B. White described the cacophony:

the roar of escaping gas from wells a few
hundreds feet away—the sound of a siren on an
ambulance tearing by as fast as traffic would
permit—the backfire of trucks and cars and
occasional pistol shots—the undefinable jargon of
human voices—a squabble between some man
and woman, neither caring who heard—the clang
of the lever of a slot machine—the continuous
grinding away of an automatic piano—the blare
of a half drunk jazz orchestra in one of the
numerous '49 dance halls—the same old tune
being constantly repeated on a phonograph—the
struggle and cries of men fighting—the voices of
the "Law"—the whack of a pistol on some poor
creature's head—the whine of some beggar
wanting the price of a bed but in most cases the
money for another drink . . . .

The Rangers were staying at the same hotel and used
the two reporters' room for their strategy sessions.

At the meetings, however, Hamer always seemed to tell
less than he knew, particularly with the reporters around.

"I didn't get along with Frank," Wilke later recalled,
"and he didn't like me."

On the other hand, Wilke was a good friend of Captain
Tom Hickman, whom he had meet in 1924 when the
Ranger escorted the Cowboy Band of Simmons College
from Abilene to England. "We were real buddies," Wilke
said of his relationship with Hickman.

That friendship proved beneficial as the Rangers went
about their work in Borger.

"Captain Hickman would tip me off," Wilke said. "Every
day we'd come out with a scoop and Hamer couldn't figure
out where we got 'em. One day Dudley and I were standing
there talking and he [Hamer] walked up and put his arms

203

around each one of us and said, 'I know how Jesus Christ felt when he was hanging on the cross between two thieves.'"

At least the reporters' Borger stories did not land Wilke and Davis in jail.

The city editor of the Borger *Herald*, Victor Wagner, was not so lucky. In early May, Ranger Private A.F. "Sugg" Cummings arrested Wagner without a warrant—and had him held without bond—for the stories he had been writing about the cleanup. When someone else with the newspaper tried to get off a telegram to the Associated Press bureau in Dallas reporting the arrest of the newsman, the Ranger prevented it from being sent. Despite the Ranger's efforts, word of Wagner's plight reached Austin.

Governor Moody did not mind that the Rangers were forcing the resignation of city and county officials and running off miscreants, but throwing a reporter in jail and then blocking coverage of the arrest was going too far.

Ranger Cummings was summoned to Austin for a personal meeting with the young red-headed governor and then ordered discharged from the service.

The governor issued a statement saying he had never intended to "meet lawlessness with lawlessness" in the Borger cleanup.

"If Mr. Cummings does not know he ought to that he has no authority to exercise a censorship over the press, and that he has no right to arrest people and place them in jail because they write things in the newspapers which are not pleasing to him," Moody said.

On May 7 Ranger Captains Hamer, Hickman, and W.W. "Bill" Sterling met with Assistant Attorney General Calloway Calhoun and the management of the Borger newspaper to smooth over things. After getting chewed out and fired by the governor, Cummings soon got a job as a Travis County sheriff's deputy in Austin.

"Rangers Make Peace With Borger Editor," the governor no doubt read with pleasure in the next day's Austin *American*. According to the AP story, "Informal plans for bringing about the fullest co-operation between rangers and the press were discussed to the end that conditions will be cleared up so that there will be no need in a short time for rangers in the county."

The Rangers would not be leaving Hutchinson County, however, until the bootleggers, crooks, and prostitutes did.

The exodus had begun shortly after the Rangers hit town in April. On April 7 the Rangers rounded up 260 undesirables. Sixty went to jail. The other 200 were told to be out of town by 6 p.m. the following day. The town's prostitutes did not even take the time to pick up their cleaning, leaving hundreds of silk dresses behind. The Rangers, confident the girls would not be needing the clothing again, at least not in Borger, donated the garments to the Salvation Army.

One of the folks leaving Borger at the suggestion of the Rangers was "Two Gun" Herwig. He went downstate to Wink, the newest oil field boom town. Forced out of Wink by Rangers there, he relocated to New Mexico, where he opened a joint and boldly proclaimed on a sign in front of the roadhouse: "Eight Miles From Texas Rangers."

Ranger Captain Will Wright, who had evicted Herwig from Wink, heard about the sign. Though noted for his sense of humor, Wright did not think the name Herwig had chosen for his latest business was very funny. Herwig obviously thought his establishment was beyond the authority of the Rangers. But federal officers know no state lines. Wright and some of his men—while retaining their state law enforcement commissions—got themselves appointed as dollar-a-year federal revenue agents. Shortly after taking on this new responsibility, the Rangers found time in their busy schedule to visit Herwig in New Mexico. Once more, "Two Gun Dick" was out of business.

Captain Sterling, newly designated commander of Company D, had been in Borger with several of his men since mid-April. That brought the Ranger contingent in Hutchinson County to twenty-one officers. For a time, all three captains and their men stayed busy. Then Hamer and Hickman left, needed elsewhere in the state on other matters.

The Rangers developed an innovative field "test" to determine if someone not actually caught red-handed in the commission of a crime needed to go to jail. After the city expended some tax dollars for a paddy wagon, Sterling later recalled,

> The Rangers helped to break in this piece of municipal equipment. They would ask a suspicious-looking loafer what he did for a living. The answer would usually be, 'I am a working man.' If an examination of his hands showed callouses or other evidence of honest toil, he was free to go about his business. But if he had the soft, white hands of a gambler or other parasite, the hoodlum wagon gained another passenger.

The Ranger hand test, while sliding past the Fourteenth Amendment, "proved to be almost infallible," Sterling said, and resulted in the apprehension of several wanted men.

"Shine" Popejoy's hands did not have to be checked to determine they belonged to the biggest bootlegger in the area. His whiskey still, hidden in a canyon in nearby Moore County, was as big a producer for Borger as any oil derrick. Sterling's Rangers wrecked Popejoy's still and took him to Dumas, the county seat, to file charges against him. But the Rangers found that there was no county jail. In fact the county—though it was thirty-six years old—had not even gotten around to building a courthouse. When the Rangers finally found the docket book to enter the complaint against Popejoy, the charge they filed was only the eighth ever lodged since the county's creation.

Back in Borger, the Rangers clearly had the situation under control. On July 26, 1927, for the first time since its construction, the Borger city jail held no prisoners. Most of the Rangers, including the captains, had turned to other law enforcement concerns elsewhere in the state.

Rangers breaking up a gambling operation. (Photo courtesy of Hutchinson County Museum)

The 1927 *Report of the Adjutant General* summed up the results of the Ranger activities in Borger that year:

The liquor traffic was broken up, many stills being seized and destroyed, and several thousand gallons of whisky being captured and poured out. Two hundred and three gambling slot machines were seized and destroyed. Numerous gambling resorts were placed under surveillance and forced to clean up, and in a period of twenty-four hours it is assumed that no less then 1,200 prostitutes left the town . . . the Mayor, City Commissioners, Chief of Police, and practically all of the Police Force of Borger resigned and were replaced by citizens pledged to enforce the laws.

A few Rangers stayed on in Borger until February 1929 when the last man left. A month later a magazine published by the Santa Fe Railroad reported Borger was "slowly but surely erasing all traces of the bad reputation it had thrust upon it during the mad rush incident to the boom."

The Rangers definitely had an impact on Borger, but like a burning oil well finally capped and cooled down, there was no guarantee that it would not blow out again. A few months later, it did. But that is another story.

Sources

Jones, John P. "Slim." *Borger: The Little Oklahoma*. n.p., n.d.

Krenek, Harry. *The Power Vested*. Austin: Presidial Press, 1980, p. 85

Report of the Adjutant General of the State of Texas For The Year Ending August 31, 1927. Austin: 1929, p. 19.

Sinise, Jerry. *Black Gold & Red Lights*. Burnet: Eakin Press, 1982.

Sterling, William Warren. *Trails and Trials of a Texas Ranger*. Norman: University of Oklahoma Press, 1968, pp. 97-114.

White, John H. *Borger, Texas*. Waco: Texian Press, 1972, p. 38.

"The Wild West Is Still Fairly Dusty," New York *World*. n.d., ca. 1927.

Wilke, L.A. Interview with author, 1971.

Rx for Keeping the Peace: Laxatives and a .45

A.E. Bennet was walking out of the Harris County courthouse in Houston when oilman Bob Smith stopped him.

Bennet had been a Texas Ranger and still carried a Special Ranger badge, which gave him limited law enforcement powers—and the ability to tote the .45 he had become pretty used to over the years.

Years later, at 89, Bennet sat in front of his retirement home at Lago Vista on Lake Travis and recalled that meeting with Smith in downtown Houston.

"He wanted me to go to Freer," Bennet said, "and clean it up for him."

Freer, in Duval County, had become typical of the oil patch boom towns in the mid-1930s as the South Texas oil fields were opening up. What had Smith particularly worried was the open gambling.

"He said the men weren't getting home with enough money to buy their groceries," Bennett said. "So I said, 'Okay, I'll go down there and clean it up for you.'"

The former Ranger moved to Freer and became the town's chief of police. He had a force of five men.

"There was gambling everywhere, all over," he said. "You know, Duval County was an outlaw county to start with."

209

The county was controlled by George Parr, the so-called Duke of Duval. "They [one of Parr's men] came to see me, but there was no run-in about it," Bennet said. "I said that was the way it was going to be, and that's the way it was. I told them [Freer] was going to be cleaned up."

Bennett got right to work, visiting each of the various gaming establishments. He courteously gave their operators a ten-day grace period to get out of town.

"They didn't pay no attention to me," Bennett said.

On the eleventh day after issuing his shutdown order, Bennett borrowed a big oil field truck and repeated his visits. No one interfered with Bennett and his officers as they confiscated cash and smashed and burned all the gaming paraphernalia they could find.

"I gave the money to the churches," he said. "They had to count it, I didn't."

Although Bennett stayed in Freer for about a year, "there wasn't nothing to do" after his first two weeks on the job, he said.

The Freer cleanup came midway in Bennett's law enforcement career. Born to a farming family in the Lee County community of Lexington in 1894, Bennett spent his childhood in the Laredo area where his parents operated an onion farm. Most of their workers came from Mexico, and Bennett picked up Spanish easily.

That knowledge came in handy when he visited Francisco "Pancho" Villa in Nuevo Laredo.

Bennett's trip across the Rio Grande was prompted by the sudden disappearance of the man working as foreman on the Bennett family onion farm.

"I rode across the river to see what was the matter with him," Bennett said. "He'd been working for me about two years and he was a good foreman."

Bennett dismounted at Villa's camp and talked for about two hours with the revolutionary leader.

"I had a long talk with him," Bennett recalled. "And I agreed with what he was doing. He said the Mexican government was robbing the poor people and he didn't like it."

Bennett told Villa he guessed his foreman could stay with the Villistas.

Bennett's transition to badge-wearing began with a visit from a doctor with the U.S. Public Health Service. At the Bennett farm to inoculate workers, the doctor noted that Bennett spoke "Tex-Mex" as well as the hands.

"He said, 'Bennett, I could sure use you. I'll give you three or four months' training and you can take care of some of these people for me. You don't have to quit your farming.'"

After the training, Bennett began driving from Laredo to the Valley to give Mexican children smallpox shots. Doctors were scarce, and before long, Bennett had learned midwifery and border country "medicine." Many of Bennett's "patients" were fight victims.

"I sewed up one Mexican who had been cut from here plum to here," Bennett said, drawing his finger all the way across his lower abdomen. "His guts were sticking out in front of him and he was sitting there holding them. He had a quart of tequila in one hand, his belly in the other. I laid him out on his back and poured about half that quart down his belly."

The procedure took more than half an hour. After sewing ninety stitches, Bennett poured a bottle of iodine over the incision.

"He got well and was eighty years old when I left that country down there," Bennett said.

But Bennett began to get discouraged by the frequency of the fights he had to clean up after. "I got tired of sewing them up. They'd get drunk and the first thing they'd grab was a knife. Whoever comes first, that's who gets it. So I decided to do something about it."

Several days before a big dance at Zapata, Bennett bought all the chewable laxative he could get from a pharmaceutical house. The day of the *baile*, he left piles of the pleasant-tasting chewables all over town, including in and around the dance hall.

No one was stabbed that night in Zapata, he said. "They went home," he laughed. "They had something else to do."

The offer of a higher salary persuaded Bennett to trade his patchin' up for a pistol.

He went to work for the Border Patrol in the mid-1920s, riding the river, helping to arrest hundreds of illegal aliens, and hauling in a few bootleggers. He worked closely with the Rangers, which eventually led him to join the state law enforcement force.

Bennett survived a gunfight or two, but was never wounded and never shot anyone.

"Funny thing...I had three boys. Two of them retired from the Houston Police Department and one from the Highway Patrol. We spent 117 years in law enforcement, and none of us ever had to kill anybody, which I'm glad of."

Bennett joined the Rangers in Austin in the 1930s, serving for a couple of years.

"I started out in Austin, but they run us all over the country," he said. "They was having trouble with Oklahoma and they sent four or five of us there for two weeks. They was having some trouble about a bridge. We went up there and talked to the officers on the other side... there wasn't no trouble."

Leaving the Rangers because the pay was too low to support his family, Bennett got a Special Ranger Commission and went to work for the old Humble Oil Company, now Exxon.

While doing security work for Humble, Bennett met Winthrop Rockefeller, who had been sent to Texas by his family to learn the oil business from the hole up. His presence drew a lot of attention, including some from the wrong kind of people.

When Bennett heard of a plan to kidnap the young Rockefeller, he quickly went to the Rice Hotel, where Rockefeller had a suite. "I stayed with him the next seven months, then carried him back to New York."

No kidnap attempt was made on Bennett's watch.

In New York, Bennett visited the Rockefeller home in Tarrytown. "They had a house down there big enough for a hotel. Winthrop's father said, 'Why don't you come up here and work for me?' and I said I'd rather pick peas. He liked to turned his chair over laughing."

Bennett spent five years with Humble before going to work for Texaco, still as a Special Ranger. That oil company had a problem with theft of gasoline from its pipeline from Shreveport, Louisiana, to Port Arthur, Texas. The line had a pressure of 700 pounds per square inch on its front end, but the gas was barely a trickle by the time it got to Texas.

The Special Ranger solved the problem. "I just followed the pipeline and everywhere somebody lived close to it, I found they were filling jars, jugs, bottles, old car tanks, buckets, and pots with gasoline," he said. He arrested about sixty-five people and the "leaks" along the pipeline were plugged.

Bennett left his job with Texaco to deal with Freer's gambling. Then former Ranger Captain Frank Hammer, who had tracked down Bonnie Parker and Clyde Barrow in 1934, wrote to tell Bennett he had a job for him back in Houston.

"They had a big dock strike down there, and the mayor of Houston called Frank and wanted him to come down there and take care of it," Bennett said. "Frank called me, and I went with him."

The strike lasted ninety-three days and led Bennett to a "temporary" job with the Port of Houston that lasted the next seventeen years. He created the port's police force.

"It was rough," Bennett said. "The longshoremen were stealing more stuff out of the ships than they were unloading. I gave them all notice that they were going to jail. I started checking all the ships as they came in and went out, and it [the stealing] stopped, just like that."

In the 1940s Bennett patrolled the wharves in Houston on horseback, just as he had ridden the Rio Grande years before.

When he retired from the Port Authority, he got a job as a municipal court judge in Missouri City, near Houston.

In 1978 Bennett and his wife moved to Lago Vista, in Travis County, Texas. He worked for a while selling ranches, but by the fall of 1983, he spent most of his time just taking it easy and listening to his wife play the organ.

As he sat in a wicker chair in front of his lake house, his mind sometimes drifted back and he heard a different kind of music—the sound of horses' hooves and the drone of insects in the mesquite along the Rio Grande—a river someone always was splashing across, for reasons ranging from honorable to evil.

His success in law enforcement, on the river and along the wharves in Houston, depended on more than toughness, though even at 89, his eyes showed he was not the kind of man who put up with much foolishness.

"My advice to a peace officer is to be honest and clean," he said, puffing on his pipe and looking at the well-worn .45 semiautomatic he had carried for so many years as a Ranger and then as a Special Ranger. "If you're honest, it won't make any difference if you're tough."

In early 1984, a few months after telling his story to a reporter, Bennett died at his lake home west of Austin.

······ ⭐ ······

Sources

Bennett, A.E. Interview with author, Oct. 7, 1983.

Cox, Mike. "The legend of a Ranger," *Onward* Magazine, Austin *American-Statesman*, Nov. 1, 1983, pp. 12-13.

Tom Mix: Famous Ranger Who Wasn't

Five days into the new year of 1992, millions of Americans read about one of the most famous Texas Rangers there ever was—Western star Tom Mix. It was in the newspapers. It had to be true!

On the inside cover of *Parade* Magazine, in Walter Scott's "Personality Parade" column, was a picture of the smiling cowboy movie idol who made some 175 Westerns in a twenty-four-year career that ended with his retirement from the film world in 1934.

An old postcard from the author's collection shows Tom Mix, star of some 400 Westerns, demonstrating a trick by his favorite mount, Tony.

216

A reader from Pelham, Alabama, had written Scott to ask about Mix. "Is it true that Tom Mix...wasn't just some celluloid cowboy but that he really had a fabulous life of adventure?"

Scott replied that Mix was indeed "the real McCoy." Not, of course, to be confused with the real Tim McCoy, a rival cowboy star. Mix, Scott informed his readers, had served in the Spanish-American War, in China during the Boxer Rebellion, and in the Boer War. Then Scott reported something that must really have helped to shape Mix's character: "Later, while a member of the Texas Rangers, Mix was shot and carried three slugs in his body for the rest of his life."

The magazine columnist's belief that Mix had been a Texas Ranger is easy enough to understand, though the assertion is patently untrue. The problem is, and Scott and other writers before him can be forgiven for falling for it, there were two Tom Mixes, a real one and one created by Hollywood. Both Tom Mixes looked alike and starred in Western movies. One died on October 12, 1940. The other Tom Mix lives on, still giving personality columnists and other authors something to write about.

Any movie buff who read the fan magazines or studio biographies of Mix knew the tale: Tom Mix was born in El Paso in a log cabin—they must have hauled the logs in from the piney woods of East Texas—on January 6, 1880. His genealogy amounted to a history of the Old West. A great-great-grandfather had been a Cherokee Indian. Mix's father had been a captain in the famed Seventh Cavalry. Riding a horse and tossing a lariat came as natural and as early to Mix as walking and talking did to most kids.

A star football player for the Virginia Military Academy, Mix dropped out of school when the Spanish-American War broke out in 1898, signed up with the army, and served with distinction in Cuba. He survived a gunshot wound to the mouth from a Spanish sniper and went on to serve his country during the Philippine Insurrection and during the Boxer Rebellion in China. Wounded again, he was ordered back to the States.

Quickly recovering, Mix went to Denver and broke horses to be purchased by the British Cavalry for use in the Boer War in South Africa. He accompanied a shipment of horses and got to the Dark Continent just in time for a little more fighting.

Back in the U.S.—this time apparently unwounded —Mix guided Theodore Roosevelt on Western hunting expeditions. Well familiar by now with both ends of a firearm, he turned to law enforcement and worked as a sheriff's deputy, U.S. marshal and, landing what many considered the ultimate of all law enforcement jobs, signed on with the Texas Rangers.

While wearing the Ranger star, Mix single-handedly captured the outlaw Shonts Brothers, surviving yet another gunshot wound. (An Indian woman plugged him in the back, but it was nothing serious.)

Still not adverse to the smell of gunpowder, Mix helped Francisco Madero during the Mexican Revolution. South of the border, he survived a firing squad (they must have all missed), but did get nicked in the leg by a rifle bullet during the Battle of Juarez.

Back on the Texas side of the river, Mix saddled up old Blue and rode west to Hollywood, where the gunfire was even more ineffectual than it had been in the real world. With a background like his, playing a cowboy in the movies would be a lot easier than standing blindfolded in front of a pockmarked adobe wall and dodging Krag bullets.

The rest, as his publicity agents would say, was history.

Mix became the preeminent Western star of the 1920s, the successor to William S. Hart and the predecessor by a decade of men like Gene Autry and Roy Rogers.

As James Horwitz wrote in *They Went Thataway*, the Tom Mix story was "wonderful and exciting... Breathless. Full of fighting and heroics and great escapes. It was a life guaranteed to inspire dreams in any Front Row Kid. It was fantastic. It was a pack of lies!"

Nevertheless, much of Mix's fictional biography has been accepted as fact. George K. Fenin and William K. Everson report the Texas Ranger story in the revised edition of their highly readable book on Western movies, though they hedge their bet a bit:

> Studio publicity has undoubtedly colored this phase of Mix's career [his purported Ranger service and other exploits] but documentary evidence does exist confirming that Mix's law enforcement activities were quite as rugged as his later movie adventures. The story of Mix's capture of the notorious New Mexico cattle rustlers, the Shonts Brothers, could have been taken from any one of his later Western thrillers for Fox.

Indeed, Mix's life story was every bit as "colorized" as the computer-enhanced prints of old black-and-white movie classics playing to a new generation of viewers on cable television. Mix was the product of studio public relations departments run amuck, the work of Hollywood flacks seeking to satisfy movie fans who wanted their screen heroes to be real heroes as well.

The real Tom Mix was born a couple of thousand miles northeast of El Paso in Mix Run, Pennsylvania, on the same date the other Tom Mix was born. His father was a lumber miller, not an Indian fighter. As for a boyhood on horseback, the closest the youngster came was Buffalo Bill's Wild West Show when it played in his part of the state. The real Tom Mix, like his Hollywood image, was an athletic young man, but he never played football for Virginia Military Academy.

Mix did enlist in the army during the Spanish-American War, but the closest he got to Cuba was the Delaware River. Mix probably could have been a Texas Ranger if he had come to Texas and signed up, but payroll records in the State Archives in Austin do not support that he ever did. And what of the notorious Shonts gang? If they ever existed, they should have had a press agent with as active an imagination as the public relations practitioners who wrote the releases about Mix. *The Encyclopedia of Western Gunfighters* lists 255 gunman and 587 gunfights up to 1924, but author Bill O'Neal does not mention any badmen by the name of Shonts.

From 1905 to 1908 Mix did work as an armed security officer at various labor camps in Kansas, Tennessee, and Colorado, rousting thieves, gamblers, and drunks. In 1909 he served as a deputy sheriff in Dewey, Oklahoma. Later that year, he was hired as a horse wrangler by a motion picture company filming on location in Oklahoma. Soon afterward, he was discovered.

The cowboy star's reported service as a Texas Ranger clearly was cooked up by Hollywood press agents, probably hard-drinking ex-reporters. As Paul Mix, one of his relatives, later wrote: "It is unfortunate that movie publicists added outlandish tales about Tom as a Texas Ranger and United States Marshal because when these stories were uncovered as shams, they tended to discredit Tom's real-life adventures as a labor camp peace officer."

Though Mix never wore a Ranger star for real, he did pin on a badge from the prop department for his leading role in *The Lone Star Ranger*, a 1923 six-reeler based on the novel by Zane Grey, the Ohio-born dentist turned Western writer. (Grey was never a Texas Ranger, either, but he did meet some real Rangers.)

Mix also got to rub shoulders with some real Rangers.

It was during the filming of *The Lone Star Ranger*, as a matter of fact, that Mix got to meet a young man who had ridden with the Rangers in West Texas, Charles (Buck) Buchanan.

Buchanan, who grew up on a ranch in Burnet County about sixty miles northwest of Austin, had served under Captain Jerry Gray at Marfa. While rangering in the Trans-Pecos, Buchanan "got the movie bug," resigned his state employment, and headed for Hollywood.

For forty dollars a week, the former Ranger worked as a stunt man and double for Buck Jones, a Western star second only to Mix in popularity with the fans. When that contract was completed, Buchanan played a Mexican bandit in *The California Romance*, a movie starring John Gilbert and Estelle Taylor. Buchanan's next gig was as a double for Mix. Over a two-and-a-half-year period, Buchanan stood in for Mix in *The Untamed*, *The Lone Star Ranger*, and *The Last of the Duanes* (1924, seven reels), another Zane Grey title with a Ranger protagonist.

Frank Hamer was the Ranger best known by the Hollywood actor. The "reel" Ranger met the real Ranger when Hamer and his wife Gladys visited California in 1918. The couple took the trip after Hamer had recovered from two pistol wounds suffered in a shoot-out in Sweetwater on October 1, 1917. Mix took the Hamers around his studio and tried to talk Frank into coming to Hollywood to join him as a Western actor. Mrs. Hamer said no, though her Ranger husband apparently had no serious intention of taking Mix up on his offer.

Mix later visited Hamer in Texas and posed with him for a photograph outside the Ranger office at the Capitol in Austin.

They remained friends, and Hamer got Mix named an honorary Texas Ranger.

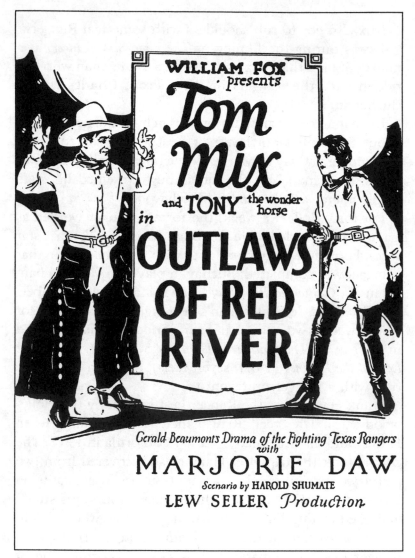

A movie poster from 1927 shows a smiling "Ranger" Mix at the mercy of a pretty, pistol-packin' rancher's daughter. (From author's collection)

In 1934, after Mix had left the movie world and started traveling with Sam B. Dill's Circus, he wrote Hamer to congratulate him on his "fine work" in tracking down the outlaws Clyde Barrow and Bonnie Parker. "We will soon be back in Texas and would appreciate a visit if you could find time to call on me," Mix wrote.

Six years later, Mix's fancy 1937 Cord Roadster—he had a pair of steer horns mounted on the hood—veered off the highway at an unexpected detour sign on a curve in the roadway near Florence, Arizona. He suffered a broken neck from a flying metal suitcase. He died with his boots on, one of them pressing too heavily on the accelerator of his white Cord.

Sources

Fenin, George N. and William K. Everson. *The Western: From Silents to the Seventies*. New York: Grossman Publishers, 1962, 1973, (Revised ed.) pp. 109-121.

Horwitz, James. *They Went Thataway*. New York: E.P. Dutton & Co., 1976, pp. 67-69.

Jenkins, John H. and H. Gordon Frost. *I'm Frank Hamer: The Life of a Texas Peace Officer*. Austin: State House Press, 1968, 1993, pp. 70-71, 74, 254.

Mix, Paul E. *Tom Mix: The Formative Years*. Austin: 1990, pp. 44-45.

Nicholas, John H. *Tom Mix: Riding Up to Glory*. Oklahoma City: National Cowboy Hall of Fame, 1980, p. 9.

O'Neal, Bill. *Encyclopedia of Western Gunfighters*. Norman: University of Oklahoma Press, 1979.

Scott, Kenneth W. *Zane Grey: Born to the West, A Reference Guide*. Boston: G.K. Hall & Co., 1979, p. 6.

"I Asked For B.M. Gault . . ."

Anyone who ever kicked in his ante, peeked at his cards, and then opened on guts hoping to draw to an inside straight knows there is more to playing poker than memorizing odds and the ranking of hands. A big part of successful poker is reading people—deciding whether someone is trying to buy the pot on a bluff or betting a sure thing.

In the early 1930s a group of men whose lives sometimes depended on the ability to judge human nature in a hurry, often with their fingers crooked on hair triggers, gathered in Austin for a weekly poker game.

The only non-gun toter sometimes allowed a seat at the table was University of Texas history professor Walter Prescott Webb, who was at work on a book about the Rangers. Webb had become friends with one of the lawmen he was writing about, Captain Frank A. Hamer.

Hamer played in his dining room with his family around. His poker chips, Webb later recalled, were "the best that money can buy, the kind that are used in professional gambling houses."

But money had not bought these chips, at least not Captain Hamer's money. They bore the initials of a rich Texan who had run a gambling joint in Houston until Hamer and other Rangers paid a visit. The captain had kept the chips as souvenirs, Webb said.

By this point in his career, Hamer's body was well scarred from bullet wounds. He had taken chances and survived, and he did the same thing at the poker table.

"These poker games show Frank Hamer at his worst," Webb recalled. "He has been known to practice deception by acting as if he held four aces when in reality he held nothing more than two deuces. Quite often he acts with such convincingness as to steal practically everything on the table . . ."

Another player at these games was a Ranger named Benjamin Manny Gault. He went by Manny.

In their service together in the Rangers, and at these weekly poker games, Hamer had ample opportunity to take the measure of Gault. In the spring of 1934 Gault was the man Hamer picked to join him in tracking down Bonnie Parker and Clyde Barrow, Texas' most notorious Depression-era outlaws.

Barrow was a small-time hood raised in Dallas who specialized in car theft, burglary, and armed robbery. Bonnie was his red-headed girlfriend. The couple traveled the nation's midsection in stolen cars, stealing, robbing, and killing. They advanced to gangster stardom on the strength of an unfortunate and vicious character flaw of Barrow's: a propensity when pulling even petty stickups to shoot and kill gratuitously. They survived two gunbattles with police. On a foggy winter morning in 1934 they brazenly raided the Eastham unit of the Texas state prison, killing a guard and springing the notorious Raymond Hamilton and three other inmates.

A couple of weeks after the bloody January 16 breakout at Eastham, prison director Lee Simmons commissioned Hamer to track the young killers down. Hamer went to work on February 10.

Bonnie and Clyde already were the most wanted outlaws in modern Texas history when, on April 1, they killed two

Texas highway patrolmen, E.B. Wheeler and H.D. Murphy, near Grapevine in Denton County.

WANTED FOR MURDER
JOPLIN, MISSOURI

F.P.C.29 - MO. 9
26 U 00 6

CLYDE CHAMPION BARROW, age 24, 5'7",130#,hair dark brown and wavy,eyes hazel,light complexion,home West Dallas,Texas. This man killed Detective Harry McGinnis and Constable J.W. Harryman in this city,April 13, 1933.

BONNIE PARKER CLYDE BARROW   CLYDE BARROW

This man is dangerous and is known to have committed the following murders: Howard Hall, Sherman, Texas; J.W.Bucher,Hillsboro, Texas; a deputy sheriff at Atoka, Okla; deputy sheriff at West Dallas, Texas; also a man at Belden, Texas.
    The above photos are kodaks taken by Barrow and his companions in various poses,and we believe they are better for identification than regular police pictures.
    Wire or write any information to the

Police Department.

On April 10, Hamer called L.G. Phares, chief of the Texas Highway Patrol, to give him the license plate number and description of the latest car the outlaws were driving. Phares told him the Highway Department—which then had responsibility for policing Texas roadways and had just lost two young officers at the hands of Bonnie and Clyde—wanted an additional lawman in on the hunt.

"I asked for B.M. Gault," Hamer later related to his friend Webb—the only person who ever got a detailed interview with Hamer regarding Bonnie and Clyde. "[Gault] had served with me in the Headquarters Ranger Company. Gault met me in Dallas on April 14, and traveled with me until the chase ended."

The man who hired Hamer remembered the circumstances of Gault's involvement a little differently. Twenty years later, in a book on his career with the Texas prison system, Simmons wrote that despite Phares' desire to put another man on the case, he at first had been reluctant.

"I wanted secrecy maintained for Hamer's protection," Simmons wrote, "as well as for the success of his undertaking."

But the prison director told Hamer to do as he saw fit, as long as "you run the show."

Simmons wrote that it was Phares who recommended Gault to Hamer. The prison director knew Gault "fairly well," he recalled, and was satisfied that as a Ranger "his judgment and reliability had been tested."

"You want him?" Simmons asked Hamer.

"Yes," Hamer said, "I'd really like to have him."

"Well, you're running things," Simmons replied.

Hamer knew he had made a good choice in picking Gault to help him with Bonnie and Clyde and so did others who knew the two men: "They made a good pair," former Adjutant General W.W. "Bill" Sterling later recalled.

Gault was born on June 21, 1886, in Travis County, the son of John M. and Minnie Gault. His father operated a dairy on Slaughter Creek Hill, southeast of Austin. Manny Gault's first career was working at a furniture manufacturing plant in South Austin. He married Rebecca Johnson and had two children, a son, Johnson Gullet Gault, and a daughter, Leona. Gault attended the Baptist Church, was a Mason and a member of the Woodmen of the World.

"I'm not sure how they met," recalled Hamer's son, Frank Hamer Jr., "but Manny did undercover work for my dad before he became a Ranger. He had a knack for inserting himself into auto theft and bootlegging rings and helped my dad make a lot of cases."

A killer tornado struck South Austin in May 1922, destroying the plant where Gault worked, Woodward Manufacturing. The Gaults lived at 1606 Nickerson, not far from where the twister hit, and Mrs. Gault suffered a serious leg injury from a piece of flying lumber.

"Gault told my dad, 'I'm out of a job,'" Hamer Jr. recalled. "But Dad said, 'You've got a job. I want you to come to work for me.'"

However, the manufacturing plant went back into operation after the tornado and Gault stayed on as an employee. Records show Gault finally went on the state payroll on the first day of 1929. He was listed as a mechanic, but that may have been a matter of budget juggling. Hamer's son said Gault went with his father to Sherman when a race riot was developing in May 1930, though the record does not show Gault listed on the payroll as a "State Ranger" until January 1, 1931.

Gault was not a big man, but he had a big smile and blue eyes which could twinkle or pierce. He wore a plain, single-breasted suit and a straw hat, and, as one writer put it, "looked more like an insurance salesman or a grocer than a fearless peace officer."

A month after joining the Rangers, Gault was one of ten Rangers dispatched to Texas' latest oilfield boom town, the wild Gregg County city of Kilgore in East Texas. *Time* magazine reported that:

Within two hours they had rounded up some 300 suspects and bad characters. Then ten Rangers herded the lot of them into the Baptist Church, and booked them from the pulpit. They were a measley collection. Forty were cut out for detention, the rest were hustled out of town. Two of those detained were wanted for murder, three for bank robbery.

Though Gault was diminutive compared with many other Rangers, he made up for it with a forceful character.

One of Gault's sisters, Barbara, later told this story about her Ranger brother: A man ran for sheriff in a West Central Texas county on a platform of cleaning up the county. That would consist mainly of taming three local toughs, a fellow named Doolittle and his two sons.

The candidate was elected and later sworn into office. The day after the new lawman moved into the sheriff's office, Doolittle and his boys visited the courthouse to "congratulate" the man on his new job. They beat the sheriff so badly that he contacted the governor's office in Austin to report that he intended to resign and that the governor would need to call a special election.

"Don't do that," the governor told the sheriff. "Just wait until I can send someone out there."

The next day, Ranger Gault arrived in town. The first person he came to, he asked: "Where can I find a Mr. Doolittle?"

"Well," the citizen considered the question, "this time of day, he'd be in the saloon."

Gault went to the saloon and asked for Mr. Doolittle. A big man looked up from his drink and headed toward the smallish Ranger.

"Are you Mr. Doolittle?" Gault asked.

Doolittle allowed that he was.

Gault explained why he was in town and added, "I hate violence." He then slapped Doolittle so hard his face turned as red as watermelon pulp. The Ranger quietly emphasized a few more points to the hardcase and slapped him again.

Soon, local residents were watching something they had never seen before. A small man walking behind Doolittle down the main thoroughfare, headed out of town. Every five steps or so Gault kicked him in the rear end.

Before Gault left town, he found Doolittle's sons and imparted similar messages to them.

Six months later, the story goes, Gault decided he had better see how the sheriff was doing in his new job. The Ranger called him and learned that the county was peaceful. Doolittle, the sheriff said, was currently serving as an elder in the church and had caused no further problems.

The Gaults and Hamers were close, Hamer's son recalled. The two families were together frequently for games of pitch and dominoes in addition to the weekly poker game.

"We had picnics and went on dove hunts," Hamer Jr. said. "Dad and Gault hunted with Hays County Sheriff George Allen on the Kuykendall Ranch. There was a huge oak tree on the ranch, near water. That's where we hunted."

Hamer Jr. remembered Gault as a quiet man, but he had a wry sense of humor. Both Rangers also shared a musical bent. "Manny played a guitar and my dad played the fiddle," Hamer's son said. "Dad bought a fiddle in Sheffield, when he was spending time along the Pecos recuperating after the first time he'd been shot. He used to tell me he 'tortured the cowbrutes' playing that fiddle until he got good at it."

Gault served as a Ranger until resigning January 16, 1933, following the election of Miriam "Ma" Ferguson to her second term as governor. Hamer and most of his colleagues also quit.

"Dad would never work for the Fergusons and most of the other old Rangers wouldn't either," Hamer Jr. recalled. "Gault had no use for the Fergusons."

For a time after leaving the Rangers, Gault worked as a Travis County sheriff's deputy. He left the county to take a commission as a Highway Patrolman, though he did not serve as a uniformed officer.

Gault met Hamer in Dallas shortly after Simmons gave his go-ahead for him to join in the search for Bonnie and Clyde. At a cafe shortly after their rendezvous, Hamer briefed his friend on what he had learned about Bonnie and Clyde.

"I compare these outlaws to wild horses that move around on an open range," Hamer said. "They always go in the same circle. I've traced their route from Dallas northeast through Oklahoma and Kansas to Joplin, Missouri, south to the northeastern part of Louisiana, and back to Dallas."

Gault had listened intently. "And what we have to do is break the circle."

"That's the way I see it," Hamer agreed.

Since both Barrow and Parker were from Dallas and were wanted there, Dallas County Sheriff Smoot Schmid assigned two of his deputies, Bob Alcorn and Ted Hinton, to help the former Rangers. Both of the Dallas deputies knew the outlaw couple and could easily recognize them.

Two things led the Texas officers to Bonnie and Clyde: Hamer's extraordinary attention to detail—he knew what kind of whiskey they drank and that Bonnie favored Camel cigarettes—and the cooperation of a Louisiana farmer, Iverson Methvin, whose son, Henry, had been running with the couple. The last time Hamer entered Louisiana before finally catching up with the pair, he carried a letter from

231

Governor Ferguson agreeing to pardon the boy if Methvin cooperated in Bonnie and Clyde's capture. The elder Methvin told Hamer where the outlaw couple would be picking up their mail, a spot off a rural road near Arcadia, Louisiana. Hamer, Gault, Alcorn, Hinton, and two Louisiana officers—the parish sheriff and one of his deputies—went to the place and set up an ambush.

Hamer's account of the events of May 23, 1934, based on an interview by Webb a little more than a month later, remains the best:

> We agreed to take Barrow and the woman alive if we could. We believed that when they stopped the car, both would be looking towards the post office [the place where Barrow and Parker picked up mail left for them by friends] and away from us; such action on their part would enable us to escape observation until we demanded their surrender.

> With everything ready, we had nothing to do but wait about seven hours, without breakfast or coffee. Waiting is the hardest thing an officer has to do. Many men will stand up in a fight, but lose their nerve completely if required to wait long for the excitement. On this occasion I did not detect the slightest nervousness on the part of a single man.

About 9:10 a.m. Hamer heard a car approaching fast, "singing like a sewing machine." When the car stopped near the officers' place of concealment, the Dallas officers could see that the pair inside were Bonnie and Clyde.

The lawmen stepped out of the brush along the side of the dirt road and commanded the couple to "stick 'em up!" Bonnie and Clyde:

both turned, but instead of obeying . . . they clutched the weapons which they either held in their hands or in their laps. When the firing began, Barrow's foot released the clutch and the car, in low gear, moved forward on the decline and turned into the ditch on the left. I looked at my watch and it was 9:20.

When it was over, the officer's ears were ringing from the blast of the high-powered rifles. One hundred sixty-seven rounds, most of them from the .30-06 Browning automatic rifles and Hamer's .35 caliber Remington, had been fired.

Hamer started walking to the car when it quit moving. "Be careful, Cap!" Gault yelled. "They may not be dead."

The big man approached the car with his .45 raised and the hammer back, but as soon as he could see inside the bullet-riddled Ford, Hamer stuck the pistol inside his belt and propped his rifle against the car. Bonnie and Clyde would not be doing any more shooting.

When Hamer opened the front door, Clyde fell to the road, his shotgun and Hamer's rifle clattering down on top of him. Bonnie's head was down between her knees.

"I would have gotten sick," Hamer said later, "but when I thought about her crimes, I didn't."

Years later, Hinton, the last survivor of these lawmen said, "I did not feel anything, least of all rejoicing. The grim job was done . . . . "

The officers obligingly posed for news photographers after Barrow's bullet-punctured car and the bloodied bodies of its two occupants were taken into nearby Arcadia. Gault looked tired as he stood with Hamer and the other officers who took part in the ambush. In another shot, the former Ranger managed a smile as Chief Phares of the

Texas Highway Patrol stood next to him in front of Barrow's car with his arm around his shoulders.

Car Bonnie and Clyde were driving when Texas and Louisiana officers ambushed them in 1934 near Arcadia, Louisiana.

A group of Austin citizens quickly planned a gala celebration to honor Hamer and native son Gault for their role in the demise of Bonnie and Clyde. The Austin *Statesman* boldly announced "Hamer-Gault Hero Day Is Set!" and detailed elaborate plans for a testimonial dinner scheduled for May 28, only four days after the shooting. But Hamer turned down the invitation and the party was canceled. If Hamer had not done so, Gault probably would have done the same thing.

Gault and Hamer were only two years apart in age. Killing a dangerous man as he reached for his gun was one thing. But killing a woman was not covered by the unwritten code the two men had lived by as Rangers. The grim scene must have been burned into Gault's memory. For the remaining thirteen years of his life, he refused to publicly discuss the case.

After the shooting of Bonnie and Clyde, Gault left the Highway Department payroll and went back into the Rangers, stationed in Austin. The last roster of the Rangers as a force under the Adjutant General's Department listed Gault and thirty-three other men on the payroll as of July 31, 1935. On August 10, 1935, a new state law enforcement agency, the Department of Public Safety, began its

...anger Company C outside the Lubbock County Courthouse in 1940. ...aptain Gault fourth from left. (Photo from author's collection)

existence. The legislative act creating the DPS moved the Highway Patrol from the Highway Department to the new agency, and took the Rangers from the Adjutant General's Department.

Hamer, on the other hand, never rejoined the Rangers. In 1935 he went to work for the Port Authority of Houston as a special officer. He and Gault remained friends for as long as both of them were alive, though they never again worked together on a major case.

Not all of Gault's experiences as a Ranger ended as spectacularly as the Bonnie and Clyde case, of course. Gault's sister Barbara later recalled the time her brother identified a murder suspect after a long investigation. Once he felt he had enough evidence, Gault went to the man's residence and confronted him.

"I guess it's time for it to be over," the man shrugged, admitting the killing.

The man then made an unusual request: Would the Ranger come in for dinner before taking him to jail?

Gault thought for a second and then took the suspect up on his offer.

At the table, the man lowered his head and invited Gault to say thanks. The Ranger refused to join the man in the blessing, but enjoyed the meal.

"I've got $3,000 buried in a can in the back of the house," the man blurted out. "It's yours if you don't take me in."

This time Gault did not have to think about his answer.

"No, I've been after you a long time," the Ranger replied. "You're going to jail."

Later, Gault told his sister he supposed the suspected murderer thought that since he had refused to pray with him, he was a man who could be bribed. But that refusal had not been based on any lack of faith on the part of the

Ranger. "I was not about to put my head down and close my eyes around that man!" Gault told his sister.

On May 8, 1937, Gault was ordered along with six other Austin-based Rangers to College Station to be part of the bodyguard for President Franklin Roosevelt, who stopped there May 11 on a visit to Texas.

Gault was promoted to sergeant of the Austin headquarters detachment on September 1. A year later he rose to captain and was transferred to Company C in Lubbock.

The Lubbock *Avalanche-Journal* ran a short feature article on Gault in the summer of 1941, but the reporter who interviewed him did not have much luck getting any information out of him.

The captain was "as taciturn as a turtle in a drought— until he gets to knowing you," the story said. Gault must not have felt he knew the reporter who wrote this article. The best the journalist could come up with was: "Behind the impassive mask of the captain's weathered face . . . is many a story that other officers will tell." Unfortunately, the reporter did not offer those stories to his readers, though his story did note that "it was Captain Frank Hamer and [Manny] Gault who did the work in running to earth Clyde Barrow and Bonnie Parker a few years ago."

Gault was ordered to El Paso to clean up gambling operations early in 1942. On March 11 the captain and two of his Rangers, Pete Crawford and Pat Tolliver, "visited" three downtown gambling establishments, the Plaza Club, the Knickerbocker Club, and the Van Dyke Club. No arrests were made at these places, but Gault and the other Rangers seized a dice table and a poker table, along with some chairs and stools, from a truck parked in an alley behind a suspected fourth downtown gambling location.

"I have been instructed to close up gambling in El Paso," Gault told a reporter. "That's partly why I'm here now."

John Wood met the Ranger captain when Wood came to the Lubbock area as a rookie Highway Patrolman in 1942. Being a young officer, Wood had only occasional encounters with Gault. Still, Wood was around the captain enough to form an opinion of him.

"He was a nice fellow," Wood recalled. "He was soft-spoken. Didn't talk too much, but his men respected him."

Wood, who himself later became a Ranger captain, never heard Gault talk about Bonnie and Clyde.

"There was a cattle theft west of Brownfield, where I was stationed, and the captain sent two Rangers down there," Wood said. "I helped them some. Later I went to Lubbock to testify, but turned out I wasn't needed. The captain thanked me for my help."

Company C was spending much of its time "running down cattle thefts," as Gault put it. Writing for the DPS employee newsletter in 1942, Gault said, "We have recovered lots of lost instead of stolen cattle. The ranchmen are short of help and when they miss some of their cattle after roundup, they report them stolen. On numerous occasions we have been able to locate these cattle but we are having our [share] of the thefts too."

Gault and his Rangers faced other problems on the South Plains. "It seems that people like to rob our banks out here," he wrote. "I don't know whether it is the wide open spaces or whether they think we are easy. But whatever the case is, they cause us lots of worry and in most instances we cause them a little trouble too."

Cattle theft and bank robbery were not Gault's only challenges as captain of Company C. On August 22, 1942, someone attacked Dr. Roy Hunt on a country road near Littlefield, thirty-eight miles northwest of Lubbock in Lamb County. He had not yet fully recovered from the gunshot wounds he suffered in the attempted murder when someone broke into his house late on the night of October

25, 1943, or early on the morning of October 26. The doctor and his wife, Mae Franks Hunt, were found brutally murdered later that morning when one of their two young daughters fled to a neighbor's house and sobbed, "A big bad man killed Mommy and Daddy."

The murder investigation—which eventually led to the conviction of another physician in the first attack and the conviction of ex-convict Jim Thomas as the triggerman in the double murder—was headed by Gault. Thomas was tried and convicted in the case twice, each time receiving a death sentence, but in both instances his conviction was overturned by the Texas Court of Criminal Appeals. Finally, on October 21, 1946, in a crowded courtroom in Sweetwater, Thomas was convicted a third time and sentenced to life imprisonment. That case still was on appeal when an argument between Thomas and another man in Durant, Oklahoma, was permanently resolved with a shotgun blast in Thomas' face.

Gault began experiencing some health problems in November 1947. He took sick leave to come home to Austin, where he and his wife had maintained their home on Nickerson Street. He died at 5:20 in the morning on December 4 at Seton Infirmary, apparently of a heart attack. Gault was sixty-one years old.

"He was one of the most courageous men I have ever known," DPS Director Colonel Homer Garrison said of Gault.

The first name on a long list of honorary pallbearers included in Gault's obituaries was Frank Hamer. The year before, Hamer had shattered his shoulder in an accidental fall on the Houston waterfront and could not serve as an active pallbearer for his old friend.

According to Hamer's son, the shooting of Bonnie and Clyde never weighed heavily on Manny Gault or his father, who lived until 1955.

"Harrison [one of the elder Hamer's brothers] and I sat on the bed with Dad the night he died," Hamer Jr. recalled. "I said, 'Dad, did it ever bother you that you used your gun so much?'"

"Boys," the old Ranger said, "I've killed fifty-two men and one woman. I killed them all right [legally] and I go to sleep every night knowing I did right."

A short time later, Hamer died.

Harrison put his arm around his nephew and said, "Let's go outside and look at the stars."

•••••• ⭐ ••••••

Sources

"Capt. Maney [sic] Gault Of Texas Rangers Could Tell You Many Stories," Lubbock *Avalanche-Journal*, June 22, 1941.

DPS News, Vol. 2, No. 4, Dec. 1942, p. 15.

Hamer, Frank Jr. Interview with author, Dec. 8, 1996.

Jenkins, John H. and H. Gordon Frost. *"I'm Frank Hamer" The Life of a Texas Peace Officer*. Austin: State House Press, 1968, 1993, pp. 209-249.

McCarthy, Chuck. Interviews with author, Sept. 13, 1996, and Dec. 18, 1996.

Milner, E.R. *The Lives and Times of Bonnie and Clyde*. Carbondale and Edwardsville: Southern Illinois University Press, 1996, p. 125.

Sterling, W.W. *Trails and Trials of a Texas Ranger*. Norman: University of Oklahoma Press, 1968, pp. 229, 428.

"Texas Rangers Clamp Lid On El Paso Gambling," El Paso *Herald-Post*, March 12, 1942.

Wood, John. Interview with author, July 29, 1996.

Notes

* The late historian and book dealer John H. Jenkins, coauthor of what has remained the definitive biography of Frank Hamer (see Sources) maintained that this weekly poker game went all the way back to the days when that gambling shootist Ben Thompson was city marshal in Austin. Jenkins, who was known to place a bet now and then himself, later was a member of this weekly game.

** The other original DPS Rangers were Quartermaster Captain R.W. Aldrich, Senior Captain Tom R. Hickman, J.B. Wheatley, Headquarters Co., Austin; M.V. West, San Antonio; Leo Baldwin, Mansion Guard, Austin; Lee Mundrick, Mansion Guard, Austin; C.P. Robinson, Mansion Guard, Austin; F.W. Albright, Mansion Guard, Austin; A.Y. Allee, Co. D, Hebbronville; W.L. Wright, Co. D, Harlingen; Leo Bishop, Co. D, Del Rio; M.E. Trejo, Co. D, Laredo; F.D. Holland, Co. D, Austin; E.T. Neal, Co. D, Austin, Levi Duncan, Co. D, Del Rio; F.L. McDaniel, Co. B, Fort Worth; F.O. Green, Co. B, Fort Worth; Dick Oldham, Co. B, Fort Worth; J.W. McCormick, Co. C, San Augustine; Dan Hines, Co. C, San Augustine; H.B. Purvis, unattached, Lufkin; J.E. England, Co. C, Palestine; J.F. Vannoy, Co. C, San Augustine; Sid Kelso, Sergeant, Headquarters Co., Austin; Z.A. Smith, Co. C, Houston; M.W. Williamson, Houston; E.M. Davenport, Houston; R.C. Hawkins, Captain, unattached, Del Rio; D.B. Burns, unattached, Austin; and R.G. Phillips, unattached, Tyler.

"Pappy" Davenport Invented Phone Raids

*L*ong before telephone advertising popularized slogans like "Let your fingers do the walking" and "Reach out and touch someone," an enterprising Texas Ranger invented telephonic gambling raids.

Though E.M. "Pappy" Davenport and his colleagues had kicked in many a door to shut down gambling joints, the Rangers could not be everywhere at once.

Some time in the late 1930s, the exact date was not reported, Davenport and other Rangers were working to shut down gambling in Houston.

The problem, Davenport knew, was that word spread quickly when the Rangers showed up. By the time the state officers hit the first joint, or certainly by the time they got to their second target, the other places would be shut down—the money, evidence, and gamblers fading faster than a sucker's hopes of filling a four-flush in a high stakes poker game.

The Ranger was particularly concerned about one joint. So Ranger Davenport picked up the phone and placed a call.

He did not have to identify himself to the man on the other end of the line.

"Bill, I know that you've got twelve men in there. Now close the place up and sit tight. I'll be there in a few minutes."

When the Ranger arrived, he found Bill had done as told. But there were only ten gamblers awaiting the lawman, not twelve.

"Don't kid me," Davenport said. "I know there were twelve."

The Ranger was right. Bill reluctantly produced the other two men, and all ended up paying fines for gambling.

The story has become part of the Ranger legend, though history also records a few instances when someone called a gambling joint with a tip before the Rangers got there.

Born in the Jackson County town of Edna in South Texas on February 22, 1884, Everard Mead Davenport began his law enforcement career as a deputy sheriff. On November 2, 1920, he was elected as Jackson County sheriff. Elected to a second term on Nov. 7, 1922, he served until Jan. 1, 1925. He joined the Rangers in September 1931 and served for two years, resigning—as did many other Rangers—following the election of Miriam "Ma" Ferguson as governor.

On March 13, 1935, Davenport went back in the Rangers and stayed on with the force when it became a part of the newly created Department of Public Safety in August 1935. On Oct. 13, 1938, he was promoted to sergeant and assigned to Company A in Houston. On Sept. 1, 1939, due to budget cutbacks during the administration of Governor "Pappy" Lee O'Daniel, Davenport was demoted to Ranger private, remaining in Houston. His salary as a private was $200 a month.

Davenport was a hard-working lawman, but he was not the stereotypical towering Ranger. Mild-mannered, with a big smile and thinning gray hair, he barely weighed in at 120 pounds with his boots on, but criminals respected him. A few even became his friends.

"He wouldn't let you walk a red light for $30,000," one gambler said of Davenport.

Reporter R.L. Wade, who had covered criminal cases investigated by Davenport, called him "a man of tireless energy."

The Ranger once complained, Wade wrote, that "24 hours is not enough for a day; when I get control of the universe I'm going to make the day 35 hours long so I'll have time enough to get my work done and drink a cup of coffee now and then."

But as Wade pointed out, the Ranger drank coffee more than "now or then." He sipped coffee "incessantly," interrupting his coffee drinking only to work a case or light up a cigarette.

In September 1940 Davenport was transferred to Corpus Christi. His orders, the newspapers reported, were "to suppress gambling which has been on the increase since start of construction on the $25,000,000 naval air training station."

Davenport's first move after hitting town was to order businesses to get rid of "marble table payoff machines, dice games, and punch boards."

Cleaning up illegal gambling in Corpus Christi was the Ranger's last big job. The years of hard work, coffee, and cigarettes did what no vengeful out-of-business gambler ever did. Ranger Davenport died of a heart attack in Corpus Christi on December 16, 1940.

"He was one of the most sincere and conscientious officers I have ever known," DPS Director Colonel Homer Garrison said after the Ranger's death.

More fitting was a tribute paid him in life, when he had been stationed in Houston.

Every time Davenport walked in one particular Bayou City night spot to arrest gamblers, the orchestra struck up the tune "Lights Out" in his honor.

Sources

"Gaming Drive in Corpus Set." San Antonio *Light*, Sept. 14, 1940.

Texas Department of Public Safety. Austin, Texas. Inactive Personnel Records.

Wade, R.L. "Death Strikes Colorful Texas Ranger Who Originated Gambling Raids by Phone." Dallas *Journal*, Jan. 3, 1941.

Lone Wolf Versus the Phantom

*T*he car moved slowly down the dirt road that cut through the pine trees about a mile-and-a-half northwest of Texarkana, Texas. It stopped and its lights went out.

It was Saturday night, February 22, 1946.

The couple in the automobile, twenty-four-year-old Jimmy Hollis and his nineteen-year-old date, Mary Jeanne Larey, assumed they were alone in this secluded spot, a local "lover's lane." But someone was watching.

The couple settled into each other's arms, talking softly, until they heard footsteps coming toward them from the darkness. The stars and the distant glow from the city provided the only light on this moonless night. Just before the flashlight beam temporarily blinded them, they saw a tall man, wearing a white handkerchief over his face. He had cut holes for his eyes.

The man gruffly ordered the couple out of the car. Now they could see that he held a pistol and was pointing it straight at them.

"I don't want to kill you, fellow, so do what I say," the man said.

The masked gunman told Hollis to drop his pants. When the young man hesitated, Mary Jeanne told him to do what the man said. She thought if they complied with his orders they would not be hurt. At that, the terrified man did as he was told.

"The man hit Jimmy twice on the head," the girl later told a reporter. "The noise was so loud I thought [he] had been shot."

When the unconscious man did not respond to a brutal kick, the attacker may have thought he was dead.

"Then he hit me," the victim said. "He knocked me to the ground but I managed to get up."

The man then told her to start running. She turned and fled, tripping and stumbling in her high-heeled shoes. Ordering her to run may have been some sort of perverse play, the predator toying with his prey. He caught up with her, threw her to the ground, and began sexually abusing her with the barrel of his pistol.

"Go ahead and kill me!" she pleaded during the attack.

Something—perhaps the sound of a car in the distance—suddenly caused him to run, leaving the young woman crying in pain and fear. She hid in the pine trees for a while to make sure the man was gone, and then walked toward a distant light until she reached a house and began pounding on the door, screaming for help.

"I ran to the back of the house and woke the people and they called the sheriff," she said later.

Bowie County Sheriff's deputies rushed to the location and found her companion unconscious at the scene of the attack. His skull had been fractured.

Later, both victims told deputies that the man in the dark was tall and had on a mask. "I would know his voice anywhere," the girl told a reporter. "It rings always in my ears." Neither victim, however, could offer a detailed physical description of their attacker. They could not even agree on his race.

The story of the attack ran under a one-column headline in the Texarkana *Gazette*. The sexual molestation of the woman was not reported. No arrests were made in the case, which did not garner much attention from the public.

Four weeks and two days later, late on the night of March 23 or shortly after midnight, another young couple drove down South Robison Road, due south of the site of the first attack. Like the first couple, they were seeking the sort of easy privacy in a romantic setting that an automobile made possible.

Twenty-nine-year-old Richard Griffin turned his 1941 Oldsmobile off the gravel road, less than 100 yards from Highway 67 West. With him was his seventeen-year-old date, Polly Ann Moore.

At 8:30 that Sunday morning, a passing motorist noticed someone slumped over inside a parked car. Maybe the person was sleeping, but it did not look right. The motorist hurried on to call the police. When the operator realized the location was outside the city limits, the sheriff's department was notified.

Sheriff W.H. "Bill" Presley happened to be talking with Texarkana Police Chief Jack N. Runnels when the call came in. They both drove to the scene. Soon, the lawmen realized the earlier incident had presaged a far more serious threat to the public than they had first thought.

Griffin, a veteran who survived World War II, was on his knees in the front seat of the car, his head resting on his hands. His date, an employee of Red River Arsenal, was face down on the back seat. Both had been shot in the back of the head.

The two officers surveyed the crime scene. Both victims were fully clothed. The couple must have been snuggling under a blanket in the back seat when they were confronted. A .32 caliber shell casing was found in a fold in the blanket. The man's pockets had been pulled inside out, suggesting robbery as a possible motive.

About twenty feet from the blood-splattered Oldsmobile, the officers found a bloodsoaked spot on the ground, indicating at least one of the victims had been shot there and moved back to the car. Overnight it had rained, destroying any tracks around the parked car.

During the war, Texarkana had been full of military and civilian personnel assigned to the busy arsenal northwest of the city. The Texas side of the city was wet—alcohol sales being legal—and the soldiers could play rough. Barroom shootings and cuttings were one thing, but a double murder with no obvious suspects was highly unusual. Sheriff Presley knew he was going to need help with this one, and he asked for it.

Ranger Jim Geer arrived in Texarkana on Monday. Soon another Ranger came to help. The couple had not died at the hands of anyone they knew, the state and local officers concluded. The attack had apparently been at random. Whether the killer was a gunhappy robber or a sex offender who robbed Griffin as an afterthought remained an open question. The Justice of the Peace acting as coroner in the case had released Polly's body to a funeral home before it could be checked for any evidence of sexual assault.

Despite a $500 reward offered by the sheriff and the Texarkana police chief, none of more than two hundred leads checked by the Rangers and other officers went anywhere. The Rangers transported a possible suspect—a woman—from San Antonio to Texarkana for questioning, but she was quickly cleared.

The lover's lane murder of the young couple was big news in Texarkana, but the story did not attract much attention outside Northeast Texas. Not for another three weeks.

On Saturday night, April 13, a local musical group—Jerry Atkins and the Rhythm-Aires—played for a dance at the Veterans of Foreign Wars club. Fifteen-year-old Betty Jo Booker, a short, round-faced brunette, was one of three girl saxophone players Atkins had recruited for his band.

Waiting to pick her up after the gig was seventeen-year-old Paul Martin, a friend Betty had known since they were in kindergarten together. They left the VFW Post about 2 a.m. in Paul's brand new coupe, one of the first new models produced since before the war. Though they had gone to school with each other, Paul had moved to Kilgore. Their families later told officers that they were sure the young couple knew of the murder of the other couple in the park only three weeks earlier. Springtime, hormones, the adolescent's false sense of invincibility, all made it easy for Paul and Betty Jo to head to the well-known lover's lane that morning. Bad things only happened to other people.

Four hours after Paul and Betty were seen leaving the VFW Post, a family driving through Spring Lake Park discovered a body lying in a ditch off the side of North Park Road, one of several winding roads behind the park. They sped to the closest house and asked the couple who lived there to call the police.

The first officers to reach the scene found a young man who had been shot to death. As soon as his identity was established as Martin and it was learned that Betty Jo was missing, a search party was organized to scour the remote park. The body of the pretty young saxaphone player was found behind a tree about 11 o'clock that morning. She, too, had been shot to death. And raped.

Since it was Palm Sunday, many in Texarkana were in church that morning. Still, word of the latest murders spread quickly. Many of those not in church, and a good number of those getting out of church, went to the park to see firsthand what was going on.

The two Rangers who had worked the first double murder reported to one of the best known lawmen in the state, Captain Manuel T. "Lone Wolf" Gonzaullas. Gonzaullas, who first joined the Rangers in 1920, commanded Company B, headquartered in Dallas. He had seven Rangers to cover fifty-eight Northeast Texas counties with a combined population of more than 2.2 million—thirty-four per cent of the state's total population. When the captain learned of the Martin-Booker murders, Gonzaullas ordered every Ranger in Company B to Texarkana. In addition, four technicians were dispatched from the crime lab at the Department of Public Safety headquarters in Austin.

Also rushed to Texarkana from the state capital was a mobile two-way communications center. Four patrol cars equipped with new two-way radios, seven Highway Patrolmen, and one Highway Patrol sergeant were dispatched to Texarkana from various cities in East Texas.

Highway Patrol Chief W.J. Elliott, in a memo to DPS Director Homer Garrison Jr., said he had received a telephone call from Gonzaullas requesting the additional manpower because "the people in Texarkana and vicinity [are] all scared to death."

The Rangers and extra Highway Patrolmen descended on Texarkana along with news reporters from elsewhere in the state and nation. Since the Rangers and other officers on the case had not yet managed to come up with the name of the killer, the press obligingly gave him one on April 16: The Phantom.

In what has become a classic in newspaper folklore, one wire service reporter wrote: "I have arrived in Texarkana, the home of the Phantom Slayer. I have just talked to a newspaperman named Graves. I am quartered at the Grim Hotel, and the hair is rising on my neck."

Though it reads like a bad joke, Texarkana really had a Grim Hotel. The newspaperman named Graves was a sports reporter for the Texarkana *Gazette* the wire guy probably had been drinking with, and whether the hair really rose on the reporter's neck is anyone's guess.

If the wire service reporter was exaggerating his own concerns about being in what was quickly becoming the

Manuel T. "Lone Wolf" Gonzaullus. (Author's collection)

Phantom's town, plenty of local residents were genuinely terrified. A teenage curfew was imposed. Many adults, particularly women, flatly refused to go out at night. Business at local cafes, taverns, theaters, and bowling alleys dropped dramatically. Even the many additional police officers patrolling the streets had concerns: They worried some jumpy citizen might shoot and kill one of them by accident. One nervous homeowner did pop off a round in the general direction of someone walking across his yard after dark. Fortunately, the innocent man was not hit.

The Phantom was still the one doing any killing in the Texarkana area. At 8:30 on Friday night, May 4, Virgil Starks, a thirty-six-year-old farmer, sat near a window in the living room of his rural home reading that day's Texarkana *Gazette* and listening to the radio. The banner headline in the newspaper said a man picked up by police in Corpus Christi had been cleared as a suspect in the Phantom murders.

Someone outside was watching.

Maybe the peeper had been looking in the window long enough to have seen Mrs. Starks, wearing a nightgown, go into the couple's bedroom to lie down. From their bed, she called to her husband to turn the radio down. She thought she had heard something outside. But there was no response.

The radio covered the sound of the .22 pistol that sent a bullet into the back of her husband's head, but she did hear the breaking glass. Rushing into the living room, she saw her husband standing by the chair, his body reacting by impulse after being shot. As she watched in horror, Starks slumped back down into the chair, blood soaking into the upholstery.

She ran to their old-style wall phone, cranked it twice, and then went to her husband. He was dead.

Someone was still watching.

Before she could get back to the telephone, two bullets tore into her face—one hitting her left cheek near her nose, the other going into her jaw beneath her lip.

The terrified woman still had the presence of mind to drop to the floor, realizing that whoever was outside could not see her to shoot again. Bleeding heavily, she crawled back into the bedroom, intending to get the .45 semi-automatic she knew was in a dresser drawer. Then, thinking she was probably going to die, she decided to write a note.

But now the person who had killed her husband was trying to get into the house. Blinded by blood and panic, Mrs. Starks ran through the house and made it out the front door. The killer, meanwhile, was inside their house. He stayed long enough to look at Starks' body, then left. For some reason, he chose not to follow the wounded woman.

A neighbor called the sheriff's office and then drove Mrs. Starks to the hospital. She would recover from her wounds, though she bore physical and mental scars the rest of her life.

Dozens of law enforcement officers from Texas and Arkansas rushed to the farm house, which was about ten miles from Texarkana off Highway 67 in Miller County, Arkansas. Bloodhounds were brought from the state police office at Hope, Arkansas, to aid in the search for the killer. The dogs picked up two trails, both ending at the highway. The officers surmised one trail was the killer's initial path to the farm house, the other his route of escape.

This time, the killer left some physical evidence—a .22 caliber shell, bloody footprints, and a red metal flashlight.

But the crime scene was not adequately protected. Additional evidence, including good latent prints, likely was lost.

The weapon used in the Starks murder was different from the handgun that killed the two couples in Texarkana, but most of the investigators believed the Arkansas crime also was the work of the Phantom. They theorized he had ditched the .32 after reading in the newspapers that investigators knew that was the caliber of the murder weapon in the lover's lane cases. A few officers were skeptical of a connection, but not the citizens of Texarkana.

"Murder Rocks City Again; Farmer Slain, Wife Wounded" blared the next day's Texarkana *Gazette*.

Asked by the local radio station what Texarkana citizens should do to protect themselves, Gonzaullas replied: "I'd tell them to check the locks and bolts on their doors and get a double-barreled shotgun to take care of any intruder who tried to get in."

One Texarkana housewife constructed a Rube Goldberg-like homemade burglar alarm system that seems ludicrous in retrospect but was simple and effective, and understandable considering the panic that settled over the city that spring. Strings tied to doorknobs led to metal pots on a bric-a-brac table. On the floor, beneath the pots, were vases. If someone opened the door, the pots would fall and shatter the vases, making a lot of noise. But just in case that did not wake up the occupants, the table itself was balanced precariously on an ashtray. Nails were scattered on the table, so that when it toppled, the nails would rain down on a metal pan on the floor, again making a considerable racket.

Life magazine ran a six-picture, double-page spread on the "Texarkana Terror." The most striking photograph looked like a Norman Rockwell painting commissioned for April Fool's Day. Mom is sitting in a lounge chair with her feet up and ankles crossed, reading a magazine. Dad, wearing a tie, is on the couch, his arm around a toddler. Next to them is the family pet, Spot. It is a classic scene of domestic tranquility, except for the pump shotgun leaning against the wall not far from Dad. The couple apparently had taken Gonzaullas' advice, though the shotgun in the picture was not double-barreled.

But when that June 10, 1946 issue of *Life* hit the newsstands, the Phantom Killer case was history, though no one thought so at the time, even though the killer was already off his every-three-week schedule. Months would pass before the people of Texarkana settled back down to their usual routine again. The Phantom did not kill again, at least in the Texarkana area. Maybe he moved on, scared off by all the publicity and beefed-up law enforcement, including an entire company of Texas Rangers. Maybe he went to jail for some other crime. Maybe he underwent some sort of self-exorcism and became free of the compulsion to kill. Or maybe he was the dead man found on the railroad tracks in Texarkana four days after the Starks murder. That body was never identified.

Gonzaullas and the Rangers of Company B did not catch the Phantom, but they probably kept him from striking again. The captain coordinated the search for the killer from a second-story office in a downtown business building. He divided all of Bowie County into patrol districts, but concentrated on areas within a few miles of Texarkana. Black-and-white Highway Patrol cars roamed the county roads and city streets at night under Gonzaullas' direction, while some Rangers and Highway Patrolmen in unmarked cars tried something else.

The captain nightly set traps for the Phantom, assigning some of his Rangers and some of the Highway Patrol officers to sit in parked cars on lonely roads. Some officers even wore wigs. Rangers working alone snuggled up to borrowed show-window mannequins.

One of those men was Henry Peacock, who in 1996 was an eighty-one-year-old retired Highway Patrolman living in Austin.

"I was stationed in Longview when Captain Guy Smith called and told me and my partner, Lloyd Webb, to go to Texarkana," Peacock recalled. "Webb and I were put out in a plain car to try to entice the killer to do something. But no one bothered us."

The officers, armed with their service revolvers and rifles, would park their car somewhere between 9 and 10 o'clock at night and stay out until 3 or 4 o'clock in the morning, Peacock said.

"We just sat and talked," he said. "It was pretty lonesome."

While the decoys waited for the Phantom to strike, "Lone Wolf" lived up to his name, roaming the county alone at night with two elaborately engraved pistols on his hip, hoping to catch the Phantom in the act.

"We tried to keep what we were doing quiet," Peacock said. "I don't think the public knew about the decoys."

...angers from Company B were called to investigate the Phantom ...ller. Note the horse and horse trailer, still in use by Texas Rangers in ...e 1940s. (Author's collection)

But the Phantom surely saw the numerous marked police cars in town, and the newspaper and the radio played up the increased number of law enforcement officers in Texarkana. He may have been smart enough to realize that with all the publicity, young couples would not be out spooning at night.

As the weeks went by with no additional murders, and with no solid leads to pursue, the law enforcement presence in Texarkana returned to normal levels. Gonzaullas went back to Dallas and his Rangers turned their attention to other crimes, though Ranger Stewart Stanley, stationed in Clarksville, continued to focus almost entirely on the case. Highway Patrolmen Peacock and Webb went back to routine duties in Longview.

With the third anniversary of her son's death approaching, Paul Martin's mother wrote a pleading letter to DPS Director Garrison asking that more be done to solve the murder of "my little boy."

Garrison replied, "Captain Gonzaullas and the Rangers under his command, have spent many days and travelled thousands of miles in this investigation. We will continue to do so until the culprit is brought to justice . . . we never quit the investigation of a case until it is finally solved."

Indeed, more than 400 persons were questioned and eliminated as suspects in the murder. In July 1946 Gonzaullas tracked down a thirty-four-year-old escaped mental patient who had been charged with raping his stepdaughter but adjudged criminally insane. The man had been at large during the Phantom murders, but after a thorough investigation the captain reported to Garrison that he was convinced the man was not the killer. Ranger Stanley went to Chicago to interview another possible suspect. He, too, had a history of violence and was from Texarkana, but the Ranger concluded the man could not have been the killer.

Gonzaullas retired from the Rangers on July 31, 1951, but for years afterward he was periodically consulted by his successors when some new development in the case occurred, usually a bogus confession on the part of someone mentally unstable or seeking publicity.

The retired captain told his friends and colleagues that the local officers in Texarkana had made a bad mistake in letting people crowd around the crime scenes, possibly destroying vital evidence in the cases. Too, some of the locals chaffed at the presence of Gonzaullas and his Rangers. J.Q. Mahaffey, retired editor of the Texarkana newspaper, later recalled a local officer telling him: "Mahaffey, you can quote me as saying that the Phantom murders will never be solved until Texarkana gets rid of the big city press and the Texas Rangers."

On the first day of 1962 a Houston man who drunkenly bragged to his wife that he was the Phantom Killer found himself explaining his boozy boast to a decidedly sober Ranger. After talking with the man, Ranger Ed Gooding was convinced he had had nothing to do with the case, though he had lived in Texarkana at the time of the murders. The man had just been trying to scare his wife. Just in case, Gooding had the man's fingerprints compared with three unidentified latent prints found on the car in the second double murder. They did not match.

A decade later, in 1971, the Texarkana *Gazette* marked the twenty-fifth anniversary of the Phantom murders with a seven-part series. The articles ran at the beginning of the decade in which a new descriptive term in criminology would develop: the serial killer. The definition developed by psychologists and criminologists is someone who kills three or more persons over a period of time, driven by some inner compulsion relieved only by the act of murder. Work done by behavioral scientists in the years preceding the fiftieth anniversary of the Phantom murders reveals much more about the killer than the Rangers and other officers saddled with trying to find him ever knew.

Psychologist Joel Norris, whose 1988 book *Serial Killers* remains a standard reference on the subject, listed 21 "symptoms of episodic aggressive behavior." These symptoms, based on the study of numerous cases, probably describe many of the Phantom's traits. They are: ritualistic behavior, masks of sanity, compulsivity, search for help, severe memory disorders and a chronic inability to tell the truth, suicidal tendencies, history of serious assault, deviate sexual behavior and hypersexuality, head injuries or injuries incurred at birth, history of chronic drug or alcohol abuse, alcohol- or drug-abusing parents, victim of physical or emotional abuse or cruel parenting, result of an unwanted pregnancy, product of a difficult gestation period for the mother, interrupted bliss or no bliss of childhood, extraordinary cruelty to animals, arsonal tendencies without obvious homicidal interest, symptoms of neurological impairment, evidence of genetic disorders, biochemical symptoms, and feelings of powerlessness or inadequacy.

Though Gonzaullas and the other officers who tried to catch the Phantom did not have the benefit of this research, the captain and other veteran officers certainly knew some of these things by experience and instinct.

In 1977 Warner Brothers released *The Town That Dreaded Sundown*, a liberally fictionalized treatment of the events of that spring in 1946. Director Charlie Pierce was from Texarkana and filmed much of the low-budget thriller there. Actor Ben Johnson played the Texas Ranger brought in to solve the murders. Not long after the movie came out, "Lone Wolf" Gonzaullas, the old Ranger captain who had tried to track down the real Phantom, died in Dallas on February 13, 1977, at eighty-five.

None of the other Rangers who searched for the Phantom was still living in the mid-1990s, but since there is no statute of limitation for homicide, the case remains in the unsolved murder files of the DPS Crime Analysis Section in Austin. One person whose name is on many of the letters in that file is Glen H. McLaughlin, chief of the DPS crime lab at the time of the Phantom murders.

"It was a puzzling case," the eighty-three-year-old retiree recalled as he sat in his West Austin home fifty years later. "We ran all kinds of leads out, but nothing ever developed."

For years, anytime a peace officer in Northeast Texas seized a .32 caliber pistol in connection with a criminal case, the weapon routinely was sent to Austin to be checked by DPS firearms experts. None of the pistols ever was linked to the projectiles recovered at the Martin-Booker crime scene. In 1956 a set of men's clothing bearing suspicious dark stains was found in the attic of an old school being torn down in Texarkana not far from Spring Lake Park. The clothes were shipped to Austin for analysis, but the crime lab determined that the stains were not blood.

A year before the Phantom murders began, McLaughlin went to Chicago to learn how to use a newly developed law enforcement tool, the polygraph machine—commonly known as a lie detector. The DPS bought a Keeler polygraph, named after its developer, a short time later.

During the Phantom investigation, McLaughlin ran "three or four" persons on the machine, including "one I never did eliminate as having been involved."

This person was a woman. McLaughlin remembers her as a strawberry blonde who claimed she had been with her boyfriend when he killed the two couples in Texarkana.

"I thought she had some involvement, that she had some additional information," McLaughlin said.

He questioned her one-on-one as Rangers and other officers in an adjoining room watched through a two-way mirror. As the machine monitored her blood pressure, respiration, and electrical currents, McLaughlin believed she was being deceptive, holding something back. But not telling the truth or withholding information was not sufficient basis to file murder charges.

The chain of events that led to McLaughlin's polygraph examination began with an observation by a young Arkansas State Police officer who, with his partner, had been the first lawmen to reach the Starks' farmhouse the night of May 4.

Max Tackett, who later became chief of the Texarkana, Arkansas city police force, had noticed that a car was stolen in Texarkana after each of the Phantom killings. He suspected a connection, though, as he later recalled, "I was still a rookie . . . not one of my ideas was accepted [by the lead investigators]."

Then the Arkansas State Police got a routine complaint involving a minor crime. A witness provided a license plate number. Checking the registration, Tackett found the vehicle had been reported stolen in Texarkana. When the car was spotted in a parking lot, Tackett and other officers staked it out. Eventually, a woman approached and started to get in the vehicle. She was arrested, but did not have much to say until Tackett finally took her twenty-nine-year-old boyfriend into custody at the bus station.

"Please don't shoot me!" was the first thing the boyfriend said, Tackett recalled.

"I'm not going to shoot you for stealing cars," Tackett reassured the man.

"Mister, don't play games with me," the man replied. "You want me for more than stealing cars!"

After the man's arrest, his twenty-one-year-old girlfriend gave a statement: The man was the Phantom Killer and she was afraid of him. This is the woman McLaughlin examined on the DPS's new polygraph in Austin. She led officers to where Martin's car had been parked. She gave three different statements, and some of the things she said were contradictory, but essential elements of her story checked out. At some point in her conversations with investigators, however, it must have dawned on her that even though she had not pulled the trigger, as an accomplice she was dangerously close to the electric chair herself. She suddenly became less cooperative.

Other than the suspicious remarks he made at the time of his arrest, her boyfriend never talked. A doctor at the State Hospital in Little Rock, Arkansas, bungled an attempt to interview the suspect under the influence of sodium penathol, the so-called "truth serum." The woman who had given the statements in the case, despite her professed fear of the man, had married the suspect a short time before his arrest. That eliminated her from being compelled to testify as a witness against him.

In one of her statements, she had said her boyfriend had owned a .32 caliber automatic, but sold the weapon to cover losses in a crap game. Tackett was never able to track the weapon down, though he did submit several pistols to the DPS for comparison. None could be matched with the bullets in evidence.

Interviewed in 1971 by the Texarkana *Gazette*, Tackett said he was convinced the murders had been solved with the identification of the woman and the man she married, though there had not been enough evidence to file charges. Some other officers still had their doubts, though Gonzaullas, after his retirement, said officers "had a good idea who the perpetrator was" but lacked conclusive evidence. The prime suspect got a life sentence as an habitual criminal and remained in prison for more than a quarter century. Paroled in 1973, he soon ended up in prison again on another charge. He was released in 1987 and died in a nursing home in Dallas in 1994. No one knows what happened to the wife after she was released by authorities in the summer of 1946.

"Max [Tackett] was always one hundred percent sure it was him," former Miller County, Arkansas, chief deputy Tilman Johnson told the Texarkana *Gazette* in the spring of 1996, a half century after the Phantom murders. "I think we had him on at least one of the shootings."

McLaughlin was philosophical about his role in the unsolved case. "You always wish it had turned out differently," he said, "but there's not much I can do about it now."

•••••• ⭐ ••••••

Sources

Biffle, Kent. "Phantom still raises hackles after 50 years." *Dallas Morning News*, Aug. 18, 1996.

_____. "Folklorist has filled a file on the Phantom." *Dallas Morning News*, Aug. 25, 1996.

The Chaparral. Austin: Texas Department of Public Safety, Aug. 1949, p. 119.

DPS Paisano. Austin: Texas Department of Public Safety, April 1996, p. 11.

Keirsey, Tex. "Riding With the Rangers on a Phantom's Trail." Amarillo *Globe-Times*, Feb. 7, 1956.

McLaughlin, Glen H. Interview with author, Nov. 8, 1996.

Malsch, Brownson. *Captain M.T. Lone Wolf Gonzaullas, the only Texas Ranger captain of Spanish descent*. Austin: Shoal Creek Publishers, 1980, pp. 159-161, 163-166, 168.

Norris, Joel. *Serial Killers*. New York: Anchor Books, 1988, pp. 222-223.

Peacock, Henry. Interview with author, Dec. 18, 1996.

"The Phantom At 50: A Retrospective." Texarkana *Gazette*, March 31-April 7, 1996.

Rosenfield, Paul. "Town's memories return." *Dallas Times-Herald*, Feb. 9, 1977.

Stephens, Robert W. *Lone Wolf: The Story of Texas Ranger Captain M.T. Gonzaullas*. Dallas: Taylor Publishing Co., 1979, pp. 71-72.

The Story of the Silver Star

Study almost any existing photograph of a group of nineteenth-century Rangers and it is easy to understand how these men upheld law and order in Texas even without wearing badges on their chests.

They wore no uniform either. Just big hats, collarless shirts, vests, woolen trousers held up by suspenders, and high-topped cowboy boots. They may have carried their Ranger commissions—forms signed by the governor and the adjutant general—in their saddlebags, but the single-action Colt .45s on their hips, the two ammunition belts around their waists (one belt for their pistols, one for their rifles), the wide-bladed Bowie knives, and the lever-action Winchesters in the scabbards on their saddles stood as sufficient indication of authority for most people.

When Jim Gillett looked back on his first day as a Ranger, he made no mention of putting on a badge as a symbol of his newly bestowed police power.

"On June 1, 1875, at ten o'clock we were formed in line, mounted, and the oath of allegiance to the state of Texas was read to us by Captain [Dan W.] Roberts," Gillett wrote. "When we had signed this oath we were pronounced Texas Rangers."

The hostile Indians Gillett and his fellow Rangers soon rode against did not recognize civil authority. Raiding Comanches did not ask for identification when they came into contact with Rangers.

266

Neither did the Rangers very often find it necessary to offer proof of identity as they went about their business of enforcing criminal laws. When confronted by a Ranger with a hunch and maybe a warrant, most felons kept their eyes on the cavernous opening at the end of the .45 in the lawman's hand. This may have led to the observation that "You can see a graveyard in the end of a Ranger's gun."

The sixgun came to be an icon in its own right, but the strongest symbol of Texas was the lone star that first graced its flag back when Texas was still an independent republic. The first documented use of a star as a symbol of Texas was in 1835, when Charles Stewart, secretary of the convention meeting to form a provisional government, used a pearl button in the shape of a star to impress in wax the first seal of Texas. The seal was placed on the commissions of three men sent to treat with the Indians.

On March 12, 1836, George C. Childress, a signer of the Texas Declaration of Independence, offered a resolution at the general convention that "a single star of five points" be recognized as the "peculiar emblem" of the republic. Also included in his resolution was the proviso that "every officer & soldier of the army and members of this convention, and all friends of Texas, be requested to wear it on their hats or bosoms . . . ." Later that year, after Texas prevailed in its revolution against Mexico, interim President David G. Burnet submitted a design incorporating the star into the official seal of the new republic.

As historian Richard V. Francaviglia wrote in his book *The Shape of Texas: Maps As Metaphors*:

> The Lone Star is a classic symbol in that it conveys both the state's history and its geographic identity in an abstract form: the star signifies brilliance, isolation, distance, and many other things as an abstract form; through the

process of association, these become the qualities we associate with Texas the place.

Long before the New World was settled, the badge (from the Norman term *cognoissance*, meaning a mark or token by which something is known) was used in heraldry. Knights in combat were able to identify each other by their badges, which might fly on their flag, be sewn to their clothing or stamped into metal and attached to their clothing. The badge, as one author explained, alluded to its wearer's "name, office, or estate...."

Collar and badge of the Order of the Bath.

At some point—there is no known record of when it happened or who did it—a Texas Ranger, perhaps following the request in Childress' resolution that officers and soldiers of the army wear a star, fashioned a homemade badge of authority by taking a Mexican silver coin and cutting a star in it. The coins were common and the metal soft enough to carve by hand. The resulting icon, which has become known as the star-in-a-wheel badge, took on a double symbolism: Since Texas had just been wrested from Mexico by Anglo-Americans and native-born Tejanos, a star cut from a Mexican coin represented a near perfect metaphor.

If a Ranger wanted to wear a piece of silver on his vest, that was up to him. The Texas government certainly did not provide a badge. During the days of the Republic, and for a good while after statehood, all the government furnished was food for man and horse, ammunition, and what Gillett referred to as "medical attendance."

Though the eastern coast of the United States had been populated for two centuries by the time of Texas' break from Mexico, the use of a badge as a symbol of law enforcement authority developed at about the same pace both in Texas and in the longer-settled areas. In New York City, police reluctantly began wearing blue uniforms in 1844, but with a change in political parties, the uniforms were dropped a year later. However, officers were supposed to wear "stars of office" while on duty. But the officers, still chafing at having had to wear uniforms, which they felt made them look like liveried servants, also were reluctant to wear badges, at least conspicuously. This caused problems, since, as one police scholar put it, "Citizens could not recognize policemen when either party was in need of help." By 1853 police uniforms were again required in New York, and by shortly before the Civil War, they had gained general acceptance among the officers in New York and other major American cities. Badges commonly were made of copper to match the buttons on their uniforms.

In Texas, though the Rangers were evolving from a paramilitary force to a law enforcement body, the state did not place the men in uniform. After the creation of the Frontier Battalion in 1874, each Ranger was issued a rifle and a revolver, but the cost of the weapons was deducted from his salary, which was forty dollars a month, paid quarterly. Rangers had to provide their own horse and tack, but the State of Texas magnanimously paid for any horse shot out from under its rider.

Judging from vintage Ranger photographs, badges did not begin coming into vogue until late in the nineteenth century. Some Rangers, ex-Confederates who had served in Colonel B.F. Terry's Eighth Texas Cavalry (also called Terry's Texas Rangers) during the Civil War later used their leftover star-shaped hat pins as badges. A photograph of Frontier Battalion Ranger Walter Durbin taken in 1888 shows a star-in-a-wheel badge on his chest. Another photograph taken some time after 1893 shows eleven Company E Rangers in Cotulla, but only one of the lawmen has a visible badge: a small, five-point star.

Rangers may have been slow to adopt badges because of the shields worn by Texas' short-lived Reconstruction era law enforcement entity, the State Police. Though twentieth-century scholarship based on a study of existing records shows the State Police were more effective than they generally have been given credit for, they were not popular among most of the citizenry. Their badges were the traditional shield-shape, with a small star pressed into the metal. Above the star were the words "State Police" and beneath it "Texas." Beneath that was a number, attached in copper.

Created in 1870, the force was abolished in 1873. When the Legislature did away with the State Police after overriding a gubernatorial veto, the editor of the Dallas *Herald* wrote: "The people of Texas are today delivered from as infernal engine of oppression as ever crushed any people. . . . The damnable police bill is ground beneath the heel of an indignant legislature."

W.D. Myres and Capt. Hughes, circa 1938. Badge shown here is probably an honorary shield issued by then El Paso County Sheriff Chris Fox. (Photo by L.A. Wilke, Austin, Texas)

In addition to their general disdain of the State Police (even though some ex-State Police officers became competent Rangers, including famed Captain Leander H. McNelly), some Rangers felt a shiny star on the chest made too tempting a target. Other Rangers preferred to operate incognito, or at least as inconspicuously as a steely-eyed fellow with a .45, two gunbelts, and an Arkansas Toothpick on his hip could be.

The oldest surviving Ranger badge is a shield worn by Frontier Battalion Ranger Ira Aten in the 1880s. A star rises in a circle in the middle of the badge. Above the circle is the word "Texas" and beneath it "Ranger." Believed to be one of a kind, the handmade badge was presented to

Aten in 1880. On the back, it is inscribed, "IRA ATEN FROM W.H.K. REALITOS 1880." "W.H.K." was William H. King, Texas' Adjutant General.

The first state-issued Ranger badge was ordered in 1900, but according to rancher and gun collector Charles Schreiner III of Mountain Home, Texas, not many of these badges were issued. This badge was a star bearing the words "Texas State Ranger."

For the next three decades, several varieties of the star-in-a-wheel badges were worn by Rangers. True to tradition, Rangers provided the badge themselves or received it as a gift.

Captain John R. Hughes wore a distinctive star-in-a-wheel badge obtained in 1902. Inside the star was the designation "Co. D" atop the letters "F.B." for Frontier Battalion. At the top of the wheel, on a curved raised base with a notch at each end, is the word "Texas." The word "Ranger" is stamped on a similar base at the bottom of the wheel.

In 1909 someone presented Captain Frank Johnson with the most ornamental of the known Ranger badges. It is a star-in-a-wheel set in laurels. Laurels also wrap around the star inside the wheel. At the top of the wheel is "CAPT. FRANK JOHNSON." Beneath are the words "TEXAS RANGER FORCE."

The only non-star-in-a-wheel badge identified from the twentieth century is a shield-shaped badge dating from about 1910, in the hands of a private collector, which has a star cut in its center. The badge has "TEXAS" on its top, "RANGER" on the bottom. The letters T-E-X-A-S are inside the star, one letter in each of the five points. Stamped in the middle of the star is a smaller star. The badge probably was custom-made for its owner.

Ranger Adrian Murry in 1917 wore a badge that looked like the classic sheriff's badge, a star with small rounded tips. On a raised circle in the middle of the star are the words "TEXAS STATE RANGER," each word separated by a line on either side of a dot (– · –).

From the late 1910s through the mid-1930s, as badge-wearing became more routine with the Rangers, several varieties of the star-in-a-wheel badge were made. Ranger M. "Red" Burton had a nickel badge with "State Ranger" above the star and "Texas" beneath. On each side of the wheel, at roughly its middle, were stamped two small crosses. Ranger S.O. "Sod" Durst had a badge that said "State" above the star and "Ranger" beneath. Inside each point of the star were the letters T-E-X-A-S. Stamped on each side of the wheel was a small diamond design. Another variety of badge from this era, one which belonged to Ranger George Glick, has "Texas" at the top of the wheel, "Ranger" on the bottom, and the letters T-E-X-A-S in the star. The wheel is marked with an indented inner and outer ring, and two small stars are stamped in the wheel on each side of its midline.

In the 1920s a St. Louis businessman gave Company A Captain Jerry Gray and his Rangers a badge with "Ranger Force" on the top of the wheel and "Texas" on the bottom. Inside the star was the word "Company" and beneath it the letter "A" on a small shield. The blank places on the wheel and star bore fancy filigree work.

When the Texas Department of Public Safety was organized on August 10, 1935, the Texas Rangers became a part of the new state law enforcement agency, moving from the control of the Adjutant General's Department. For four years, from 1935 to 1939, the Rangers used a simple round badge with a raised star in the center. The wording at the top of the badge said "TEXAS RANGERS" and beneath was the designation "DEPT. OF PUBLIC SAFETY."

A new Ranger badge adopted by the DPS in 1940 retained a star as its primary focus, but it was placed inside a slightly elongated circle, with wreaths on either side of the star. The letters T-E-X-A-S are distributed inside each angle of the star. As with the original DPS badge, the words "DEPT. OF PUBLIC SAFETY" are on top, with "TEXAS RANGER" on the bottom. The badge was the same as issued to the uniformed Highway Patrol, except for the wording "TEXAS HIGHWAY PATROL" on the bottom. On the Highway Patrol badges, a number on the inside of the star identified the officer to whom the badge was issued.

On July 1, 1957, the DPS began issuing an enamel-on-polished-metal badge. The Ranger badge had the traditional five-pointed star on a royal blue enamel background. The letters T-E-X-A-S were on the blue, each letter between one of the points of the star. At the top of the badge were the words "DEPARTMENT OF PUBLIC SAFETY." On the bottom the badge were the words "TEXAS RANGERS."

According to police badge historian Frank Latham Jr., the Sputnik-era badge was not popular with the Rangers. They "did not like wearing the same badge as highway patrolmen and other D.P.S. officers," he wrote. Many of the Rangers also thought the enamel badge was too serious a break with the service's Old West tradition.

In 1962 Ranger Hardy L. Purvis and his mother presented the DPS with enough *cinco peso* Mexican, Cuauhtamoc .900 silver coins for each of the sixty-two Rangers the agency had at the time to have a traditional star-in-a-wheel badge. This gift to the state, made in honor of Ranger Purvis' late father, Ranger Captain Hardy B. Purvis, also included underwriting the cost of having the new badges manufactured. Rangers began wearing the badge in October 1962.

The Ranger badge has had only one change since that time: When the silver badges were first issued, the center of the star bore the designation of the Ranger company the wearer belonged to, as in "CO D." Since Rangers sometimes are transferred from one company to another, the company designation was dropped from the badges in 1970.

Modern Texas Rangers receive two badges when they are promoted to the Ranger Service, a silver badge made from a Mexican *cinco peso* coin to wear and a bronze, silver-plated flat badge to carry in their leather identification case along with the DPS ID card. The badge they wear is slightly convex, while the ID badge is flat for an easier fit in the fold-out badge case. Both styles of badges are manufactured by the Southern Badge Company of Houston.

Each Ranger—with the Senior Ranger Captain's approval—may order at his own expense personalized coin badges bearing his or her own name. Badges for Ranger sergeants and lieutenants are silver, with gold for captains.

Though only duly commissioned Rangers and Special Rangers can legally wear the silver star (using the badge for dramatic purposes is legal, of course), the badges are highly sought by collectors. But because of their intrinsic and sentimental value to those who have worn them and to their family or descendants, genuine Rangers badges are hard to come by. They tend to stay in the Rangers' families or go to museums. That, obviously, has led to a proliferation of reproductions. Some badges foisted off on unsuspecting buyers at flea markets and gunshows are not even accurate representations—nothing like them was ever worn by a real Ranger.

The problem is further compounded by the fact that there are believed to have been as many as one hundred varieties of genuine Ranger badges over the years. Some of these real badges occasionally do reach the marketplace, but they are expensive, and they usually come with proof of their provenance.

Someone offering a Ranger badge for sale without good proof of its authenticity should be viewed every bit as suspiciously as a man trying to sell a "genuine" Rolex watch.

Sources

Arrington, Chester W. "'Texas Ranger' Collectibles Catalog #1." Austin: 1987, pp. 4-5.

"Badges With History." Austin: Texas Department of Public Safety, 1957, pp. 1-3.

Casteel, Senior Captain Bruce. Interview with author, Nov. 12, 1996.

Eckhart, Jerry. "Texas Ranger's Badge," *True West*, Sept. 1993, pp. 46-49.

Emsley, Clive. *Policing and its Context, 1750-1870*. New York: Schocken Books, 1984, pp. 111-112.

Francaviglia, Richard V. *The Shape of Texas: Maps As Metaphors*. College Station: Texas A&M University Press, 1995, p. 81.

Gillett, James B. *Six Years with the Texas Rangers*. Lincoln: University of Nebraska Press, 1976, (Reprint of 1925 ed.) p. 25.

Latham, Frank Jr. "Badges of the Texas Rangers," *Police Collectors News*, June 1988, pp. 6-17.

The New Handbook of Texas. Austin: The Texas State Historical Association, 1996, Vol. 5, p. 950.

Palliser, Mrs. Bury. *Historic Devices, Badges, And War-Cries*. Detroit: Gale Research Company, 1971, pp. 1-2.

Schreiner, Charles III, et al., compilers. *A Pictorial History of the Texas Rangers*. Mountain Home, Texas: Y.O. Press, 1969, pp. 222-224.

Spain, Charles A. Jr. "The Flags and Seals of Texas," *South Texas Law Review*, Vol. 33, No. 1, Feb. 1992, p. 244.

"Texas Rangers Now Wear New Badges," *Texas Public Employee*, Nov. 1962, p. 11.

Virgines, George E. "Heraldry of the Texas Rangers," *Passbook*, Vol. 37, No. 2 (Summer 1992), pp. 83-88.

Rangers Make 'em Die Laughing

Retired Company D Ranger Jerome Preiss' smile spreads across his face as big as South Texas.

"You show me a man who doesn't have a little tinge of humor in his makeup and I'll show you a man who's got a problem," Preiss said. "That goes for a Ranger or anyone else."

Preiss' sense of humor made national news back in 1964. The Outdoor Writers of America was having its national convention that year in the Rio Grande Valley city of McAllen. L.A. Wilke, an Austin writer who was coordinator for the convention, asked the governor's office if a Ranger could drop by the gathering at some point so the writers attending from out-of-state could see one of these legendary lawmen in person.

The request trickled down to Captain A.Y. Allee, who assigned Preiss to pay a friendly visit to the writers. Preiss showed up with his horse Noche, patiently posing for pictures with children and their parents.

This was in June, and Noche ended up with a glistening film of sweat over his pretty coat. At the end of the photo session, Preiss saddled up and headed Noche to a nearby service station.

"How much to wash my horse?" Preiss asked the station attendant.

"Two dollars," he replied.

Preiss unsaddled Noche and the horse went through the station's outdoor carwash.

One of the writers picked up on the story and the Associated Press carried it nation-wide. The AP reported that Preiss used his state-issued credit card to pay for the horse wash, but Preiss insists he paid the two dollars with his personal credit card.

Unlike the horse-through-the-carwash incident, Ranger humor tends toward the dry. In modern times, researchers have concluded that humor, particularly its end result of laughter, relieves stress. Being a Ranger can be stressful, and humor seems to have been used as a coping mechanism long before someone actually proved its value in scientific studies. Humor also can be a useful management tool, though the old Rangers would not have known what the word management meant, at least not in the context of supervisory techniques. Finally, a little humor—then as now—can be just plain fun.

Some of the earliest examples of Ranger humor come from N.A. Jennings, who served as a Ranger under Captain Leander H. McNelly in South Texas and wrote a book about it twenty years later.

"One of our most popular forms of amusement was playing practical jokes on each other," Jennings wrote, "and some of them were of a pretty rough character."

The old "snipe hunt" trick was particularly popular with the Rangers, at least until one of their victims got the last laugh.

A McNelly Ranger named Rector, called "Reck" by his comrades in arms, was invited to be the honoree at a snipe hunt. As the Rangers excitedly explained, snipe "were as thick as hops" in the vicinity of a marshy area near the Nueces River. Successful snipe hunting boils down to beating the birds out of the brush and driving them toward someone holding a gunny sack open, the Rangers explained to Rector. A candle is placed in front of the sack to attract the birds. The flame blinds them when they get close. In a panic, the hapless snipe run right into the sack. Being the sack holder takes much less work, the Rangers continued, and is considered the prestige hunting position.

After reaching the mosquito-infested marsh, the "honoree" was left holding the bag—literally—as the other Rangers went off supposedly in search of snipe to drive back toward Rector. Where they actually went was back to camp, to get some sleep until the gullible Ranger finally figured out he had been duped.

Back at camp, Jennings wrote, "the boys howled with wicked delight as we drew graphic pictures of poor Reck holding on with both hands to that sack, while every mosquito in the swamp within sight of the candles made a bee line to the spot."

Around midnight, it dawned on Reck that the other Rangers were not coming back. On the way back to camp, he got lost, but when he tripped and fell into an ant bed, he got an idea.

When he finally found the camp, he went straight to the bedroll of the Ranger who had invited him on the snipe hunt.

The Ranger sat up at the sack holder's approach.

"Hello, Reck! Did you get any snipe?"

"You bet your boots I did!" he said, shaking the contents of his sack all over the Ranger.

The bag held about two quarts of black ants Reck had managed to collect after stumbling on their mound. Now they were all over the Ranger and marching toward the other bedrolls.

"That was the last 'sniping' party we ever had in the Rangers, but it was far from being the last practical joke played," Jennings wrote.

Another stunt practiced by McNelly Rangers included creating sudden chaos by tossing live ammunition into the camp fire (the experienced Rangers knew the ammunition would not explode immediately and could be raked out in time). Jennings also got good at working his tongue in such a way as to perfectly imitate the dreaded buzz of a rattlesnake, a talent that sent several of his comrades jumping into the air.

Rookie Rangers made particularly satisfying targets for pratical jokes.

James B. Gillett, writing about his days in the Frontier Battalion, fondly recalled:

> One of the favorite diversions of the old rangers was to make a newcomer believe that the state furnished the rangers with socks and start him off to the captain's tent to demand his share of the free hosiery. The captain took these pranks in good part and assured the crestfallen applicant that the rangers were only playing a joke on him, while his tormentors enjoyed his discomfiture from a safe distance.

Ranger Captain Dan W. Roberts of the Frontier Battalion took his new bride with him on some of his scouts in the 1870s. Years later she wrote a book about their experiences on the frontier. Since she was the captain's wife, and older than most of the Rangers, she became somewhat of a surrogate mother to the men of Roberts' company.

Her memoir demonstrates that the Rangers, while tough on Indians and outlaws, could be a tad gullible.

"Practical jokes varied camp life," she wrote. "Even I caught the spirit. The Rangers were always on the anxious seat when the Legislature assembled to make biennial appropriations. Would the appropriations for the Rangers be continued? Would they all be continued in service? The mail was looked forward to with great eagerness at such times."

One day, while her husband was away from camp, the mail brought a letter for the captain from the adjutant general.

"The Rangers came to me to know what the letter contained," she continued. "I read it to them correctly that the appropriation had been made, but I added, 'Discharge every man under five feet ten.' Then there was some measuring."

Not until the captain returned and reread the letter to his men did they realize, to the great relief of the short to average-sized men in the company, that they had been duped by Mrs. Roberts.

In the aftermath of the bandit troubles in South Texas, the Rangers came under criticism for excesses in their use of force. A legislative committee held hearings on the Rangers, and there was talk of doing away with the service.

Among the papers of longtime Ranger Captain R.W. Aldrich, who served on the border in 1915, is a two-page typewritten, single-spaced document styled, "Rules and Regulations Governing New Rangers." Whoever wrote the official-looking memorandum obviously was a fairly literate individual, which suggests the bookish Aldrich as a prime suspect.

"General Qualifications" for getting a job as a Ranger included being "versed in ... Theology, Sociology, Astronomy, Osteopathy, Theosophy and Domestic Science" as well as being a college graduate; being "accomplished Bridge Players ... finished Ping Pong Players, [who know] the Language of Flowers and the Rules of Handkerchief Flirtation" and being "able to stand satisfactory examination in all the higher branches of mathematics and domestic economy in order to be able to figure out how to make both ends meet on $50.00 per month, and to be able to dress in the latest style."

Eight rules of conduct also were specified, including a prohibition against cursing, "bad thoughts," and "bad dreams."

In addition, the chaplain "will be used for your model of daily life." Divine services on Sunday as well as the weekly prayer meeting had to be attended.

As for attire, the rules went on, "Rangers will at all times dress modestly and in the latest New York styles. Boots, spurs, especially big hats, and pistols and rifles over .22 caliber are prohibited." The rule pertaining to dress further required that each Ranger "equip himself with low quarter shoes (pumps preferred), derby hats, and walking sticks and riding crops." Silk underwear "with here and there a little showing of lace [to] indicate gentility" also was advised.

Two of the rules, reflective of the criticism the Rangers were experiencing, amounted to biting sarcasm: "Rangers must be meek and humble at all times and if anyone ... strikes him he must say 'beg pardon' and turn the other cheek;" and "If an outlaw attempts to harm a Ranger, he must by no means arrest him or lay heavy hands upon him until he [the outlaw] has first indicated his intentions by shooting." The rules continue with a proviso that if the Ranger is not killed outright by an outlaw he has confronted, "he has the option of getting a warrant of arrest from the Justice of the Peace (provided the said J.P. is sober and willing and not a friend of the outlaw) or giving him a moral lecture on the rights [of] alien enemies and disloyalists...." If a lecture did not work, the final force option was to "display your indignation by stamping your foot on the ground and exclaiming in soft, well modulated voice, 'O Fudge,' three times. Otherwise, duck, sidestep or skidoo."

The "rules" ended with a disclaimer, "(THE ABOVE IS WRITTEN JUST TO 'POOK' A LITTLE FUN)."

Whoever wrote this was a much better writer than most Rangers. Their official reports tended to be short and to the point. Sometimes, however, they demonstrated a certain dry wit. A few examples:

☆ Ranger James D. Dunaway, sent to Groveton in East Texas in 1907 to keep things settled during a hotly contested wet-dry election, got in a gunfight and was shot seventeen times. Dragged to a grocery store for medical treatment, the Ranger asked for a pencil and paper and then scribbled a wire for Governor T.M. Campbell: "Shot all to pieces, but not serious." He was right. He survived.

☆ An incident in the brush country caused this report to be sent to Austin: "Run up on some cattle thieves. Expense to State, 18 rounds."

☆ When a Ranger reached headquarters without the prisoner he had been traveling with, he reported: "Left to escort prisoner to Austin. Norther hit right after we crossed

the Pecos. That night he kicked his blanket off and froze to death."

☆ Another Ranger explained the outcome of a border gunfight: "Made him a naturalized citizen."

☆ The result was the same in this incident: "We had a little shooting match and they lost."

☆ Telegram from Ranger Jeff Milton: "Send two coffins and a doctor."

Starting in the late 1910s, Ranger paperwork increased. The adjutant general's office designed a fill-in-the-blank report that Rangers were to complete after each scout they made. The Rangers did not appreciate the added work, nor did their supervisors. "One of my men is going to get killed behind a typewriter yet," some Ranger captain is reputed to have said in disgust after the state saddled him with more paperwork. One of the blanks on the new report form was labeled: "Disposition of Prisoner." On May 10, 1920, Ranger Kiowa Jones duly noted the disposition of one prisoner as: "Mean as Hell. Had to kill him."

Rangers over the years have not been afraid to laugh at themselves, either. The old border Rangers used to tell this tale about one young Ranger who took himself too seriously but quickly got straightened out:

Back in the days when Rangers alternated between Model Ts and horses, but still preferred the horses, a new Ranger, all duded up, showed up at a Ranger camp upriver from Del Rio.

This young man was all full of himself, proud to be wearing the Ranger badge and the heavy six-gun on his hip. He was not in camp long before, just to show how tough he was, he pulled his pistol and plugged a hole in the camp coffee pot.

At that point, an older Ranger drew his sixgun and proceeded to empty it into every other pot and pan in the camp, several of the shots whizzing dangerously near the young Ranger.

"What'd you go and do that for?" the startled rookie asked.

"Well," the older Ranger replied, "when my partner gets in a gunfight, I'm going to back him up!"

Rangers over the years have gotten plenty of good laughs in retelling what has come to be known as the Mustard Incident. It occurred in a West Texas county in the 1960s, usually not named to protect the guilty.

A Ranger was investigating a simple murder case. He knew who the victim was and already had the killer in custody. All he lacked was the murder weapon, a pistol.

The cooperative suspect said he had tossed the pistol off a local landmark known as the Old Iron Bridge as he drove across.

After getting a good description of the gun in question, the Ranger concluded it probably weighed 16 ounces.

Then the Ranger had an idea: If something that also weighed 16 ounces were tossed from a moving car at the same spot on the bridge where the killer had pitched the weapon, chances are it would land about where the gun had landed. And then maybe he could find the missing piece of evidence.

The only thing the Ranger could find in a hurry that weighed 16 ounces was a jar of mustard. But that was perfect, because the mustard jar would doubtless break, spreading mustard all over. That would make the spot much easier to find.

So, with the helpful killer along to show just where he had tossed the gun, the Ranger drove across the bridge and hurled the mustard jar when his prisoner told him to.

Leaving the man handcuffed in his state car, the Ranger hurried beneath the bridge to find where the mustard jar had hit.

Unknown to the Ranger, at the precise moment that he threw the jar, a couple seeking privacy beneath the country bridge had been actively engaged in a most friendly act. The couple were married, but not to each other.

When the Ranger got under the bridge, he found a partially attired gentleman covered in mustard and detected that a woman was hiding in the nearby brush.

"Some fool hit me with a mustard jar and I want to report it," the man blurted, not stopping to wonder why a Texas Ranger just happened to be patrolling under the Old Iron Bridge.

The Ranger took a notebook from his pocket and politely took all the information down, solemnly promising he would do everything possible to locate the assailant.

Depending on the occasion, Rangers could take sure aim with bullets or leave a person dying with laughter. (Author's collection)

Sources

Aldrich, Roy W. Papers. Sul Ross State University, Alpine, Texas.

"Credit Card Cleans Up Texas Ranger's Horse," Orlando *Sentinel*, June 27, 1964.

Gillett, James B. *Six Years With The Texas Rangers*. Lincoln: University of Nebraska Press, 1976, (Reprint of 1925 ed.) pp. 26-27.

Hudson, Lou. "Spiced-up tale has a jarring end." Fort Worth *Star-Telegram*, April 3, 1991.

Jennings, N.A. Ben Proctor, ed. *A Texas Ranger*. Chicago: R.L. Donnelley & Sons Company, 1992, (Reprint of 1899 ed.) pp. 219-225.

Preiss, Jerome. Interview with author, Oct. 10, 1995.

Roberts, Mrs. Dan W. *A Woman's Reminiscences of Six Years in Camp With the Texas Rangers*. Austin: 1928, pp. 29-39.

Snow, Bob. Interview with author, 1976.

Appendix

Writing Rangers:
A Bibliographic Essay

The Texas Rangers have been arresting the imagination of readers since the 1840s. Few other law enforcement agencies, with the possible exception of England's Scotland Yard, have been the focus of as much writing as the Rangers. Their derring-do has been celebrated in scholarly studies, biographies, popular fiction, pulp Westerns, motion pictures, radio, and television.

But of all those who have worn the silver Ranger star since the force's beginning in 1823, when empresario Stephen F. Austin hired ten men to "range" his colony as a protection against hostile Indians, only a handful have left a legacy of personal narratives—their own lives and adventures in their own words.

As the late bookman Jeff Dykes put it in one of his rare book catalogs, "Only a few of the Rangers got around to writing their memoirs—they were fighters, not writers —but we are especially grateful for those few eye-witness accounts."

Indeed, the handful of Ranger narratives published prior to 1930 constitutes a very small body of work in comparison to the number of men who served as Texas Rangers in the nineteenth century. Unfortunately, the exact number of pre-1900 Rangers probably will never be known. Record keeping was not all that precise in frontier Texas. Two capitol fires destroyed many records.

Muster rolls and payroll data maintained at the Archives Division of the Texas State Library list more than 15,000 names of men who are carried in the records as either minute men, militia members, home guards, Indian fighters, or Texas Rangers. Given that many men served their communities in the role of Ranger on a volunteer, as needed basis, 15,000 is a conservative figure.

Still, not one man in a thousand bothered to put down his Ranger recollections for the sake of posterity. Why?

Nineteenth-century Rangers for the most part were not highly educated men. A Ranger needed a good gun, not good grammar. Many were most likely illiterate. Others, those who generally rose in rank, could read and write well enough to handle orders for supplies and report writing, but only a few were as facile with a pen as they were with a horse or sixgun.

Another factor is the unwritten Ranger code, something that exists to this day. One aspect of the code is, in today's parlance, "Keep a low profile." Rangers who bragged of their exploits were seen as self-promoters. They were subject to harassment from fellow Rangers and superiors.

This part of the code matches the stereotype of the Ranger as a loner (consider the Lone Ranger of radio, comic book, television, and movie fame)—a single, strong individual who faces danger armed only with his Colt, his courage, and his convictions.

Whatever the reason for their scarcity, Ranger narratives have proven enormously popular with readers, researchers and book collectors. To some extent, these books are popular simply because they are Texas Ranger items. To a Ranger collector, the literary quality of the book is not as important as the fact that it has something to do with the Rangers.

Following is an evaluation of ten selected Ranger narratives published between 1847 and 1928. The books are considered alphabetically by author, not in the order of their literary merit.

Banta

Banta, William. *Twenty-Seven Years on the Texas Frontier*. Austin: Ben C. Jones & Co., Printers, 1893.

When Captain William Banta sat down to write his memoir, he was sixty-six years old. He had been a Ranger in the 1850s and '60s, trailing and fighting Indians who raided into Central Texas. Like most Rangers of this era, he had served voluntarily.

In the preface to his book, self-published in 1893, Banta admitted he was "no experienced book-writer." He was not looking for fame, he said. "What I have done for the state as a ranger and a ranger captain, was done gratuitously, not expecting pay or receiving it. I write this biography that the rising generation may know what the pioneers of Texas suffered."

Despite Banta's disclaimer about not being a "book-writer," his narrative is interesting and revealing of the frontier mindset. Though Banta promises to write the truth, "plain and unvarnished," given the passage of time between the events described and the writing of the book, the failings of memory and the likelihood of some embellishment must be taken into consideration in evaluating Banta's narrative.

Added to Banta's recollections are those of J.W. Caldwell, another former Ranger captain. Caldwell's story was put together by his son, who said in his prefatory remarks that he had had "the assistance of rangers who were companions and eyewitnesses of my father...."

Like many other privately published narratives, the Banta-Caldwell book did not stay in print very long. In

1933 Banta's grandson, L.G. Park, issued a second edition of the book, "Re-written and Revised." He added a photograph of Banta and an introduction, which included Banta's date of birth and other biographical data, though he omitted his grandfather's date of death. Since Park, too, may have polished his grandfather's narrative, the very rare first edition should be considered the most accurate. Both editions are necessary, however, for a complete evaluation of Banta's memoir.

J. Frank Dobie notes the Banta-Caldwell book in his *Guide to Life and Literature of the Southwest*, but makes no comment on it. Likewise, the title is listed without comment in Wright Howe's *U.S.iana* (B109). The book is out of print.

Gillett

Gillett, James B. *Six Years With The Texas Rangers, 1875 To 1881*. Austin: 1921. Revised edition, New Haven: Yale University Press, 1925.

By all evaluative standards, and by one other—the pure pleasure derived in reading it—the Ranger narrative of J.B. Gillett is the best of this small genre.

First self-published by Gillett in 1921, his *Six Years With the Texas Rangers* was so well thought of that a revised edition was brought out by Yale University four years later. Two years later, the World Book Company (Yonkers-on-Hudson, N.Y. and Chicago) produced an illustrated edition for use as a textbook, *The Texas Ranger, A Story of the Southwestern Frontier*. In 1943 Gillett's narrative was published as part of the Lakeside Classics Series (No. 43) by the Lakeside Press, R.R. Donnelley & Sons Co. The book remains in print, available in paperback from the University of Nebraska Press.

Dobie beatified the work with these words in his *Guide to Life and Literature of the Southwest*: "I regard Gillett as the strongest and straightest of all Ranger narrators... He wrote in the sunshine." Dykes wrote: "Jim Gillett was one of the greatest storytellers your bookseller ever knew—and he wrote the way he talked."

The *Dallas Morning News* said in 1936 that Gillett's book "bears the stamp of authenticity in its straightforward, matter-of-fact narration of events, which moved fast and furious during the years between 1875 and 1881." Indeed, that was the period in which the Rangers of the Frontier Battalion assured their permanent place in history. In six years time, the threat from hostile Indians in Texas was ended and many notorious outlaws were either dead, in prison, or no longer living in Texas. Gillett participated in much of the action that brought all that about and wrote of it in his book.

In his *Best Books On The West: A Guide to a Core Collection*, compiler Richard Morrison, an Austin book dealer, listed Gillett among 121 titles recommended by three or more bibliographers. The top book on the list has been recommended by nine authors. Gillett is one of 32 books with four significant bibliographic recommendations to its credit.

Writer-historian A.C. Greene includes Gillett in his *The 50 Best Books on Texas*, applauding the fact that Gillett "never succumbs to the deification process" in writing about the Rangers. The book, Green wrote, "is superb, and truthful; its dramatic color coming from the events themselves, not Gillett's manner of telling them."

John Jenkins, in his *Basic Texas Books* (Gillett is No. 76), suggests that Gillett's book was written with the help of an unknown editor, but he offers no source for that conclusion.

However, an examination of other writings of Gillett indicates definite growth in his literary skills and makes a strong case that Gillett had not needed as much help as Jenkins thought. As he proudly proclaimed in his book, "When school closed in the early summer of 1868 I went fishing, and never attended school an hour thereafter." A letter Gillett wrote ten years later, as a young Ranger, certainly supports that: "I dont know hoo is on the scout yet. Their was 4 men killed at Junction City while we ware gone to Austin."

Forty-four years later, one year after publication of his book, Gillett penned a letter to John Holman, managing editor of *Forest and Stream* Magazine in New York. Only one modest misspelling is evident in the two-paragraph letter, which has an organization that demonstrates Gillett had learned considerably since leaving school to go fishing. Describing his book, he wrote: "It is a true storey [sic] of the Texas frontier and all old Texas rangers during the time (six years seven mo) I was with them. I hope it may interest you."

In addition to his book, Gillett wrote magazine articles. Two articles published in the 1930s are well written and organized. It appears that Gillett, known to have been an avid reader and book collector, was a self-educated man. His Ranger memoir is probably his work, not someone else's.

Gillett's book is frequently cited in other works, including Walter Prescott Webb's classic history of the Rangers, *The Texas Rangers: A Century of Frontier Defense*. But the book is not perfect. As Ramon Adams pointed out in his *Six-Guns and Saddle Leather*, the definitive bibliography of lawman and outlaw books, "Though considered one of the better Ranger books, the author makes many mistakes, especially in his chapter on Sam Bass."

Still, if a person wanted to read only one book on the Rangers of the Frontier Battalion, Gillett would be the best choice.

Jennings

Jennings, Napoleon Augustus. *A Texas Ranger*. New York: Charles Scribners Sons, 1899.

Of all the Ranger narrative writers, Jennings was the only one who was a professional author. He had a long career as a reporter and press agent after his adventuring days were over. Unfortunately, he was a reporter in an era when the emphasis on accuracy and ethics was not as strong as it would become in the twentieth century. Inventiveness and the ability to tell a good story no matter the true facts were highly marketable job skills.

A Texas Ranger is certainly a very readable book, full of insight into the mindset of the Ranger of the 1870s and conditions along the Texas-Mexican border. It has been reprinted seven times. But it does contain inaccuracies and, worse, outright fiction.

In a review, Webb said the book was of "doubtful authenticity" and "abounds in errors and in misrepresentations."

Dobie addressed the question in his foreword to the 1930 printing of the book (Dallas: Southwest Press). First of all, he pointed out, there was no question that Jennings had been a Texas Ranger. Official records bore that out. Those records showed, however, that Jennings did not spend as much time in the Ranger service as he indicated in his book.

But even Jennings admitted that. Dobie quoted from a letter from Jennings to Captain Leander McNelly's widow in which he said that in his book he had made himself a member of McNelly's company a year before he actually joined. "I did this to add interest to the recital and to avoid too much of a hear-say character," Jennings wrote. "Told in the first person adventures hold the attention of the reader much more closely than at second hand."

Dobie said that if Jennings had not seen everything he described, his material came from eyewitnesses. Jennings came back to Texas in the mid-1890s to do research for his book and looked up some of his old comrades for interviews.

"He probably telescoped some events; space and the exigencies of narrative necessarily prevented his giving credit to every individual Ranger who took part in the exploits recorded," Dobie wrote. "Every writer who expects to be read must be selective, and many a historian who wanted to make the truth live has buried it in a dismal swamp of unselected facts."

Though Jennings owned up to the use of literary license in his letter to McNelly's widow, he did not do so in his book. In his narrative's first paragraph, Jennings wrote that he had "endeavored to set down, plainly and truthfully, events as they actually occurred." The only thing he admitted doing was "in some instances" changing the names of some persons mentioned in the book because they had since become respectable citizens of the state.

One of Jennings' former colleagues did not have much use for *A Texas Ranger*. George Durham, who rode with McNelly, related his Ranger experiences to Clyde Wantland in the 1940s. Durham said Jennings had been taken on by McNelly in Laredo as field clerk to "do the writing" for the company. "Later on he sure wrote," Durham said in his memoir, which was published in 1962. "He sold stories on McNelly to a big magazine and he put it in a book. The boy took it mostly out of his head, and it is pretty awful . . . . "

Author-historian Chuck Parsons, in a book on another of McNelly's Rangers, said Jennings "re-wrote history in his book... creating considerable fiction."

Not surprisingly, some of Jennings' fiction puts him in a better light. He has himself and another Ranger arresting the outlaw King Fisher, an outright and well-documented falsehood.

Still, Jenkins considered *A Texas Ranger* to be a basic Texas book, calling it "one of the most interesting accounts of the life of the Texas Rangers in the late 1870's."

In 1992 the book was reprinted as a Lakeside Classic (No. 90) by R.R. Donnelley & Sons of Chicago. Historian Ben Proctor annotated it and provided a new prologue, doing the best job yet of placing Jennings' narrative into proper historical perspective. Also containing photographs of individuals who figure in the book and a color map of the South Texas country patrolled by McNelly's Rangers, this is the most useful edition of the Jennings book.

Lee

Lee, Nelson. *Three Years Among The Camanches: The Narrative of Nelson Lee, The Texas Ranger, Containing A Detailed Account Of His Captivity Among the Indians, His Singular Escape Through The Instrumentality Of His Watch, And Fully Illustrating Indian Life As It Is On The War Path And In The Camp*. Albany, N.Y.: Baker Taylor, 1859.

Once considered one of the better of the Ranger narratives, Nelson A. Lee's *Three Years Among The Camanches* [sic] has suffered a decline in reputation in recent years. It still is a good read, but just how historically accurate it is has been subject to some debate.

Published in 1859, when Indians were still very much a threat to much of Texas, *Three Years Among The Camanches* had been out of print for years and considered quite scarce when the University of Oklahoma Press reprinted it in 1957.

Walter Prescott Webb wrote the introduction to the reissue of Lee's narrative, saying, "There is no better description of the life of the Texas Ranger...."

According to the original preface by an unnamed nineteenth century editor, Lee, intelligent but uneducated, told his story to someone who took it down. That person doubtless did some polishing, if not outright invention. Lee, of course, could have fabricated portions of his story in the telling.

A year after the book's reissue, a writer in *Southwest Review* said the second half of the book, in which Lee related his supposed capture by the Comanches, was an outright fraud. In 1983 Jenkins included the book in his *Basic Texas Books* (No. 123) and defended it, saying "the weight of the evidence is in favor of Lee ... although his account of his captivity may be exaggerated."

In 1991 OU Press brought the book out in paperback, with a new foreword by historian Gary Clayton Anderson. Anderson points out two significant problems with even the first half of the book, which chronicles Lee's experiences as a Ranger under two legendary captains, Ben McCulloch and Jack C. Hays. First, though Lee claimed to have come to Texas in 1840, he does not show up in any records until late in 1842, when someone named Nelson Lee enlisted in a militia company. Secondly, no extant state records show Lee to have been a Texas Ranger at any time.

"In other words," Anderson wrote, "Lee probably never saw any of the fights he described in the first half of the book."

Anderson also made several points in support of his argument that the portion of the book on Lee's supposed captivity by Comanches is spurious, having been "cribbed from other sources or adapted from observations of other, more friendly Indians . . . ."

In sum, Anderson wrote, the book is a "unique brand of fiction/history, the embellished writings of a man who experienced part of what he claimed and added the rest based upon collected information."

If Lee was not totally honest in his narrative, he was in Texas during the 1840s and his book does contain useful information based on what he saw or heard from others. In addition, it is a useful social document, giving insight into the thinking of Anglos in Texas during the days of the Republic.

Maltby

Maltby, William J. *Captain Jeff; or Frontier Life in Texas with the Texas Rangers* . . . Colorado, Texas: 1906.

In 1906, two years before his death, Jeff Maltby's narrative was published by a printer in Colorado City. However, nowhere on the title page does it say that Maltby was the author of *Captain Jeff or Frontier Life with the Texas Rangers*. Beneath a V-shaped 48-word subtitle seven lines deep, the only information is that the book is "By One of the Nine/A Member of Company "E"/Texas Rangers."

But the book is clearly by Maltby, who uses third person narration to allow him to more subjectively relate his Indian fighting experiences on the Texas frontier. At one point in the narrative, Maltby tells his wife goodbye before riding off in pursuit of a Kiowa raiding party that had killed several Burnet County settlers.

She replied, "Jeff, go and avenge the death of these noble and good people, and may God bless you and bring you safe back to me and the children." Maltby then writes,

"Such was the woman worthy to be the wife of the man who was destined to rid the bleeding frontier... of two of the most barbarous and bloody savages that ever depredated upon it...."

Occasionally, however, Maltby lapses into first person plural, the word "our" slipping into a description of some action his Ranger company had taken.

The heart of Maltby's narrative is his relentless pursuit of the Kiowa chief Big Foot and his Comanche "lieutenant," Jape. Several Indians known on the Texas frontier were called Big Foot. Dr. Rupert N. Richardson, who did the introduction to a 1967 reprinting of the book, suggested that Big Foot was a composite of several Indians, but Maltby turns him into a wily foe worthy of any Indian in Larry McMurtry's Pulitzer Prize-winning *Lonesome Dove*. The writing, as one reviewer pointed out, has "the Victorian flavor of George Ruxton and Ned Buntline."

His self-serving prose aside, Maltby clearly was a leader of men as a Ranger captain, both on a volunteer and paid basis, and did play an important part in ridding the Texas frontier of hostile Indians. His recollections, written years after the fact, give a good picture of what the life of a Texas Ranger was like in a time when every "light moon," settlers feared for their lives and property.

The book, though, is badly organized, a problem Dobie commented on with only one word in his entry on Maltby in his *Guide to Life and Literature of the Southwest*: "Amorphus." The first 96 pages of the book, which covers 17 short chapters, constitute Maltby's narrative. The rest of the book is a collection of articles by or about him, along with some letters to and from him.

Despite the poor organization and Maltby's self-glorification, his book offers considerable insight into the time when hostile Indians were still a threat in Texas. As Richardson wrote in his introduction to the reprint of the book (Waco: Texian Press), Maltby "wrote in vivid style and contributed to the history of the Texas frontier some chapters that should not be lost to posterity."

Maltby's narrative, reprinted in 1965 in facsimile and reset and reprinted in 1967, is out of print.

Pike

Pike, James. *The Scout And Ranger: Being the Personal Adventures of Corporal Pike, of the Fourth Ohio Cavalry, as a Texas Ranger, in the Indian Wars*. . . Cincinnati and New York: J.R. Hawley & Co., 1865.

First published right after the Civil War, a 1932 reprint included only the Texas portion of the book. (*Scout and Ranger; Being the Personal Adventures of James Pike of the Texas Rangers in 1859-60*. Princeton: Princeton University Press.) Carl L. Cannon edited the book and provided a new preface and introductory essay.

Dobie said Pike "drew a long bow" and called the book "interesting." Jenkins included Pike in *Basic Texas Books* (No. 162). He, too, called it an "interesting reminiscence."

Pike served as a Ranger for two years, first under John Henry Brown and then with J.M. Smith. He saw plenty of Indian fighting action during the turmoil surrounding Texas' attempt to maintain Indian reservations in the 1850s. Rangers were kept busy not only by hostile Indians, but in trying to deal with whites who adhered to the philosophy that "the only good Indian was a dead Indian."

Dobie compared Pike's narrative to Gillett's and Jennings'. The strongest parallel is with Jennings. Like Jennings, Pike had a newspaper background, which is reflected in his writing. Pike's father was a newspaper editor, and Pike had worked as a printer's assistant in his native Ohio and also in Missouri. It is not known if he did any newspaper writing, but the line between printer and writer was not as distinct in the nineteenth century as it came to be in the twentieth. Whether he came by it genetically or by experience, Pike was as handy with a phrase as he was with a Colt revolver.

A second point of similarity between Pike and Jennings is that Pike probably embellished his account. As Jenkins put it, "Pike tells the truth in his narrative, but not the naked truth." Also like Jennings, Pike seemed to deny any fictionalizing, declaring that the facts in his book held "more of the strange and heroic, than could be conceived by the fertility of a Dickens or a Dumas."

The book currently is out of print.

Reid

Reid, Samuel. *The Scouting Expeditions of McCulloch's Texas Rangers; or, the Summer and Fall Campaign of the Army of the United States in Mexico—1846* . . . Philadelphia: G.B. Zieber and Co., 1847.

The first book-length treatment of the Rangers, and also the first Ranger narrative, did much to foster their national reputation. Published in 1847, less than two years after Texas became a state and only twenty-four years after Stephen F. Austin first hired the first Texas Rangers, Samuel C. Reid Jr.'s *The Scouting Expeditions of McCulloch's Texas Rangers* is a seminal work.

Though the book primarily deals with the Texas Rangers during the Mexican War, when they served as volunteer scouts under General Zachary Taylor, it also is a rich source for material on the noted Ranger Captain John Coffee Hays and his Rangering exploits during the days of the Texas Republic. The story of Hays' solitary fight with Comanches atop Enchanted Rock, in what is now Llano

County, is told for the first time in Reid's book (pp. 111-112), only five years after it happened.*

Written while the Mexican War was still being fought, Reid's book is more important for its anecdotes than its history, which can and has been developed by historians from other sources. But Reid gives a reader a genuine feel for the times as he describes everything from Ranger camp life to practical jokes.

Jenkins, in selecting Reid's work for inclusion in his *Basic Texas Books* (No. 170), called it "the best contemporary account of the Texas Rangers in the northern campaigns of the Mexican War." Dykes called it a "highly entertaining eyewitness account."

Reid, the son of a War of 1812 naval hero, was a lawyer. When the Mexican War broke out, he joined the 6th Louisiana Volunteers and came to Texas. Discovering that his regiment would not likely see action, he resigned his commission and went to Matamoros, Mexico, where he enlisted in "the company of Texas Rangers... kept for scouting service by General Taylor."

His memoir was based on a diary he kept from June to October of 1846, though the book was obviously supplemented from other sources, probably material from newspapers. (One example begins on page 105, where Reid wrote, "we are indebted to Mr. Lumsden, of the [New Orleans] 'Picayune,' whose letter we copy entire:") Most of the text, however, is obviously based on Reid's personal observation or on events he heard about around the camp fire. The narrative is rich with this colorful material.

Reid's book also abounds in adjective-rich writing, showing that the lawyer-author was equal to any opposing attorney's flowery courtroom language. Though reprinted seven times, it currently is out of print.

Roberts

Roberts, Daniel Webster. *Rangers and Sovereignty*. San
Antonio: Wood Printing & Engraving Co., 1914.

In 1914, more than three decades after he last rode as
a Ranger, Daniel W. Roberts wrote a book detailing his
experiences in the Frontier Battalion. As Dobie pointed
out in his *Guide to Life and Literature of the Southwest*,
"Roberts was a better Ranger than writer."

Still, Jenkins considered *Rangers and Sovereignty* an essential Texas book (No. 178). Agreeing with Dobie that
the book was poorly written, Jenkins wrote that the book
"gives a remarkable, concise account of the service of one
of the most active of all Texas Ranger units."

Though badly written, Roberts' book is full of action
and is an accurate recollection of the events in which he
actually took part. However, some errors did creep in when
the old Ranger wrote of cases in which he was not an actual
participant, such as the demise of the outlaw Sam Bass in
Round Rock in 1878.

The old Ranger's writing comes to life when he describes
the range wars and Indian fights in which he took part. As
though caught up once more in the action, at these points
in the book he forgets to use the frequent breath-pause
commas that dot the narrative elsewhere.

Roberts settled into his saddle more comfortably than
into his narrative person. His changes in person are as
puzzling as they are distracting. In his seven-paragraph
"Biographical Sketch," Roberts switched from third person
("His father") to first person "my mother" and "I was
born") and finally to the editorial "we" ("we were never a
politician").

An unsuspecting reader, starting the first lines (p. 95)
of the chapter "Rio Grande Campaign," might think
Roberts had died before finishing his book and that some

other author had supplied the remaining facts of the Ranger's life:

"In 1878, Lieutenant D.W. Roberts resigned the command of Company 'D' and went to Houston.... Major Jones wrote D.W. Roberts, who was then in Houston, that if he would come back and take command of his old company, that he would insure him a captaincy, and that his pay would be better...."

Three lines from the bottom of the page, Roberts went back to first person: "I concluded to do it, came to Austin, received a captain's commission...."

Roberts' frequent reliance on third person and the editorial "we" may reflect a strong sense of modesty, but it detracts from readability.

Modern readers may also find Roberts' heavy use of apology quotation marks irritating, such as "boys" when referring to fellow Rangers. In 1914 such words as "dare devil," "cattle man," "rattler," "dead run," "war dance," "rode double," and "hard to catch" were commonly understood and inoffensive enough not to need apology.

Fourteen years after Roberts' book was published, his wife wrote a much more readable account of Ranger life, *A Woman's Reminiscences of Six Years in Camp with the Texas Rangers* (Austin: Von Boeckmann-Jones Co., 1928). Jenkins called this short work the "essential companion" to her husband's book. In 1986, evidently agreeing with Jenkins, Austin publisher Tom Munnerlyn brought out both narratives in one book. Both books had been out of print until that time.

Mrs. Roberts' book is an oddity within a rarity—a Ranger narrative written by a woman. Historically, no women served on the Ranger force in other than an honorary capacity until 1993, when two women were sworn in as Rangers. Though Mrs. Roberts was not a Ranger, she went with her husband on his company's patrols and was known among the men as "Assistant Commander." She also was a surrogate mother to them. Dobie said Mrs. Roberts was "a sensible and charming woman with a seeing eye."

The edition combining both narratives (Austin: State House Press, 1986) provides a new introduction and first-ever index, making it the best choice for convenience in reading and scholarly value. It remains in print.

Sowell

Sowell, Andrew Jackson. *Rangers and Pioneers of Texas, with a Concise Account of the Early Settlements, Hardships, Massacres, Battles, and Wars By Which Texas Was Rescued From the Rule of the Savage and Consecrated to the Empire of Civilization*. San Antonio: Shepard Bros. & Co, 1884.

Andrew Jackson Sowell may have been the only author of a Ranger narrative to have decided while still serving as a Ranger that his story was worthy of a book. His account of his Ranger experiences in 1870-1871, contained in his *Rangers and Pioneers of Texas*, is one of the best of this small genre. As Dobie said, "Sowell will some day be recognized as an extraordinary chronicler."

Dykes called Sowell a "writing Ranger." He wrote four solid nonfiction books during his lifetime, more than any other Ranger. His first was *Rangers and Pioneers*, which has twice been reprinted (1964 and 1991). The more recent edition (Austin: State House Press, 1991), with an added index, remains in print.

Written in 1883 and published the following year, *Rangers and Pioneers* is significant in that it was written while Sowell was still a young man (he was born in Seguin in 1848) and contained fresh recollections from veterans of Texas Indian fights as well as his own. Dobie said Sowell's book was "graphic...down to bedrock." Jenkins considered it worthy of inclusion in his *Basic Texas Books* (No. 192), calling it "one of the best of all first-person ranger campaign narratives."

Rangers and Pioneers of Texas is actually three books. In the first section, Sowell wrote of Indian depredations relayed to him by surviving participants. Sowell then devoted space to his own illustrious family, which came to Texas in 1829, telling stories of his father and others who took part in the Texas Revolution. The final portion of the book, which amounts to about 50 percent of its content, is Sowell's narrative of his stint as a Texas Ranger, "Campaign of the Texas Rangers to the Wichita Mountains in 1871."

As Jenkins observed, Sowell either planned from the start to write about his experiences or made up his mind as he was at it. The clue is a line in an 1876 letter from a former comrade that Sowell included in the book: "I presume you are still at work on your book."

In fact, a reader does not have to get very far into Sowell's narrative before realizing that he must have written some of it at the time he was a Ranger, probably while sitting around the camp fire after the day's "march." In several places, Sowell jumps from past tense to a line that must have been from a journal or a letter home: "We rode hard until nearly night, but could still see nothing of the company. To-day [sic] I killed the first prairie dog that I got . . . " (p. 242). That entry hardly reads like something written from memory more than a decade later. The detail and dates in the narrative definitely suggest that in 1883, Sowell was writing from a journal or letters. These apparently have not survived, or if they did, they are not known.

Sowell's firsthand account of rangering is lively and well written. "The tales that Sowell tells have the authority and authenticity found only in the reminiscences of a participant who has a good feel for history and a way with words," wrote George Ward of the Texas State Historical Association in his introduction to the 1991 edition.

Not only did Sowell have a way with words, many of those words were in the vernacular of the time, making *Rangers and Pioneers* a good source for the study of frontier language. "'Boys,' said Sergeant Cobb . . . 'what do you say to a charge?' 'All right, Ed,' came from the rangers . . . ." Judging from the number of times he uses the word, "boys" must have been in common usage among comrades in arms in frontier Texas.

Years later, writing a biographical sketch in another of his books (*History of Fort Bend County*, Houston: 1904), Sowell summed up his Ranger experience:

> I scouted, trailed Indians, suffered with cold, hunger, thirst, and witnessed many startling scenes . . . I was one of the eleven Rangers who made the fight with forty-one Indians at the Keep Ranch, and saved the women and children there; was powder burned in the face, and one arrow cut the shoulder of my jacket.

While Sowell obviously risked his life to help protect the Texas frontier, in his *Rangers and Pioneers*, as the bibliophile Dykes said in his *Rangers All!*, Sowell "rendered another, and probably greater, service to his State—he interviewed many pioneers of the Texas frontier and recorded and published their recollections."

Sullivan

Sullivan, W. John L. *Twelve Years in the Saddle For Law and Order on the Frontiers of Texas*. Austin: Von Boeckmann-Jones Co., 1909.

Like Gillett, Sullivan was a Frontier Battalion Ranger, serving in Company B. But there is no similarity between Gillett's book and Sullivan's narrative.

Dobie omitted mention of it in his *Guide to Life and Literature of the Southwest*. Dykes noted only that the first edition was "very scarce." Adams, likewise, called the volume "exceedingly rare," but did not offer a characterization of the book other than it "tells about the life of this Texas Ranger and contains chapters about the hanging of Bill Longley, the Cook gang, and some Texas feuds and bank robberies."

Jenkins selected Sullivan as a Basic Texas Book (No. 200), noting that Sullivan's narrative covered a period (1888-1900) for which "there are few surviving ranger recollections."

Sullivan's narrative, though interesting, is weakened by an episodic organization. In Chapter III, for instance, he tells of an encounter with Indians he had as a cowboy while on a trail drive to Kansas in 1871. As soon as he wraps up that story, he jumps a quarter century to 1896, when he relates an experience he had in Quanah when he was a Texas Ranger. Sullivan offers another Ranger story in Chapter V, then backtracks in the next chapter to recount a buffalo hunt in 1877.

Jenkins said Sullivan's recollections "lack flavor," but in the next paragraph of his assessment in *Basic Texas Books* he offered a quotation from the book that does not lack flavor at all. Sullivan, arresting a man who seemed reluctant to hand over his gun, told him he "would not hurt a hair on his head for the world" but that "if you do make a bad break . . . I will cut you off at your pockets."

As Jenkins points out, the book obviously was written by someone with a better education than Sullivan. The old Ranger may well have been inspired to write his memoir by Albert Bigelow Paine's biography of Sullivan's old captain, Bill McDonald. That book was published the same year as Sullivan's.

Reprinted only once, in 1966, Sullivan's narrative is out of print.

Sources

Adams, Ramon. *Six-Guns and Saddle Leather*. Norman: University of Oklahoma Press, 1969.

Conger, Roger N. "Review of *Captain Jeff.*" *Southwestern Historical Quarterly*, LXXIII (July 1969) pp. 138-139.

Cutrer, Thomas W. "Review of *Rangers and Sovereignty.*" *Military History of the Southwest*. Vol. 19, No. 2 (Fall 1989) pp. 196-198.

Dallas Morning News. "News of Southwestern Authors and Presses." April 5, 1936.

Dobie, J. Frank. *Guide to Life and Literature of the Southwest*. Dallas: Southern Methodist University Press, 1942, 1952.

Durham, George, as told to Clyde Wantland. *Taming the Nueces Strip: The Story of McNelly's Rangers*. Austin: University of Texas Press, 1962.

Dykes, Jeff. *Rangers All!* College Park, MD: 1966.

Garrett, Henry D., M.D. "Review of *Pioneers and Rangers of Texas.*" El Paso Historical Society, *Password*, Vol. 37, No. 1 (Spring 1992) pp. 50-51.

Greene, A.C. *The 50 Best Books on Texas*. Dallas: Pressworks Publishing, Inc., 1982.

Howes, Wright. *U.S.iana (1650-1950)* New York: R.R. Bowker Co. for The Newberry Library, 1962.

Hunter, J. Marvin. "A.J. Sowell, Ranger and Author." *Frontier Times*, Vol. 20, No. 12 (Sept. 1943) pp. 251-252.

Ingmire, Frances J. *Texas Ranger Service Records, 1847-1900*. St. Louis: 1982.

Jenkins, John H. *Basic Texas Books*. Austin: Jenkins Publishing Co., 1983.

Morrison, Richard. *Best Books on the West: A Guide to a Core Collection*. Austin: 1989.

Proctor, Ben. "Review of *Rangers and Pioneers of Texas*." *East Texas Historical Journal*, 1992, Vol. 30, No. 2, p. 70.

Webb, Walter Prescott. *The Texas Rangers: A Century of Frontier Defense*. Austin: The University of Texas Press, 1965. (Reprint of 1935 ed.)

White, Gifford. "Texas Ranger," *Texana*, Spring 1964, pp. 77-78.

Williamson, Robert Lee. "Review of *Three Years Among the Comanches*." *Southwestern Historical Quarterly*, LXI (April 1958) pp. 555-558.

Notes

*   Frederick Wilkins, in *The Legend Begins: The Texas Rangers 1823-1845* (Austin: State House Press, 1996), questions whether this fight ever occurred. Wilkins was unable to find any contemporary records concerning the incident (pp. 201-204, 208).

Index